BASEBALL AT THE UNIVERSITY OF MICHIGAN

BASEBALL AT THE UNIVERSITY OF MICHIGAN

Rich Adler

ARCADIA
PUBLISHING

ISBN 978-0-7385-3221-9

Published by Arcadia Publishing
Charleston, South Carolina

Printed in the United States of America

Library of Congress Catalog Card Number: 2004100476

For all general information contact Arcadia Publishing at:
Telephone 843-853-2070
Fax 843-853-0044
E-mail sales@arcadiapublishing.com
For customer service and orders:
Toll-Free 1-888-313-2665

Visit us on the Internet at www.arcadiapublishing.com

Contents

Acknowledgments

First and foremost, I would like to express my appreciation to the staff at the Bentley Historical Library on the University of Michigan campus, for their patience in helping to find what was often obscure information. Likewise, I thank the staff members of the University Graduate Library, at the Ann Arbor Public Library, and the staff of the *Michigan Daily*, especially Tony Ding, in providing access to photographs, documents and historical information. In particular, I would single out Ruth Dusenbery for her help with printing.

Other individuals who provided information, answers to questions or photographs include Peter Morris, Casey Close, Don Lund, Jim Schneider and Bruce Madej. The editing suggestions from Marc Okkonen were also of significant help.

And to my son Steven, and the girls, Sally, Rebekah, Ruth, and Rose.

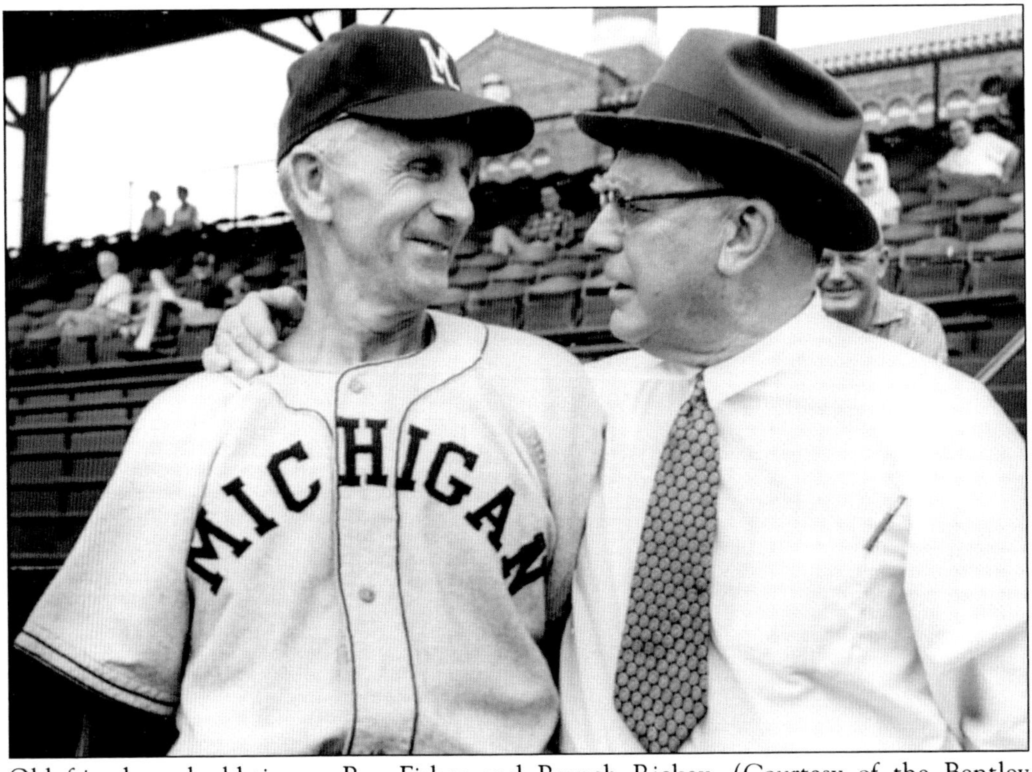

Old friends and old-timers: Ray Fisher and Branch Rickey. (Courtesy of the Bentley Historical Library.)

Introduction

The preliminary title for this book was to be *University of Michigan Baseball: The Other Sport*, reflecting its position in the "pecking order" within the athletic department. As is true at many universities, arguably including Michigan, football and basketball seem to reign supreme today in both popularity and funding; baseball, if it even continues to be an organized activity, often ranks a distant third.

Yet, baseball has been a sanctioned sport at Michigan for over one hundred thirty years, clearly preceding the other major activities as the most important sport in the mind of the student. Baseball, or as it was known during the times—base ball—began as basically a "club" sport, little more than an early version of a pickup game. The university "diamond" was an open plot of ground, north of the present-day Diag at the site of the current Chemistry Building. During the 1870s, the sport grew in popularity among the students, helped in part by a variety of athletic associations to which students could join. The squad also began to play teams outside of the university. Mostly, these were local schools or base ball clubs, with names such as the Hiawathas, Aetnas or Detroiters. During these early years, the inclusion of professionals participating in a supposedly amateur sport was often an issue, as teams sometimes added "ringers" for important games—clearly some things never really change.

There exist several "eras" into which the history of Michigan baseball can be subdivided. I have attempted to categorize these periods based upon the significance of each particular era. Among my sources were the earliest student newspapers: *The Michigan Daily*, which began publishing in 1890, and continues to the present day, and the *Michigan Argonaut*, which preceded the *Daily* during the 1880s. Reading these early files provides more than just a look into the earlier history of the U. The writing of the period provided an informal look into those events of the day which affected or concerned the students. Anecdotes and stories abound, not only those associated with the Ann Arbor campus, but from campuses throughout the East and West; in the eastern-centric mindset, there was only the East (New York State or the "coast"), and everything else constituted the "West." Hence we have a Michigan fight song, written during this period, the lyrics of which state we are indeed the "champions of the West."

Some anecdotes were often too enjoyable to not be included. Particularly in the first sections, I have included stories or quotes which seem apropos, not only to the contemporary story, but even find a present day meaning. I trust the reader will find these as amusing as I do.

Chapter One: The Early Years: 1869–1895. This represents the period during which baseball grew from being a "club" sport, to one in which distant schools were challenged for a mythical "supremacy." The year 1895 represented the last year in which Michigan was an "independent." The following year represented the beginning of the Big Ten Conference.

Chapter Two: From Manager to Coach. The earliest squads were led by either a captain or a manager, generally students who served to organize both the team and a schedule. Practices were informal. With the addition of more challenging opponents, actual coaches were hired, most often professionals who used the time during their off-season to work with the colleges.

Chapter Three: The Conference Era: 1896–1920. Michigan is well noted for its role in the "Big Ten." The conference, originally nine schools, was formed as a means to highlight the quality of western schools. From the beginning, the "Big Nine" encountered controversy, even losing Michigan for a decade.

Chapter Four: The Fisher Era. Few people have had the influence on college baseball as that of Ray Fisher at Michigan, coach from 1921 to 1958.

Chapter Five: Champions: Not Just "of the West." In the 1950s, Michigan graduated from being a power in the Big Ten, to becoming a major player at the national level. Led first by Fisher himself, and then by coaching successors who learned under Fisher, Michigan twice emerged as the champion of the NCAA College World Series, and participated an additional five times.

Chapter Six: Scandal and Rebirth: 1980–2003. Under Bud Middaugh, Michigan continued its dominance of the Big Ten, with six titles in his first eight years as coach. But scandal led to Middaugh's firing in 1989, and it was a decade before the team could recover.

Chapter Seven: "Maize and Blue" Diamonds. The sites and history associated with the athletic fields have mirrored the growth of the University of Michigan itself.

Records, of course, can be misleading. Nineteenth-century records are often incomplete, and the nature and quality of the team's opponents varied considerably. Newspapers sometimes provided conflicting accounts. Using both information from the University's Athletic Office's Media Guide, as well as primary sources from the period, I have attempted to reproduce data such as team records as accurately as possible. In some cases, the records of contemporary sources do not correspond with those from the Athletic Department. In those circumstances, I have tried to utilize the original source as my guide, sometimes discovering that the Guide is incorrect. Most errors were minor; scores or the spelling of names may have been inaccurate. Some errors were more significant, as in the Media Guides' listing Charles Watkins as coach in 1899 and 1901. I have tried to correct such errors in this book. As well, hitting and pitching records were sometimes incomplete, particularly through the early decades of the twentieth century. I have tried to incorporate such records in as accurate a fashion as possible.

The question of what constituted "competition" was also subject to change. The opponents in the 19th or early 20th centuries often included known professionals, in which case these would be considered as practice games. Sometimes this was obvious, as when Michigan played Minor League teams, or even exhibitions with the Detroit Tigers. In some instances, organizations like the Detroit Athletic Club might utilize professionals one year, and amateurs in other years. I have tried to include only those games in which the opponents were strictly amateurs.

ONE

The Early Years

1866–1895

College baseball in a form reasonably close to something the modern fan would recognize is considered to have begun July 1, 1859. On that date, a game between Amherst and Williams Colleges was played at Pittsfield, Massachusetts; Amherst won, 73-22. The Amherst "thrower," Henry Hyde, pitched the first complete game in college history.

Despite the advent of the Civil War two years later, baseball, or base ball as it was generally written, proved almost uniformly popular among college students. Rules tended to vary. Indeed, the 1859 match between Amherst and Williams was played using the "Massachusetts rules:" 13 men on each side, a diamond of 60 feet, and a "thrower" only 25 yards from the batter. Over the next decade, New York Rules superceded the earlier version, and a game more comparable to that of modern baseball evolved. In general, the college game was to follow the same rules as later defined by professional teams.

The earliest college teams could more properly be defined as informal "clubs." Students elected officers whose jobs included record keeping as well as finding suitable opponents. While the eastern schools often played each other in natural rivalries, Harvard vs Williams in 1865 as one example, mid-western schools generally played teams from local clubs or organizations, and even from high schools. The popularity of the sport meant different classes—freshman, sophomore, etc., often had their own teams, and even Colleges or departments within the larger university might field their own teams. It wasn't long, given the issue of pride in defeating a worthy opponent, that a varsity "nine" would be formed.

In 1863, John Hinchman, former member of a Detroit baseball club, and Emory Grant ('66) organized the first team comprised of students at the University of Michigan. Grant ordered the necessary equipment, and with two other students, Oscar Bills ('65) and Edward Page ('66), was also instrumental in having a diamond laid out in the northeast area of the campus, near the present-day Diag. The University agreed to maintain the diamond for use by the students.

The following year, the University Base Ball Club was established, with Hinchman as president. Hinchman also served as captain and catcher for the squad. In 1866, a university team twice defeated the Ann Arbor Baseball Club, first by a score of 33-11, and again by 13-5. To complete its first "undefeated" season, Michigan also defeated a team from Jackson, 61-41. Such scores were far from unusual. A year later, the "blue and yellow" along with 70 "supporters" traveled to Detroit, where in a three-and-a-half hour game marked by six home runs, Michigan was victorious by a 70-18 score. Catcher George Dawson ('70) hit four of those home runs, and scored 11 runs for Michigan. The Detroit club had been considered state champions, and the Michigan team was justifiably proud of their triumph. Dawson later became the principal at Flint High School. Detroit had a measure of revenge later that fall. In a return match they defeated Michigan 36-20.

"What is the object of a college nine? The average college student does not take up base ball with an idea of following it as a profession; but weary with study, he seeks fresh air . . . by wielding the willow"
– Michigan Argonaut, *Feb. 16, 1884.*

In theory, members of sports teams were "student-athletes" in a literal sense. However, the popularity of the sport inevitably opened the way to betting on college games, and the occasional use of ringers or questionable "students" as part of the "nine:"

"The Amherst College senate threatened to withdraw the base ball nine from the league if betting on the game becomes as prevalent as it was last spring."
– Michigan Argonaut, *April 4, 1885*

"There is a probability that Taylor, the first baseman of the Louisville club who has been taking a course in the U of M law department, will cover first base for the Ann Arbor boys."
– U of M Daily, *May 7, 1891 (quote from the Detroit Tribune)*

The university during this period consisted of several departments or colleges, the identities of which fluctuated slightly over the decades: Medical, Law, Homeopathy (later divested) and Literary [Liberal] Arts and Engineering, a Dental College, and School of Pharmacy. Despite the professional degrees offered by each department, students were in effect considered undergraduates and could participate, if in good academic standing, in any sport. The varsity teams were often designated as the "Universities" in media references. Each department, and indeed each class, fielded their own teams in individual sports.

"Smoking will be prohibited in the grandstand; we hope to see it graced by larger numbers of young ladies; as it costs them nothing to enter there should be more in attendance."
– Michigan Argonaut, *May 3, 1890.*

"There is no prettier or more enjoyable sight in athletic circles than a crowd of collegians and their fair lady friends, attired in university colors [blue and yellow], and wildly cheering."
– U. of M. Daily, *May 7, 1891*

Enrollment during this period averaged some 2,500 students in the "universities", approximately a quarter of whom were women. Popularity of the sport among college women varied, but they were encouraged to attend and root for the team. While students in general paid an admission charge of 50 cents, or purchased through the Athletic Association ($1.00 for a membership) a season ticket which varied in cost from $2.00 to $2.50, women were admitted free to athletic events, at least until 1894. In that year, admission was first charged equally to women, though one or two "Ladies Days" still appeared on the schedule:

"The college woman is always the first to demand her rights, and wishes to enjoy all the privileges of the other sex. . . . Rights imply duties, and it is the duty . . . to lay aside feminine prejudices."
– U. of M. Daily, *April 26, 1894, in reference to the new admission charge.*

This is not to say student publications embraced full equality:

"Prof.: Give an example of a highly compressible solid.
Stud.: The female form."
– Michigan Argonaut, *March 7, 1885.*

In one area, however, the University was in the forefront of equal opportunity. African-Americans, while not in significant numbers, nevertheless constituted a proportion of the student body. Most notable among the athletes during this period were the Walker brothers: Moses Fleetwood and Welday. Each played on the varsity nine during the early 1880s. Each in turn went on to play professional baseball, Fleet Walker as a catcher with Toledo of the American Association, then a Major League, and Welday as an outfielder on the same team. Though neither graduated from the university, each was accepted as a member of the student body. Such was not always the situation at other schools:

"There has been a good deal of criticism about the exclusion from a recent Harvard University dinner here of colored graduates. There was a dinner tonight of alumni of the University of Michigan. . .

. Three of the alumni present were colored men. Thus Harvard was put to shame by the western university."

– New York Herald, *quoted in* Michigan Argonaut, *Feb. 28, 1885.*

While student managers and coaches during this era were unpaid, endorsements among the faculty were even then accepted as part of the norm, albeit with some modicum of acceptance:

"One of the professors at Yale is said to be worth a million dollars. So long as professors' salaries at the University of Michigan retain their present microscopic dimensions there is little danger of any member of our faculty attaining a similar distinction."

– Michigan Argonaut, *March 7, 1885.*

"When the professors of Michigan University *(sic) . . . give their official endorsements to soaps and baking powders, it is carrying matters a trifle too far."*

– Detroit News, *quoted in the Michigan Argonaut, April 4, 1885.*

The Argonaut's *response: "Not a little fame which every professor covets is to be acquired by having one's name on a baking product label."*

The "waxing and waning" of the popularity of base ball on campus could often be a concern; this was particularly true following the introduction of "foot ball" during the 1870s. In 1870, for example, the university team played only a single match, defeating a local club from Ann Arbor. As later pointed out within the student paper *The Michigan Chronicle* in the June 7, 1884 issue, teams were generally "organized in April, played until July, and disbanded.". It did not help that the manager, in addition to arranging transportation, as well as being an active member of the team, had to pay expenses from his own "pocket."

That there did exist a base ball club (on "paper") is attested in the student newspapers of the time; meetings were held and officers were elected. But actual matches depended upon the level of aggressiveness of the student manager. No team was formed in 1872, while an 1873 "nine" defeated the Mutuals of Jackson, 19-9. The 1873 squad was noted for another reason. Catcher Frank Bliss became the first Michigan player to advance to the Major Leagues when he appeared in two games in 1878 with Milwaukee of the National League

By 1882, the university nine began to expand its list of "usual opponents." While in previous years, local clubs such as the Jackson Mutuals, Detroit Aetnas or Kalamazoo Unas constituted the primary external opposition, the natural interest in college rivalries resulted in the periodic addition of other college nines to the schedule. That year Wisconsin, Racine and Northwestern were added to the schedule, with a May 20 match against Wisconsin representing the first intercollegiate competition for the university. The 20-8 victory over Wisconsin included a home run by Michigan's African-American catcher, Moses Fleetwood Walker. The rivalry resulted in the formation of the first conference in which Michigan would participate: the Inter-Collegiate Baseball League. Michigan was victorious in two matches against each (including a forfeit by Northwestern), becoming conference champion.

In 1884, Michigan Agricultural College, the forerunner to Michigan State, joined the schedule. In a June 14 match, the "universities" were victorious by a score of 13-3 behind the pitching of John Hibbard, and the hitting of third baseman Welday Walker. Walker went 4 for 5 that day, scoring four runs. That game is considered the first meeting between the Michigan schools. However, the game may actually have been a rematch from a contest earlier that month, won by the Lansing nine, 4-3. The teams met twice in 1887. M.A.C. defeated Michigan: 9-8 on April 29 (opening day), and again on June 11, by a score of 11-9. M.A.C. captain and pitcher Don Yerkes pitched all 18 innings in Michigan's two defeats. But Michigan would defeat the "farmers" eight consecutive times before M.A.C. won again, in 1903. The list of Michigan victories included a 19-5 punishment in 1890, in which the M.A.C. pitcher, Wheaton, was reportedly a professional who had previous experience with both the Muskegon and Saginaw Michigan League teams.

Despite some reluctance on the part of the faculty and administration, in 1890, the varsity embarked on an eastern trip, playing Cornell at Ithaca, and Colgate in Hamilton, New York.

"The crowd at the [Cornell] game was ungentlemanly, and indulged in such hooting and yelling as would shock us Ann Arborites."

– Michigan Argonaut, *May 24, 1890.*

The increased quality of the opposition also meant that self-regulated practice under the auspices of a student manager would no longer be sufficient to ensure a quality nine. In a move similar to that occurring throughout college sports, that year the university hired its first professional coach, Pete Conway, to oversee the team. Like most of the coaches hired at various colleges, Conway had been a professional. While the student manager still carried out most of the scheduling and arrangements for trips, it was the role of the coach to develop the abilities of the individual players.

Year	Won	Lost	Student Manager
1866	3	0	
1867	4	1	
1868	2	0	
1869–1871*			
1872	1	0	
1873	1	0	
1874*			
1875	2	2	
1876*			
1877	1	1	
1878	1	0	
1879*			
1880	2	4	
1881	3	3	
1882	10	3	
1883	3	3	
1884	8	1 (1 Tie)	
1885	3	1	
1886	5	2.	Rasch
1887	3	4	
1888	6	3 (1 Tie)	
1889	4	3	
1890	8	3	
1891	10	3	H. T. Abbott
1892	12	6 (1 Tie)	Ralph Stone
1893	14	4	H. G. Cleaveland
1894	11	8	George J. Cadwell
1895	19	3 (1 Tie)	E. C. Weeks

* No Complete Record Available

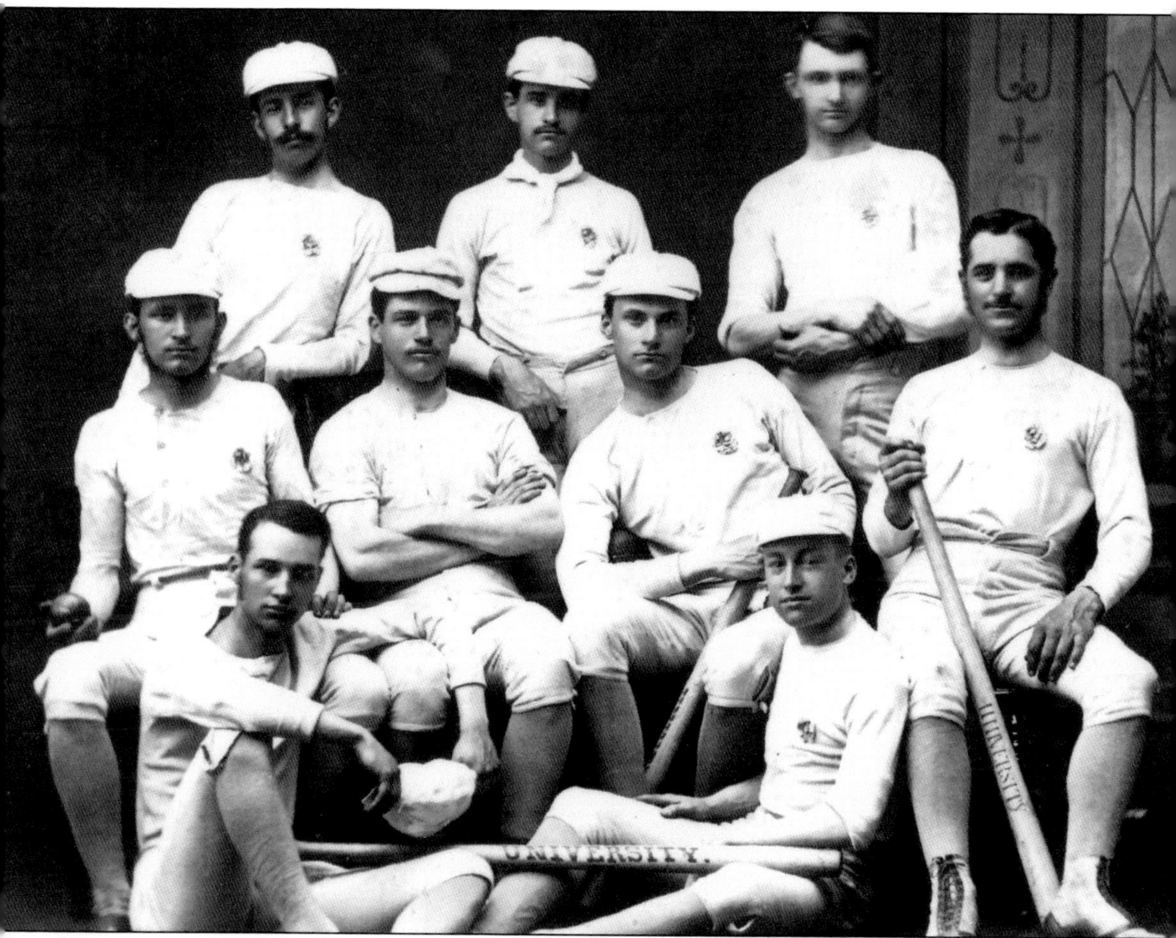

Pictured, from left to right, is the 1875 Michigan team: (front row) Frederick Stearns (2B), and William Johnson (RF); (middle row) George Abbott (P), Edgar Root (CF), Charles Burch (1B), and Oscar Shepardson (LF); (back row) Ogden Ferdon (3B), Willis Roberts (SS), and George Winslow (c). Prior to the season, the rules relating to pitching were altered, with elimination of "straight-arm" throwing. In addition, strikes could now be called on the batter even if he did not swing at a pitch. As a result, the number of runs per game was significantly reduced as compared with scores from previous years. During the season, the Michigan team finished with a record of 2-2, losing matches to the Aetnas of Detroit (7-6) and Mutuals of Jackson (7-5), while defeating the Aetnas in a second match (15-10). They also defeated the Unas of Kalamazoo, 5-2. Kalamazoo that year was considered among the best in the state, and the Michigan victory established the student team as among the contenders for that title. Several of these students also played with the Detroit Aetnas during their summer vacation, including at least one match with the professional White Stockings from Chicago. Fred Stearns (front left) attended the University from 1873–1876, but did not graduate, leaving to join his father's company. He did receive an honorary degree in 1901, reflecting his work in Detroit. During the mid-1880s, he became owner of the Detroit Wolverines, the moribund cellar dwelling team in the National League. Stearns was not averse to investing money in the team, and was rewarded with the league championship in 1887. Stearns also served as President of the Detroit Athletic Club, and was a noted musician for many years in the city. Stearns is perhaps best known as President (and son of the founder) of Frederick Stearns and Co., one of Detroit's most important pharmaceutical companies during the 19th century. Stearns died in 1924.

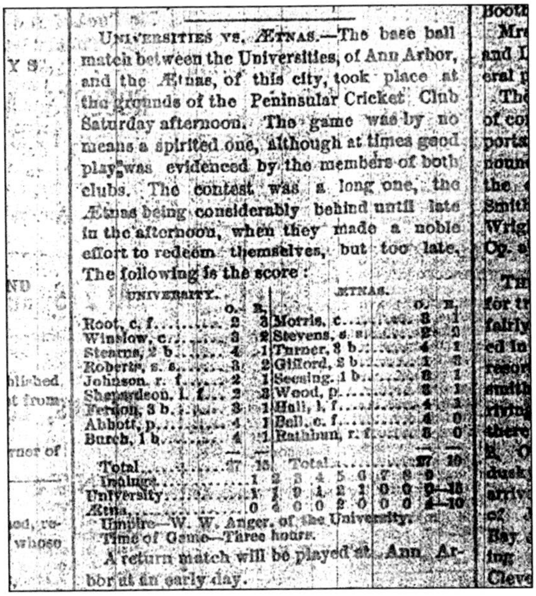

UNIVERSITIES vs. ÆTNAS.—The base ball match between the Universities, of Ann Arbor, and the Ætnas, of this city, took place at the grounds of the Peninsular Cricket Club Saturday afternoon. The game was by no means a spirited one, although at times good play was evidenced by the members of both clubs. The contest was a long one, the Ætnas being considerably behind until late in the afternoon, when they made a noble effort to redeem themselves, but too late. The following is the score:

UNIVERSITY.	O.	R.	ÆTNAS.	O.	R.
Root, c. f.	2	3	Morris, c.	3	1
Winslow, c.	3	2	Stevens, s. s.	2	2
Stearns, 2 b.	4	1	Turner, 3 b.	4	1
Roberts, s. s.	3	2	Gifford, 2 b.	1	3
Johnson, r. f.	2	1	Seesing, 1 b.	3	1
Sheppardson, l. f.	2	3	Wood, p.	3	1
Ferson, 3 b.	3	1	Hall, l. f.	4	1
Abbott, p.	4	1	Bell, c. f.	4	0
Burch, 1 b.	4	1	Rathbun, r. f.	3	0
Total	27	15	Total	27	10

Innings	1	2	3	4	5	6	7	8	9	
University	1	1	0	4	2	1	0	0	6	—15
Ætna	0	4	0	0	2	0	0	0	4	—10

Umpire—W. W. Anger, of the University.
Time of Game—Three hours.

A return match will be played at Ann Arbor at an early day.

The earliest known box score gives this May 29, 1875 description of a 15-10 victory over the Detroit Aetnas played at the Peninsular Cricket Club . Second baseman Fred Stearns would shortly leave the university to head the Stearns Pharmaceutical Company of Detroit. George Abbott ('75) pitched the entire three-hour game. The grounds were located between Cass and Woodward, behind the Whitney Mansion. Shortly, the Detroit Athletic Club would purchase the property for their first location in the city.

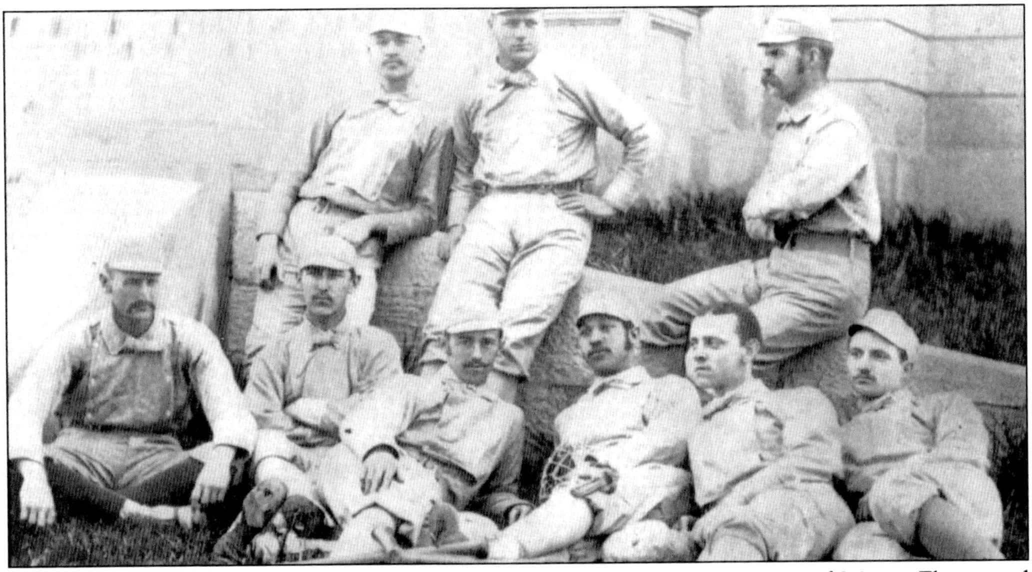

If for no other reason, the 1882 team was noteworthy for the presence of Moses Fleetwood Walker as catcher. Walker (front row, third from right) had recently transferred from Oberlin College in Ohio, becoming the first African-American to play sports at Michigan. During the winter prior to the start of the season, Michigan joined with Wisconsin, Northwestern and Racine to form the Intercollegiate Baseball League, a conference of western teams. The matches represented the first by Michigan with teams from other colleges. Albert Harvey (front left) was chosen captain. On May 20, Michigan defeated Wisconsin (20-8) in the first league match. Arthur Packard (left of Walker), also an Oberlin transfer, struck out eleven. On its western tour, Michigan twice defeated Racine. Wisconsin fell a second time, and Northwestern was beaten. With a later forfeit on the part of Northwestern, Michigan finished the conference season with a record of 6-0, and its first championship. Overall, the team had a record of 10-3. Michigan had originally planned on traveling east to play the champion of that region, but a lack of funds forced the plan to be canceled. (Courtesy of the Bentley Historical Library.)

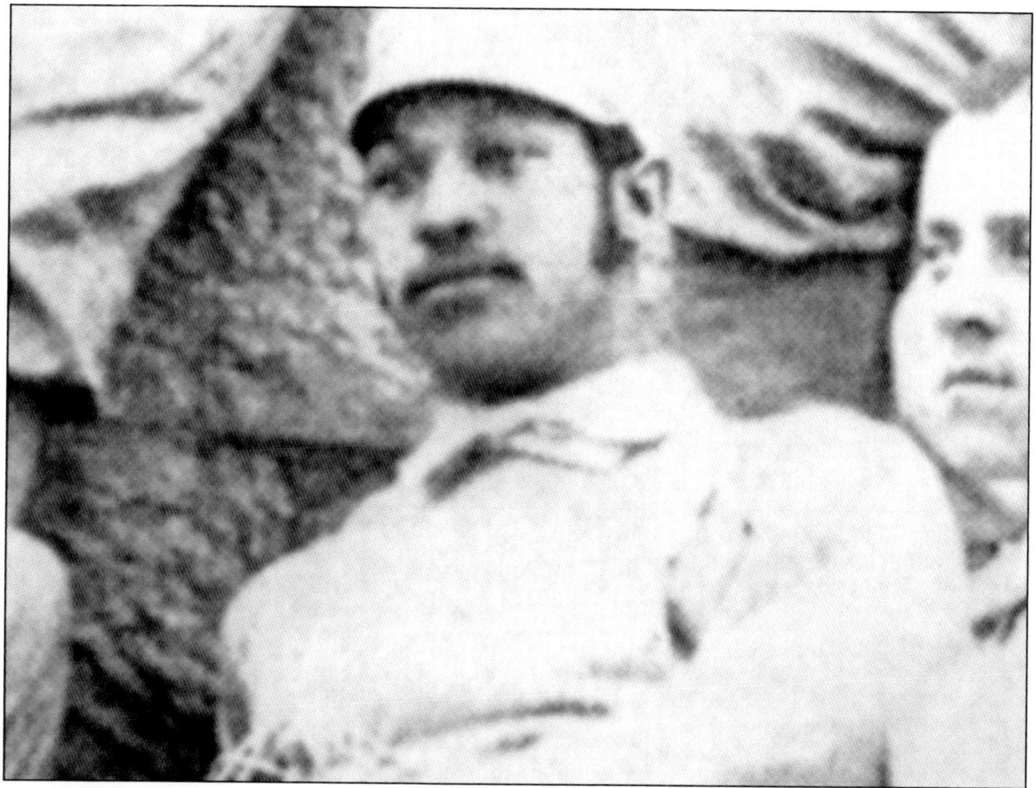

Moses Fleetwood Walker is the answer to the trivia question, "Who was the first African-American to play Major League baseball?" With his brother Welday, Walker played the 1884 season with the Toledo Blue Stockings of the American Association, then a Major League. Walker was born in Mt. Pleasant, Ohio, in 1856. In 1877, he enrolled at Oberlin College, becoming in 1881 a member of the school's first varsity inter-collegiate baseball team. Walker's hitting, as well as his impressive catching ability at a time in which protective equipment was minimal, quickly gained the attention of opponents. The reasons behind Walker's transfer to Michigan prior to the 1882 season are obscure. Michigan lacked a quality catcher, and Walker's play in a 9-2 victory for Oberlin over Michigan in the season finale may have been instrumental in the Michigan players convincing Walker to join the team. It was far from unusual for "ringers" and transfers to move from college to college during the period. In the biography of Walker written by David Zang, the author suggests more personal motives may have been behind Walker's move: his girlfriend became pregnant. Given Oberlin's rules on such actions, Walker may have found it more prudent to move to Ann Arbor, where he subsequently enrolled in Michigan's law school. Walker was not alone in transferring. Welday would subsequently follow, enrolling in Michigan's homeopathy school. Overall, Michigan went 10-3 that season, while winning the western conference championship. Walker hit .308 for the season, with 8 hits in 26 times at bat. At least two hits were home runs. In addition to marrying that summer, Walker became a professional. First playing with a team from Newcastle, Pennsylvania, and then at Toledo, Walker never seriously considered returning to Michigan to complete his degree requirements. In 42 games for Toledo in 1884, Walker batted .263. Walker's baseball career ended in 1889 with the Syracuse Stars. Restricted from organized baseball because of his color, Walker interned at several law offices before returning to Ohio where he worked for the postal service. Eventually he and Welday managed several movie theaters in Steubenville. Walker died in 1924. (Courtesy of the Bentley Historical Library.)

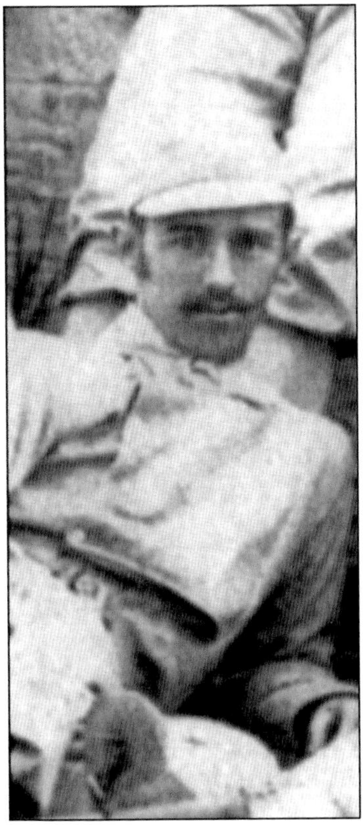

Walker's battery-mate from Oberlin, Arthur Packard, transferred as well. Much of what is known of Walker at Oberlin is found in Packard's diaries from the time. Like Walker, Packard was recruited by the Michigan players, and transferred to Michigan in time for the 1882 season. Ironically, in April 1882, Packard's pitching and Walker's home run led Michigan to victory over an Oberlin team. Packard's father was Congressman Jaspar Packard, a former general in the Civil War and a political power in Ohio. There is no question the father's influence played a role in the successful transfer of Packard, as well as the Walker brothers, Moses and Weldon, to Michigan. Eligibility rules for the time were flexible, to put it mildly. There are also hints in Packard's diaries of additional underlying reasons for the transfer besides Packard's athletic interest. Shortly after graduating in 1883, Packard moved first to Chicago, and then out west to the badlands of the Dakota Territory. He settled in the new town of Medora, where with the town's founder, The Marquis de Mores, and a local cowboy and future President, Theodore Roosevelt, he started a local newspaper, the *Bad Lands Cow Boy*. The *Cow Boy* would only be published through the end of 1886, when the office apparently was destroyed in an accidental fire. Following the loss of the paper, Packard temporarily moved to Montana. Eventually he returned to Chicago, becoming a sports editor for the *Chicago Evening Post*. Packard died in 1931. (Courtesy of the Bentley Historical Library.)

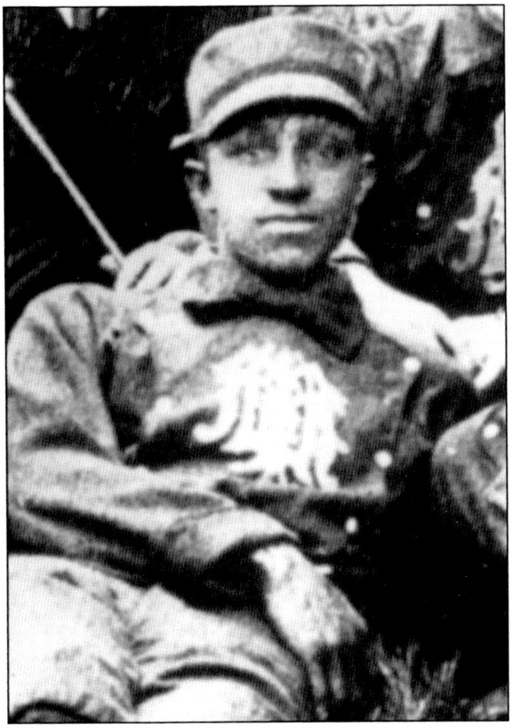

Following in the footsteps of his brother Fleet, Welday Walker initially enrolled at Oberlin College in Ohio, and then transferred to the University of Michigan in 1883. He played through the 1884 season, and again following his brother, joined the Toledo Blue Stockings of the American Association, at the time a second major league. The Walkers therefore represent the first African-Americans to play Major League baseball. Walker appeared in five games as an outfielder. He later played with the Akron team of the Ohio State league, and Cleveland of the Western League. Walker died in 1937, at the age of 78. (Courtesy of the Bentley Historical Library.)

Early box scores, like this one from the June 10, 1882 issue of *The Chronicle*, attest to the significant impact Moses Fleetwood Walker had while catching for Michigan. Michigan was undefeated in tournament play, though the expense of traveling resulted in withdrawal the following season. (Courtesy of *The Chronicle*.)

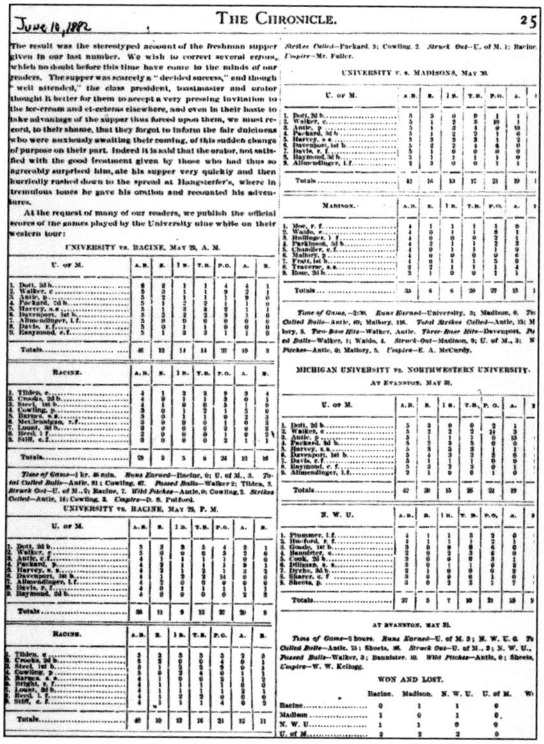

June 10, 1882

THE CHRONICLE. 25

The result was the stereotyped account of the freshman supper given in our last number. We wish to correct several errors, which no doubt before this time have come to the minds of our readers. The supper was scarcely a "decided success," and though "well attended," the class president, toastmaster and orator thought it better for them to accept a very pressing invitation to the ice-cream and et-ceteras elsewhere, and even in their haste to take advantage of the supper thus forced upon them, we must record, to their shame, that they forgot to inform the fair dulcineas who were anxiously awaiting their coming, of this sudden change of purpose on their part. Indeed it is said that the orator, not satisfied with the good treatment given by those who had thus so agreeably surprised him, ate his supper very quickly and then hurriedly rushed down to the spread at Hangsterfer's, where in tremulous tones he gave his oration and recounted his adventures.

At the request of many of our readers, we publish the official scores of the games played by the University nine while on their western tour:

UNIVERSITY vs. RACINE, MAY 29, A. M.

Time of Game—1 hr. 45 min. *Runs Earned*—Racine, 0; U. of M., 3. *Total Called Balls*—Antic, 81; Cowling, 67. *Passed Balls*—Walker 2; Tilden, 3. *Struck Out*—U. of M., 2; Racine, 7. *Wild Pitches*—Antic, 0; Cowling, 2. *Strikes Called*—Antic, 14; Cowling, 3. *Umpire*—D. S. Fulford.

UNIVERSITY vs. RACINE, MAY 29, P. M.

Strikes Called—Packard, 9; Cowling, 2. *Struck Out*—U. of M. 1; Racine. *Umpire*—Mr. Fuller.

UNIVERSITY vs. MADISONS, MAY 30.

Time of Game,—2:30. *Runs Earned*—University, 3; Madison, 0. *Total Called Balls*—Antic, 60; Mallory, 116. *Total Strikes Called*—Antic, 15; Mallory, 8. *Two-Base Hits*—Walker, Antic. *Three-Base Hits*—Davenport. *Passed Balls*—Walker, 1; Waldo, 4. *Struck-Out*—Madison, 9; U. of M., 3; *Wild Pitches*—Antic, 0; Mallory, 5. *Umpire*—E. A. McCurdy.

MICHIGAN UNIVERSITY vs. NORTHWESTERN UNIVERSITY.

AT EVANSTON, MAY 31.

AT EVANSTON, MAY 31.

Time of Game—2 hours. *Runs Earned*—U. of M. 3; N. W. U. 0. *Total Called Balls*—Antic, 75; Sheets, 96. *Struck Out*—U. of M., 3; N. W. U., [illegible] *Passed Balls*—Walker, 3; Bannister, 10. *Wild Pitches*—Antic, 0; Sheets, [illegible] *Umpire*—W. W. Kellogg.

WON AND LOST.

	Racine.	Madison.	N. W. U.	U. of M.
Racine	0	1	1	0
Madison	1	0	1	0
N. W. U.	1	1	0	0
U. of M.	2	2	2	0

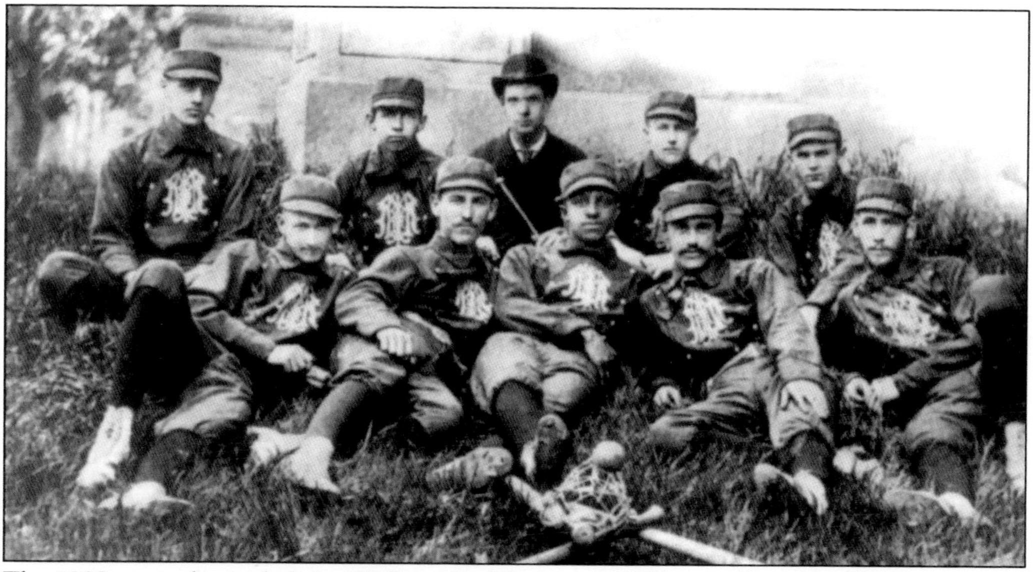

The 1883 team also included a Walker: third-baseman Welday Walker, Moses' brother (front row, center). In March, Michigan had withdrawn from the Western Collegiate League as a result of the difficulty in raising expenses. Competition for the season consisted of teams within a day's ride from Ann Arbor. After winning an exhibition against a local nine, Michigan opened their "regular" season with a 23-1 defeat of Adrian. The final record of 3-3 included a victory over the professional team from Toledo, 14-11, and two shutouts at the hands of the professionals from Port Huron. The man in the suit is Albert Miller, team manager, while Arthur Packard is to the right of Walker. (Courtesy of the Bentley Historical Library.)

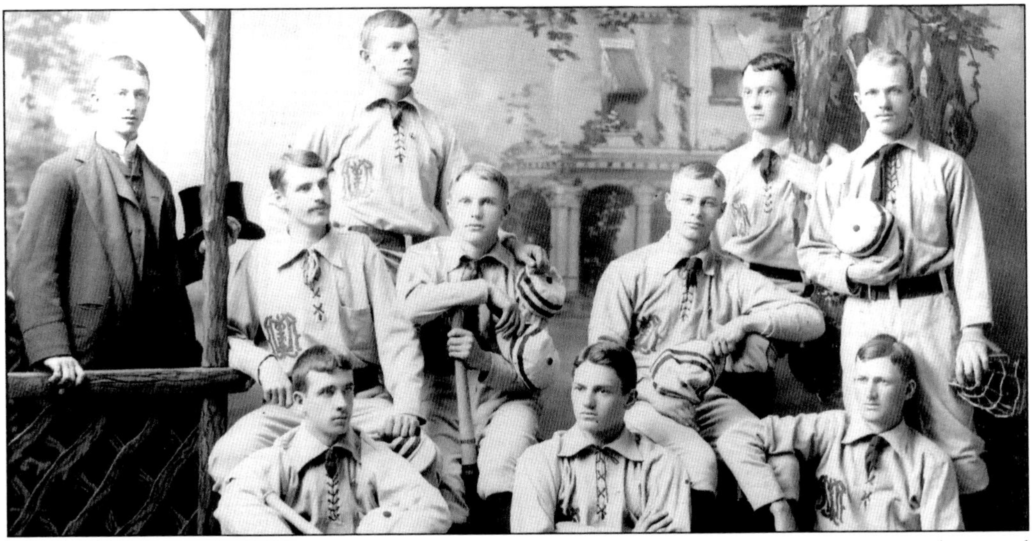

Pictured, from left to right, is the 1886 Michigan team: (front row) McDonell, McArthur, and McMillan; (middle row) Wilkinson, Miller, Smith, and unidentified; (back row) Rasch (mgr., in suit), Hibbard, (Unk.), and Muir. John Hibbard ('87) (standing, back left) was the primary pitcher for Michigan during his four years on the team (1884–1887), as well as being elected captain in both 1885 and 1886. At the time of his graduation, he was considered one of the "best players ever in the University." Few catchers "could successfully hold his swift pitching." Note the rudimentary equipment held by the catcher, Clifford Smith (standing, right). Ironically, by today's standard, Hibbard would have been considered a professional, having pitched in 1884 with the Chicago White Stockings. During this single season in the majors, Hibbard had a record of 1-1. Hibbard had a long career as a metallurgical engineer, dying in 1937 at age 72. The 1886 team had a record of 5-2, with a team batting average of .271, and a fielding average of .826. The leading hitter was second baseman Frank McDonell, with an average of .333. (Courtesy of the Bentley Historical Library.)

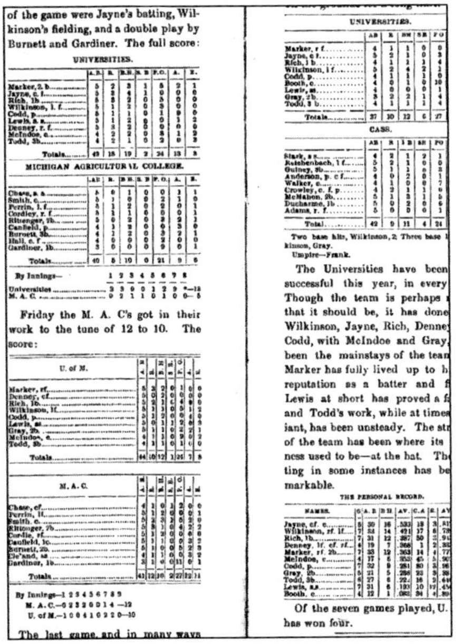

of the game were Jayne's batting, Wilkinson's fielding, and a double play by Burnett and Gardiner. The full score:

UNIVERSITIES.

	A.B.	R.	B.H.	S.B.	P.O.	A.	E.
Marker, 2 b.	5	2	3	1	5	2	1
Jayne, c. f.	5	2	4	1	0	0	0
Rich, 1b.	5	3	2	0	5	0	0
Wilkinson, l. f.	5	1	2	0	3	0	0
Codd, p.	5	1	1	0	1	9	0
Lewis, s. s.	5	1	2	0	0	1	2
Denney, r. f.	5	3	2	0	0	0	0
McIndoe, c.	4	2	2	0	8	1	2
Todd, 3b.	4	2	1	0	2	0	3
Totals	43	18	19	2	24	13	8

MICHIGAN AGRICULTURAL COLLEGE.

	A.B.	R.	B.H.	S.B.	P.O.	A.	E.
Chase, s. s.	5	0	1	0	0	1	1
Smith, c.	5	1	0	0	2	1	0
Perrin, l. f.	5	1	2	0	2	0	1
Cordley, r. f.	5	1	1	0	0	0	1
Rittenger, 2b.	5	0	2	0	3	2	1
Canfield, p.	4	1	2	0	0	3	0
Burnett, 3b.	4	1	2	0	3	2	1
Hall, c. f.	4	0	0	0	2	0	0
Gardiner, 1b.	3	0	0	0	9	0	1
Totals	40	5	10	0	21	9	6

By Innings—	1	2	3	4	5	6	7	8	
Universities	3	3	0	0	1	2	3	*	—12
M. A. C.	0	2	1	1	0	1	0	0	— 5

Friday the M. A. C's got in their work to the tune of 12 to 10. The score:

U. of M.	A.B.	R.	B.H.	S.B.	P.O.	A.	E.
Marker, rf.	5	3	2	0	1	0	0
Denney, cf.	5	0	2	0	0	0	0
Rich, 1b.	5	2	1	0	4	0	0
Wilkinson, lf.	5	1	1	0	5	1	2
Codd, p.	5	1	2	0	0	4	0
Lewis, ss.	5	0	1	1	2	0	3
Gray, 2b.	5	1	1	0	2	2	1
McIndoe, c.	4	1	1	0	9	0	2
Todd, 3b.	4	1	1	0	1	0	0
Totals	44	10	12	1	25	7	8

M. A. C.	A.B.	R.	B.H.	S.B.	P.O.	A.	E.
Chase, cf.	4	1	0	1	2	0	0
Perrin, lf.	5	1	2	0	0	0	1
Smith, c.	5	2	3	1	5	2	0
Rittenger, 2b.	5	3	1	0	4	2	2
Cordle, rf.	5	1	2	0	0	0	0
Canfield, 1c.	5	1	1	0	0	3	2
Burnett, 3b.	5	1	0	0	5	2	3
Cleland, ss.	4	1	1	0	0	3	2
Gardiner, 1b.	3	1	0	0	11	0	1
Totals	43	12	10	2	27	12	11

By Innings—1 2 3 4 5 6 7 8 9
M. A. C.—0 2 3 2 0 0 1 4 —12
U. of M.—1 0 0 4 1 0 2 2 0—10

The last game, and in many ways

UNIVERSITIES.

	AB	R	BH	SB	PO
Marker, r f.	4	1	1	0	0
Jayne, c f.	5	2	1	0	3
Rich, 1 b.	4	1	1	1	4
Wilkinson, l f.	5	2	4	2	1
Codd, p.	4	1	1	1	0
Booth, c.	4	0	1	0	10
Lewis, ss.	4	0	0	0	1
Gray, 2 b.	3	2	2	1	4
Todd, 3 b.	4	1	1	1	4
Totals	37	10	12	6	27

CASS.

	AB	R	1B	SB	PO
Stark, s s.	4	2	1	2	1
Reichenbach, l f.	5	2	1	0	0
Guiney, 3b.	5	1	1	0	3
Anderson, p. c f.	4	0	2	0	1
Walker, c.	4	1	0	0	7
Crowley, c. f. p.	4	2	1	1	0
McMahon, 2b.	5	1	3	1	5
Ducharme, 1b.	5	0	2	0	6
Adams, r. f.	5	0	0	0	1
Total	42	9	11	4	24

Two base hits, Wilkinson, 2; Three base [illegible] kinson, Gray.
Umpire—Frank.

The Universities have been successful this year, in every [illegible] Though the team is perhaps [illegible] that it should be, it has done [illegible] Wilkinson, Jayne, Rich, Denne[illegible] Codd, with McIndoe and Gray, [illegible] been the mainstays of the tea[illegible] Marker has fully lived up to h[illegible] reputation as a batter and f[illegible] Lewis at short has proved a f[illegible] and Todd's work, while at times [illegible]iant, has been unsteady. The str[illegible] of the team has been where its [illegible]ness used to be—at the bat. Th[illegible]ting in some instances has be[illegible]markable.

THE PERSONAL RECORD.

NAMES.	G	A. B	B H	AV.	C.A	E.	AV
Jayne, cf. c.	8	30	16	.533	13	3	.81
Wilkinson, rf. lf.	7	33	14	.421	37	6	.78
Rich, 1b.	7	31	12	.387	50	3	.9[illegible]
Denney, lf. cf. rf.	4	19	7	.368	1	2	.3[illegible]
Marker, rf. 2b.	7	33	12	.363	14	4	.77
McIndoe, c.	4	17	6	.352	45	5	.90
Codd, p.	7	32	9	.281	80	3	.96
Gray, 2b.	5	21	5	.238	23	3	.88
Todd, 3b.	6	27	6	.222	16	2	.64
Lewis, ss.	7	31	6	.193	10	17	.45
Booth, c.	4	12	1	.083	24	4	.8[illegible]

Of the seven games played, U. has won four.

These box scores and descriptions are of several 1889 matches, including two with the Michigan Agricultural College, forerunner of Michigan State. Pitcher George Codd, future Detroit mayor and judge, won two of the three games. (Following graduation from the University with a degree in Law, Codd began his practice in Detroit in 1893. He became a member of the Board of Alderman in 1902, and Mayor of Detroit in 1905–1906. Codd later served as Regent of the University of Michigan, and was twice elected circuit judge, a position he held until his death in 1927.) As can be seen in the "Personal record," he also batted .281 for the season. Outfielder and catcher Trafford Jayne led the team with a .533 average. Outfielder Thomas Wilkinson batted .424, and was also manager of the football team that fall. As a whole, the team averaged .328 for the season, nearly as high as the team fielding average of .846. (Courtesy of the *Michigan Argonaut*.)

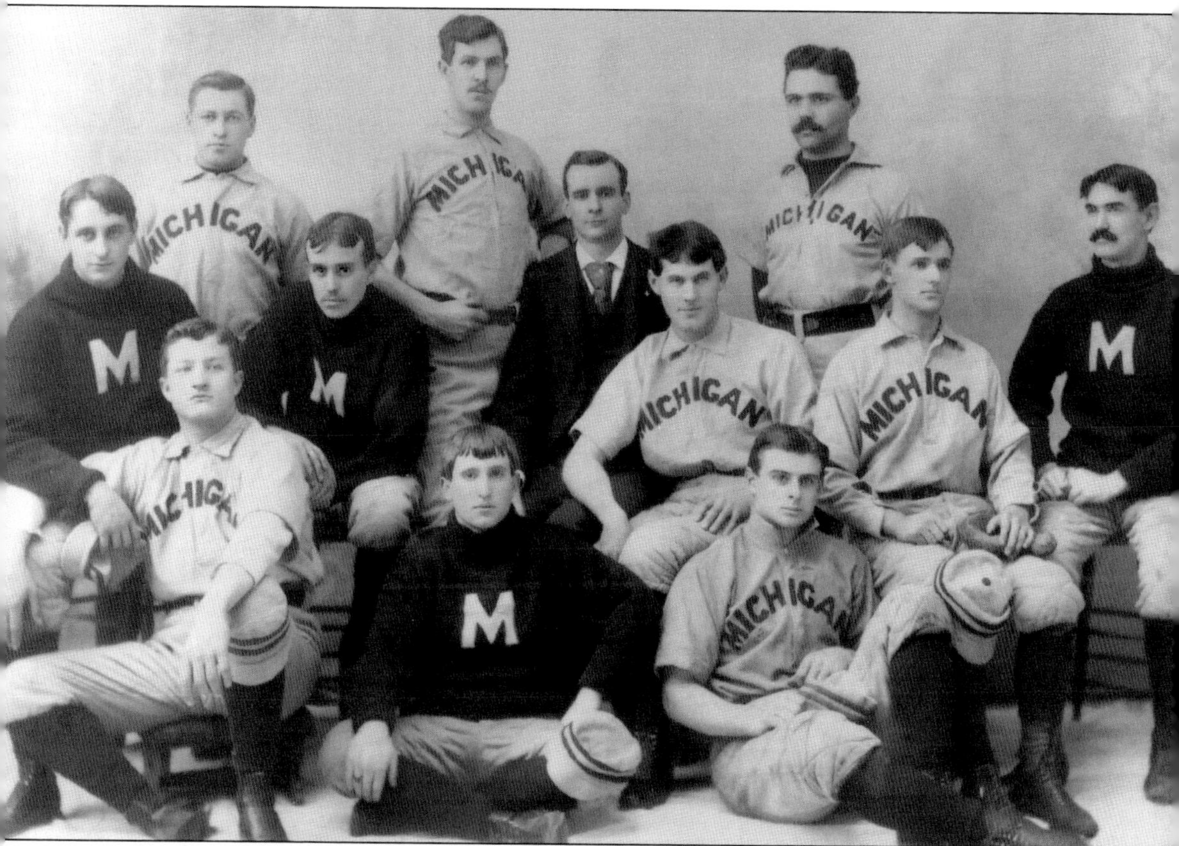

Pictured, from left to right, is the 1892 Michigan team: (front row) Spurney (2B), Pepple (3B), and Shields (CF); (middle row) Smeltzer (LF, C), Codd (P), Stone (mgr.), Robinson (P, OF), Crawford (P), and Seymour (P, IF); (top row) Spitzer (SS), Jeffries (1B), and Pearson (3B). For the second season in a row, Pete Conway served as coach. Of the twenty matches played by Michigan during the season, sixteen were competitions with other colleges. Michigan won eleven of those. The team carried out two extended trips, one to the West and one to the East. Most notable among these matches with other colleges were victories over Wisconsin (7-4) and Yale (3-2). In turn, Michigan was defeated by Eastern powerhouses Harvard (4-2) and Princeton (9-4). Three contests were held with the Detroit Athletic Club (D.A.C), including one later in the fall of the year; the D.A.C. won twice, and a third ended in a tie. The final season record for Michigan was 12-7-1. Sherman Spitzer led the team with a .315 average, while Frank Bowerman (C, not pictured) hit .305. Bowerman did not graduate from the University, but later gained fame as the favorite catcher of New York Giants great Christy Mathewson. George Codd (second from left, middle row) was finishing a long career at Michigan. Some considered him the equal of Amos Alonzo Stagg of Yale as the outstanding pitcher in the college ranks. Codd first came to public notice in June 1889, when he struck out 18 in a 25-1 victory over the Owashtonong club of Grand Rapids. Typical of the fluid nature in college sports of the time, Codd spent part of several seasons with the D.A.C., where he "practically won the championship" for that semi-professional team in 1890. He rejoined Michigan on May 19, in time for the eastern trip. The *University of Michigan Daily* reported in its April 27 issue, the formation of a Western Inter-Collegiate Athletic Association, consisting of Michigan, Minnesota, Wisconsin and Northwestern. Ralph Stone (middle row, in suit) was elected President. Another first occurred on April 30 of that year, as Michigan played their first game on the new diamond at Regents' Field. (Courtesy of the Bentley Historical Library.)

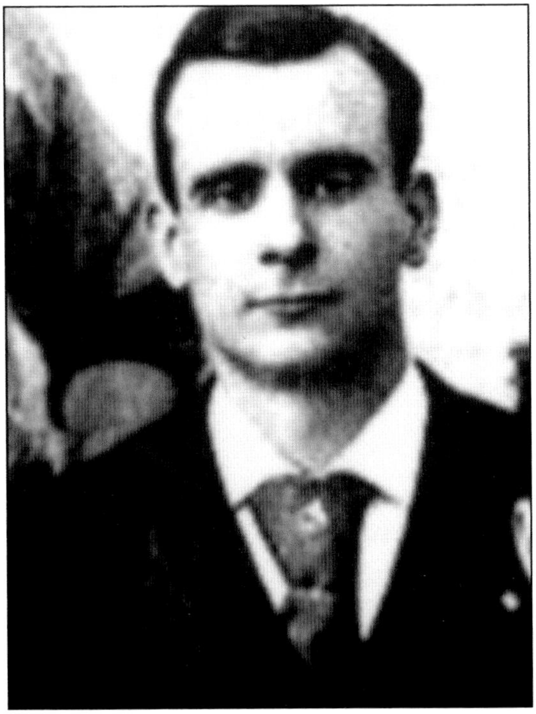

Ralph Stone was graduated from Swarthmore College in Delaware in 1889. While at Swarthmore, Stone competed in football and track, as well as in baseball. In 1890, he entered Michigan to pursue a degree in law, which he earned in 1892. That year he also served as the student baseball manager. Stone was instrumental in the drafting of the constitution of the Athletic Association, the successor to various sports associations at the University. He also helped found the *University of Michigan Daily*, serving as managing editor, as well as serving as Editor-in-Chief of the *Michigan Law Journal*. After graduation, Stone set up a practice in Detroit. There he was an organizer, and later President, of the Detroit Bureau of Governmental Research. Stone served as a Regent for 16 years for the University of Michigan, retiring in 1940. Stone died in 1956, at the age of 88. (Courtesy of *Palladium*.)

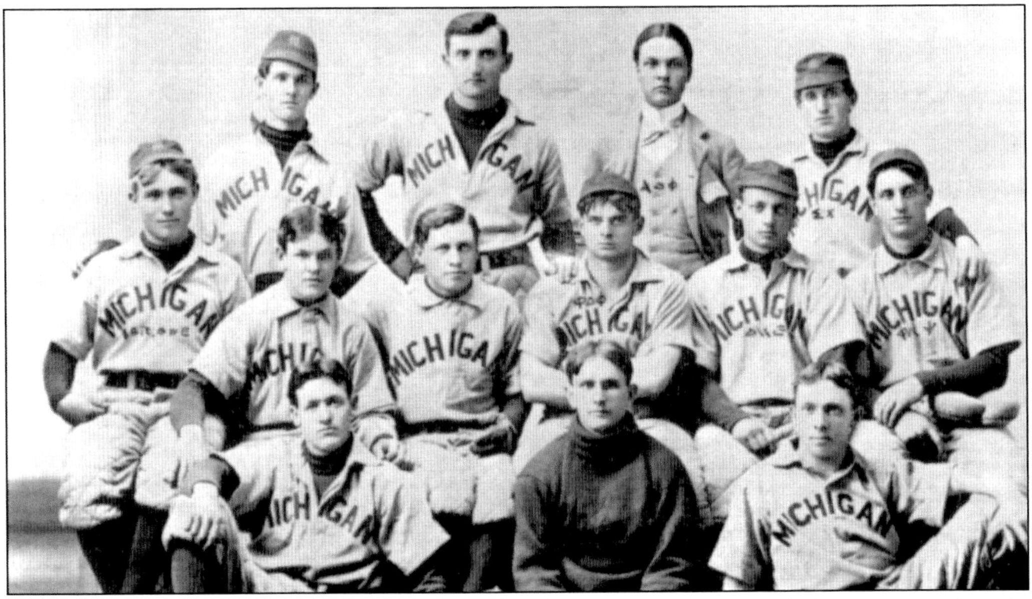

The 1894 Michigan team, with George J. Cadwell (top, second from right) as manager/coach, and centerfielder Edmund Shields (middle, third from right) as captain, finished with an 11-8 record. Michigan distinguished itself when playing opposition from the west (Ohio, Illinois and Wisconsin), but proved unable to defeat any of its eastern opposition: Vermont, Dartmouth, Harvard and Princeton, against whom it suffered a 21-4 defeat. Michigan did defeat Chicago by a score of 3-2, marking the first in a long series of matches between the two schools. Cadwell served as manager only the single season, graduating with a degree in pharmacy that year. Cadwell died in 1928. (Courtesy of *Palladium*.)

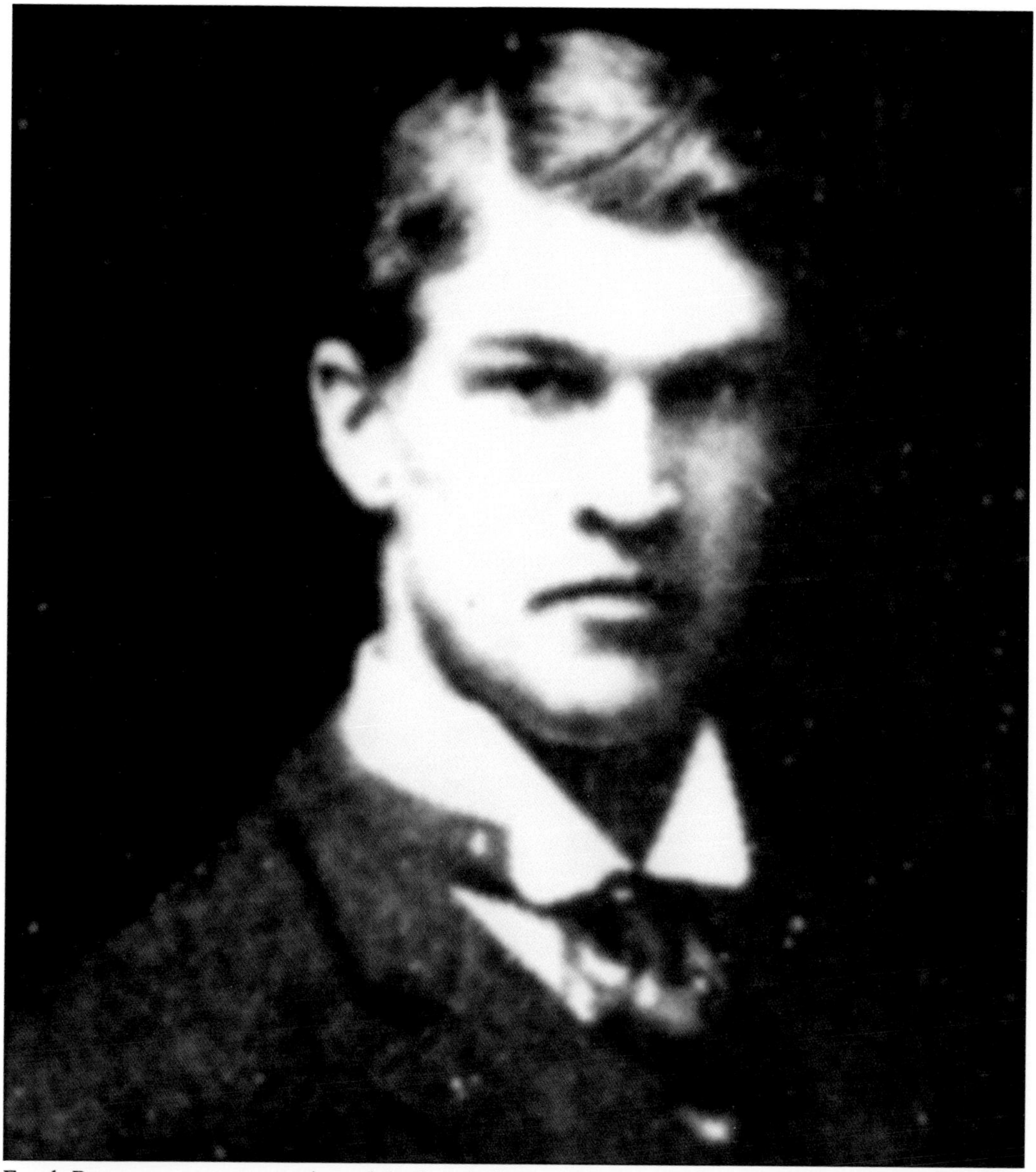

Frank Bowerman was a member of the baseball team for one season at Michigan (1892), during which he played several positions: pitcher, catcher and centerfield. The following year, he joined the Detroit Athletic Club, catching for the team that considered itself the "world amateur champion." Bowerman was a large man for his time (6'2"), and was considered one of the toughest catchers in professional baseball during a period in which use of protective equipment was the exception. After several seasons with the National League Baltimore Orioles, Bowerman moved to John McGraw's New York Giants. He was a member of that team from 1900–1907, and was considered to be Christy Mathewson's "favorite catcher." In later life, Bowerman told the story of how he "discovered Matty," a tale which may have gained additional credence in the memory of an old man. Bowerman finished his major league career with the Boston Braves. Following several seasons with minor league teams in Indianapolis and Kansas City, he retired from baseball. His later life was spent as a fruit farmer near Romeo, Michigan. Bowerman died in 1948. (Courtesy of the National Baseball Hall of Fame and Library.)

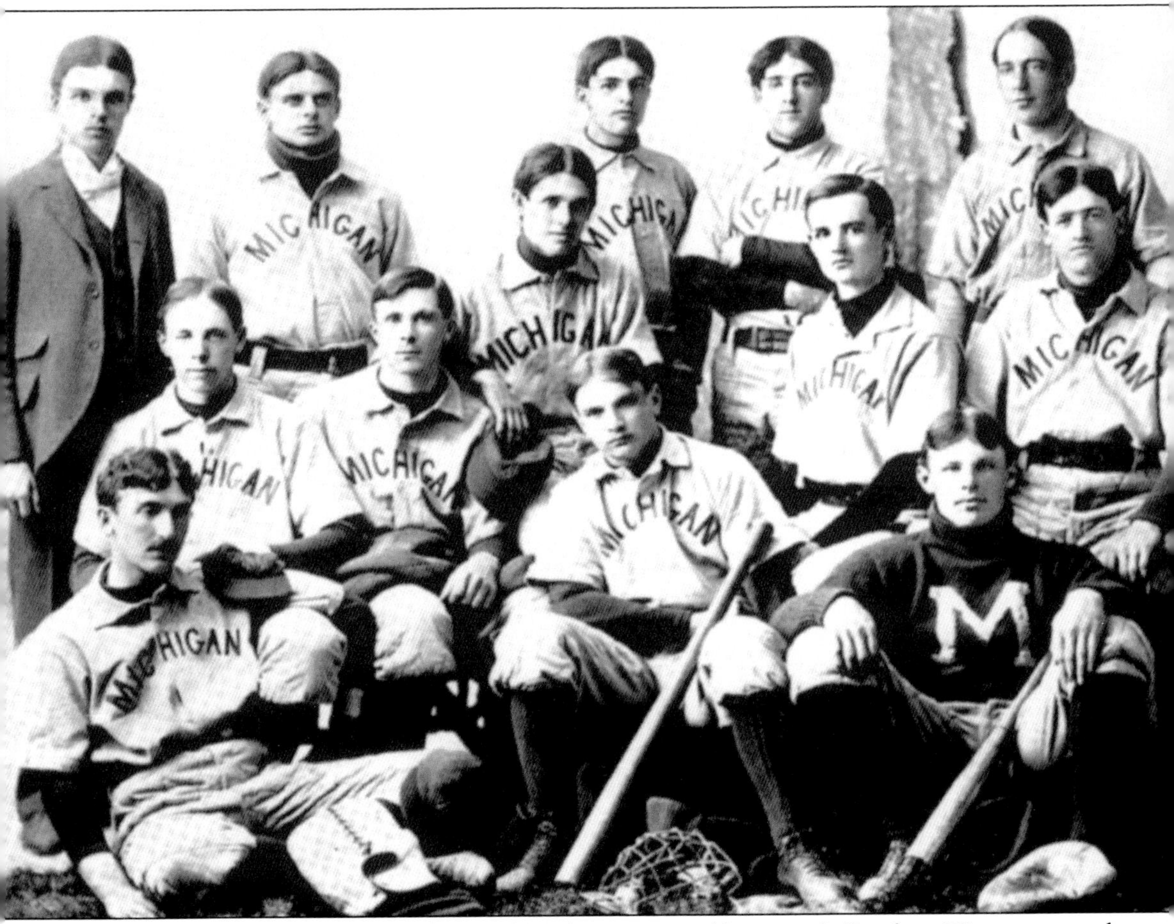

Pictured, from left to right, is the 1895 Michigan team: (front row) Condon, Waterman, and Bloomingston; (middle row) McKenzie, Watkins, Russell, Miller, and Deans; (back row) Weeks, Shields, Gallup, Sexton, and Holmes. Edward Weeks (top left) served as manager for the team in the absence of a full time coach. Edmund Shields was elected captain for the second consecutive year. The 1895 team was one of the stronger baseball squads that represented Michigan. Prior to the start of the season, the Board in Control of Athletics, which oversaw Michigan sports, allowed weekday games to take place. As a result, the number of teams scheduled increased from that found in previous years. The team finished with a record of 19-3-1, losing to Cornell from the east, and splitting with Chicago. They also lost an 18-17 slugfest to a semi-professional Detroit squad that was a member of the Western League. An April 20 tie with Illinois was highlighted by a dispute in the 9th inning. Umpire Arms called an Illinois runner safe. When Michigan could not resolve the argument to their satisfaction, they left the field. Michigan's 6-4 victory over Chicago represented the final game of the season. Since the two colleges had split the series, Amos Alonzo Stagg, Chicago's legendary coach, suggested to Weeks that the teams play a third time to decide the "Championship of the West." However, Weeks declined and the season ended with Michigan's best record to that date. (Courtesy of *Palladium*.)

Two

From Manager to Coach

Conway to Lowe

The growing popularity of base ball on college campuses inevitably led to a desire for an increased level of competition. Schedules were expanded, not only in the specific number of matches carried out by the varsity team, but in the expansion of the competition to include other colleges or professional clubs from other cities. "Road trips," while if not embraced by the faculty, were at least tolerated with the stipulation that students would maintain their grades.

"After the team was selected, no pain was spared to put the team in the best possible shape to show expert scholars of Harvard and Yale how real live persons from the west play ball. [H.T. Abbott, Manager] hopes to arrange a date with Cap Anson's [Chicago] Colts.

– U. of M. Daily, *January 28, 1891.*

Prior to the 1890s, Michigan base ball teams were led primarily by student managers. Generally, these men used their spare time to sell tickets, arrange schedules and travel arrangements, and in general prepare the squad of fifteen to twenty for practices and games.

Increasingly however, colleges hired professional players to serve as coaches to train the players for the greater degree of competition. Among the first was Northwestern, which in 1881, hired Billy Sunday, outfielder of the Chicago National League club, and future evangelist, as coach; the following year Princeton hired John Montgomery Ward as that college's first base ball coach. Tony Mullane of the Baltimore Orioles was hired at the University of Virginia. Professional coaches soon became the norm. In some instances, the coach was even able, perhaps encouraged, to enroll in classes at the same time; though noted primarily for their managerial talents, Hall of Fame members John McGraw and Hugh Jennings both coached and enrolled in classes at St. Bonaventure during the 1890s.

Apparently on the recommendation of Manager Adrian "Cap" Anson of the National League Chicago Colts, ancestor of the modern Cubs, Abbott attempted to hire either Billy Sunday from the Colts, or Charlie Bennett, a local product who had a long career as catcher for Detroit, then in the National League. Charlie Comiskey, recent member of the Chicago Player's League club, was also reportedly a candidate. None accepted any offer. The position as first official coach at Michigan was filled by Pete Conway in 1891.

Conway had been a pitcher and utility outfielder with several Major League teams. He was a thirty-game winner with Detroit in 1888, accounting for approximately half of his total sixty-one career victories. Arm problems had ended his professional career; serving as a college coach allowed him to remain associated with the game. Typical of most college coaches during this period, Conway arrived early in April, 1891, towards the end of spring practice. He remained until the end of May, covering most of the actual season. The efforts of Coach Conway were evident, as the team finished with a record of 10-3, including victories over Harvard, 4-3, and Cornell, 8-6; the team was shut out by Yale, however, 2-0.

Conway remained as coach for two seasons, to be replaced by H.G. Cleaveland in 1893. Whether Cleaveland's official position was that of coach is unclear from contemporary sources, as he is referred to only as Manager. That he was a local product is attested by his later position as head of the athletic board for the school.

For more than a decade, the Michigan coaching position could be likened to a revolving door, as coaches rarely stayed more than a year or two. Cleaveland was succeeded as manager by George J. Cadwell. Cadwell also served as a substitute player when necessary.

In 1896, Frank Sexton was hired for the first of what would be three years as coach, with an intervening period of five years. Sexton had been a pitcher at Brown University prior to a short career with Boston of the National League; Fred C. Tenney, arguably one of the better first basemen of his era, had earlier served as Sexton's catcher at both Brown and Boston. Sexton's primary purpose in coming to Ann Arbor was to enroll in courses leading to a medical degree, but his professional experience was the primary factor in becoming the new coach.

On occasion, Sexton served as umpire for the college match if a regular arbiter was unavailable. On at least one occasion, this resulted in a serious dispute. On April 17, 1896, in a game against Indiana, the score after 7 innings was an 11-11 tie. The Indiana players, and their local umpire, called the game because of darkness. Sexton, serving as a second umpire, ordered the game continued, and when the Indiana players left the field, awarded a forfeit to Michigan. Back at the hotel, a man attacked Sexton with a cane; Sexton's response was to grab him by the throat. A warrant was sworn, but Sexton left. William Holmes, catcher and team captain, was identified by the Indiana captain as Sexton, arrested and held overnight in jail. Perhaps due to a threatened $10,000 lawsuit, charges against Holmes were dropped.

On at least one occasion, Coach Sexton pitched for the Michigan squad; again Holmes was the center of the controversy. In a June, 1896, match against Chicago, Holmes was initially tossed from the game due to abusive language directed against Stage, the umpire, resulting from a call made at first base. Despite the fact Holmes was later allowed to continue in that game, the Michigan athletic board of control barred Holmes from further competition. To complicate matters for the team, both John Bloomingston the second baseman, and Joseph Lowney, the shortstop, were banned from the team because they had "played for compensation at Flint and Saginaw the previous week." As a result, the team was short handed. In the June 10 match with the Detroit Athletic Club, both the competition and the board of control allowed Sexton to take the mound for Michigan. It would appear that Sexton's best years as pitcher were behind him, as the final score was an 11-11 tie.

Following his short experience at Michigan, Sexton would serve as baseball coach at his alma mater Brown for twelve years, and at Harvard for five.

While most hired coaches were either active or retired professionals, at least one during this era was neither. Charles Watkins was hired in 1897, in part as a result of his being a "Michigan man," a former pitcher and 1896 graduate of the university. On one occasion, an April 17 match with the Detroit Athletic Club, Watkins appeared on the mound. Watkins would remain either as head coach, or as an assistant through 1901, the longest tenure of anyone during this time.

The popular Frank Sexton returned for two seasons (1901–1902). But by this time, Sexton had earned his medical degree, and had an established practice in Boston. Despite only serving as coach from April to the beginning of June each season, Sexton felt his practice was the more important job, and he returned to that city permanently after the 1902 season. To replace Sexton, another former pitcher, Rudolph "Skel" Roach, was hired for the 1903 season.

The most recognizable Michigan coach during this period was Robert (Bobby) Lowe. Lowe's principle claim to notoriety came in 1894, when he became the first player to hit four home runs in a game. By 1907, it became apparent that his career as an active ballplayer was approaching an end. He spent that year coaching Michigan baseball, finishing his Major League career with Detroit in 1908.

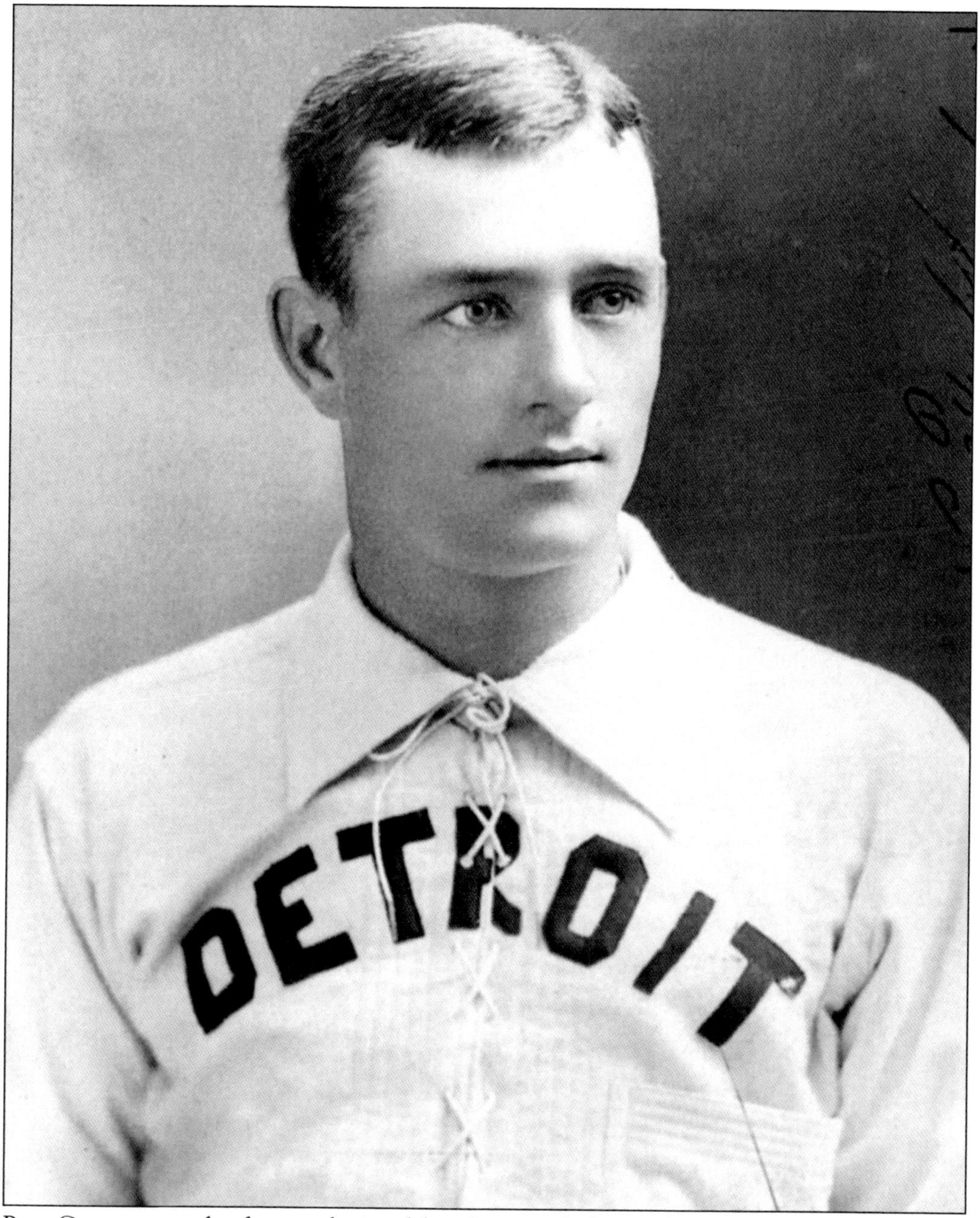

Pete Conway was the first professional hired as coach for Michigan Baseball (1891–1892). Conway had been a pitcher for several professional teams from 1885–1889: Buffalo, Kansas City, Detroit and Pittsburg, teams in the fledgling National League. His career totals by 1889 were 61-61. But arm trouble coupled with a contract dispute regarding his jumping to the new Players League brought a finish to Conway's major league career. In his two years as Michigan coach, the team record was 22-9-1. Conway's tenure was not significant in itself, as he was only present from mid-April to June each season. But it signified a growing commitment in college baseball to expand the sport from club play to one involving legitimate competition. (Courtesy of the National Baseball Hall of Fame and Museum.)

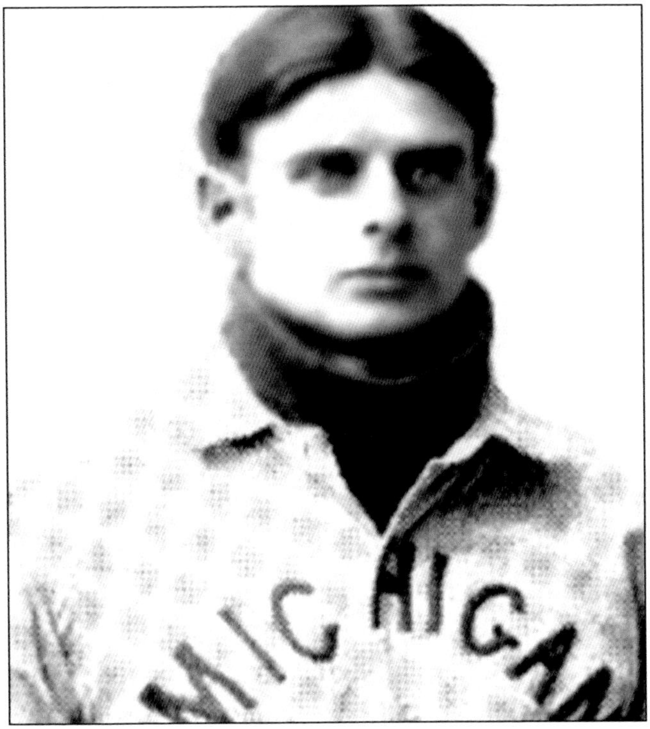

Edmund Claude Shields played centerfield from 1892–1896, rules being more flexible with regard to years of eligibility during that era. In both 1894 and 1895, he was elected captain. The following year he became student manager under Coach Frank Sexton, graduating that spring of '96 with a degree in law. In later years, Shields became a prominent attorney in the state capital at Lansing, as well as a power in state politics. He served as a delegate or alternate to the democratic Convention eight times between 1912 and 1944, as well as serving on the University Board of Regents from 1933–1935 and 1938–1945. Shields died in 1947. (Courtesy of *Palladium*.)

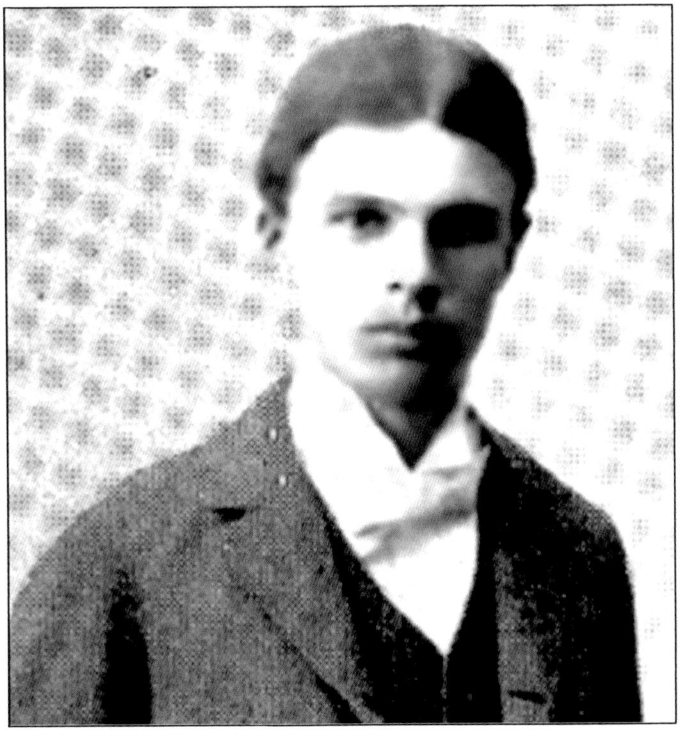

Edward Chester Weeks (right) served as manager and coach for the 1895 team, graduating that year with a degree in pharmacy. Weeks died in 1961. Pete Conway (1891–1892) and Frank Sexton (1896) were professional players and coaches hired to prepare their respective Michigan squads for competition with stronger opposition than that faced in the 1880s. In the interim, Holbrook Cleaveland (1893), George Cadwell (1894) and Weeks (1895), students at the university, carried out the jobs of preparing schedules and serving as *de facto* coaches. (Courtesy of *Palladium*.)

An 1896 graduate with a degree in Pharmacy, Charles F. Watkins both pitched and played an occasional right field for the 1895 and 1896 squads. Charles Baird, Manager of Athletics, felt "Watty's" popularity and previous strong influence on the team, as well as his being a "Michigan man," would make him an excellent baseball coach. As a player, Watkins had been a "crack pitcher" as well as exhibiting all-around baseball talent. Watkins' appointment was only one example of the wholesale changes being made by the Athletic Board. Rather than importing eastern coaches, as had been the case following implementation of expanded schedules earlier in the decade, coaching in all sports at the University would subsequently be carried out by recent graduates. Watkins served as baseball coach during the 1897, 1898 and 1900 seasons, finishing with a record of 31-23-1. He received a medical degree from Michigan in 1901, and set up practice in Montana. Walkins died in 1936. (Courtesy of the *Michiganensian*.)

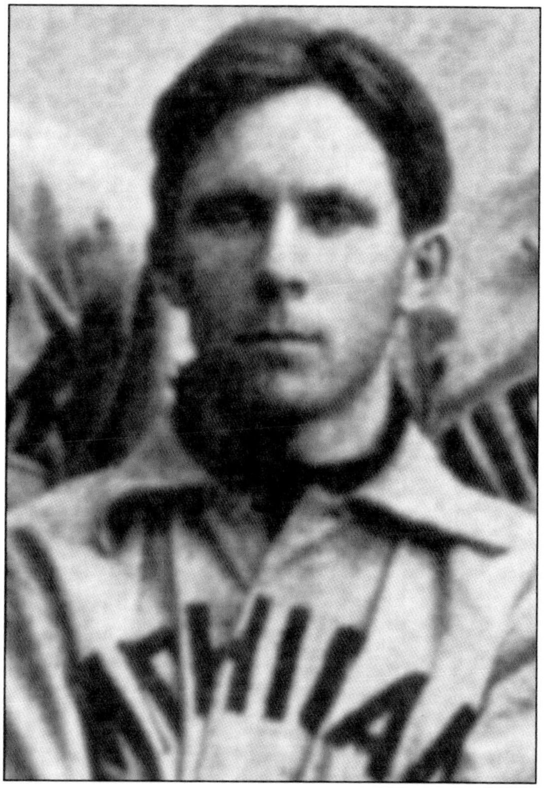

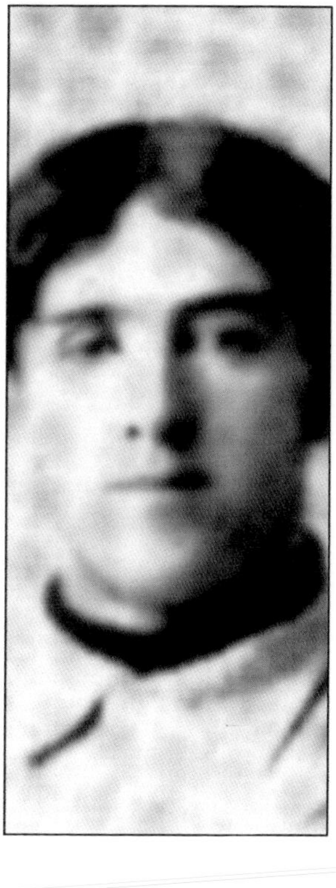

Frank Sexton originally matriculated at Brown University, where he was a pitcher on the baseball team. Fred Tenney, later reaching prominence as a first baseman with Boston, was Sexton's catcher at Brown. Interested in a medical career, Sexton transferred to Michigan in time for the 1895 season, earning a letter with the Michigan baseball squad. As a pitcher, Sexton was most noted for an 11-0 shutout he pitched against Cornell, avenging a defeat from the previous year. E.C. Shields, center fielder and captain for the team, considered this game the "most satisfactory moment" of his [Shields'] career, and that the team was the best Michigan ever had. That summer, Sexton signed with Boston of the National League, winning one of six decisions in his only season in the "Majors." It is believed Sexton may have played professionally for several clubs under an assumed name. Sexton returned to Michigan in 1896 to continue his medical training, at the same time agreeing to serve as baseball coach to earn expenses. That first year, 1896, Michigan compiled a record of 17-4-1, finishing second in conference play. Sexton completed two years of medical training at Michigan, later obtaining his medical degree at the University of Pennsylvania. He returned to Michigan as coach for both the 1901 and 1902 seasons. Following the expiration of his contract on June 1, 1902, Sexton returned to Boston where he resumed his medical practice. He later served as baseball coach at both Brown and Harvard. Sexton died in 1938. (Courtesy of *Palladium*.)

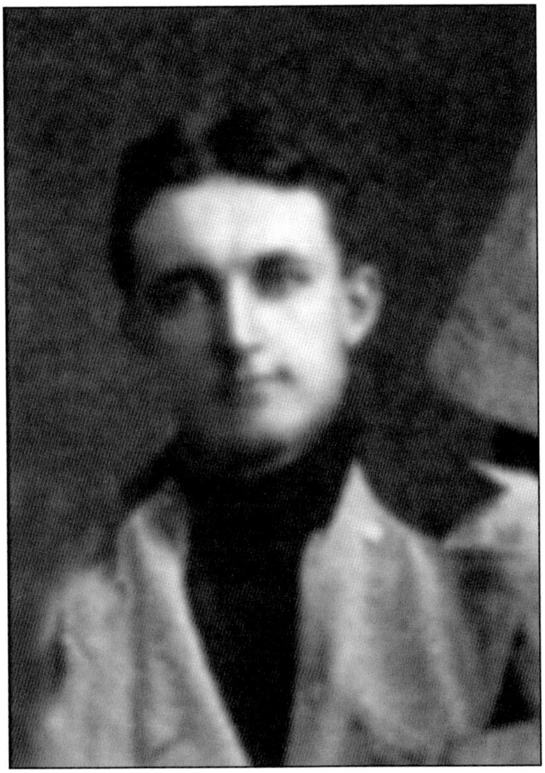

Henry Tefft Clarke, Jr.'s father was a prominent merchant who moved to Nebraska in the 1850s, becoming involved in bridge and railroad construction. It was there that Clarke was born in 1875. Clarke attended Williams College in Massachusetts from 1892–1894, where he was a pitcher on the baseball team. He transferred to the University of Chicago, graduating in 1896. Clarke briefly played Major League baseball, compiling a record of 0-4 with the Cleveland Spiders (1897) and a record of 1-0 with the Chicago Orphans (1898). Clarke entered Michigan in 1898 for pursuit of a law degree, serving as assistant baseball coach under Charles Watkins that year, and then as head coach in 1899. After graduation, Clarke returned to Nebraska, becoming a prominent attorney in a law firm with Frank Crawford. In 1905, Clarke was elected to the state legislature, where he sponsored the first child labor law among the first bills he introduced. Clarke died in 1950. (Courtesy of the *Michiganensian*.)

Rudolph Charles ("Skel") Roach (born Rudolph Charles Weichbrodt) was baseball coach at Michigan for the 1903 season. Roach had a major league career consisting of a single game. On August 3, 1899, Roach was observed pitching for the "Spaldings," a semi-amateur team playing in Chicago. Following the game, he was picked up by the police, possibly for pitching on a Sunday. At the station house, Roach was informed he was to travel to Washington, where he would pitch for the Chicago Orphans of the National League. On August 9, he won a 6-3 decision over Washington, pitching the entire nine innings. Because Roach and the team ownership were unable to agree on a salary, while Roach never pitched again in the "Big Leagues," he did have a brief career in the minor leagues. Prior to joining Michigan, he pitched at Butte, Montana, as well as for a semi-professional team in Oak Park, Michigan. Following the 1903 season, Roach played several years with Portland and Seattle in the Pacific Coast League, winning 16 games with Seattle in 1905. He used his baseball earnings to pay for law school at Northwestern University, serving as an attorney in Chicago in his later years. Roach died in 1958. Roach was an imposing figure, standing 6'2" at a time when even the Michigan football squad only averaged approximately 5'8" in height.

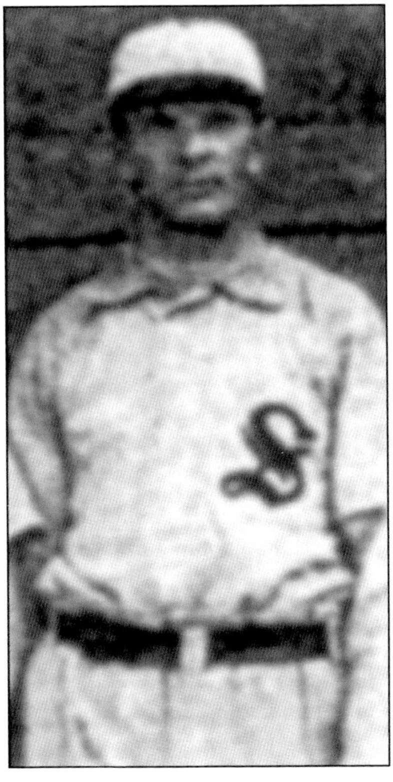

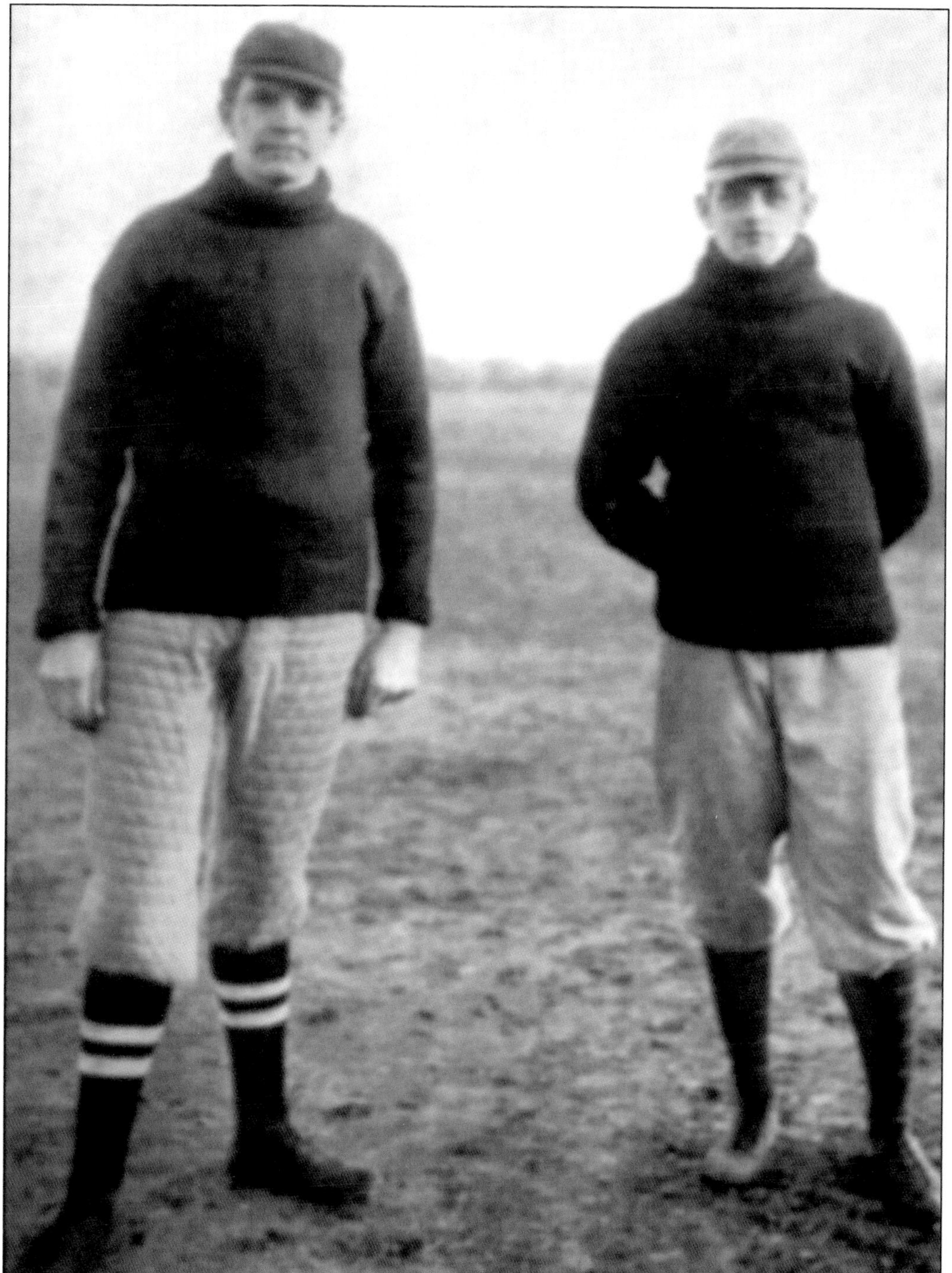

Pitcher Jerry Utley (right) played four seasons for Michigan, and was captain of the 1902 squad. He served as assistant coach under "Skel" Roach in 1903. In 1904, Utley replaced Roach as coach. The team finished that season with a record of 10-5. (Courtesy of the *Michiganensian*.)

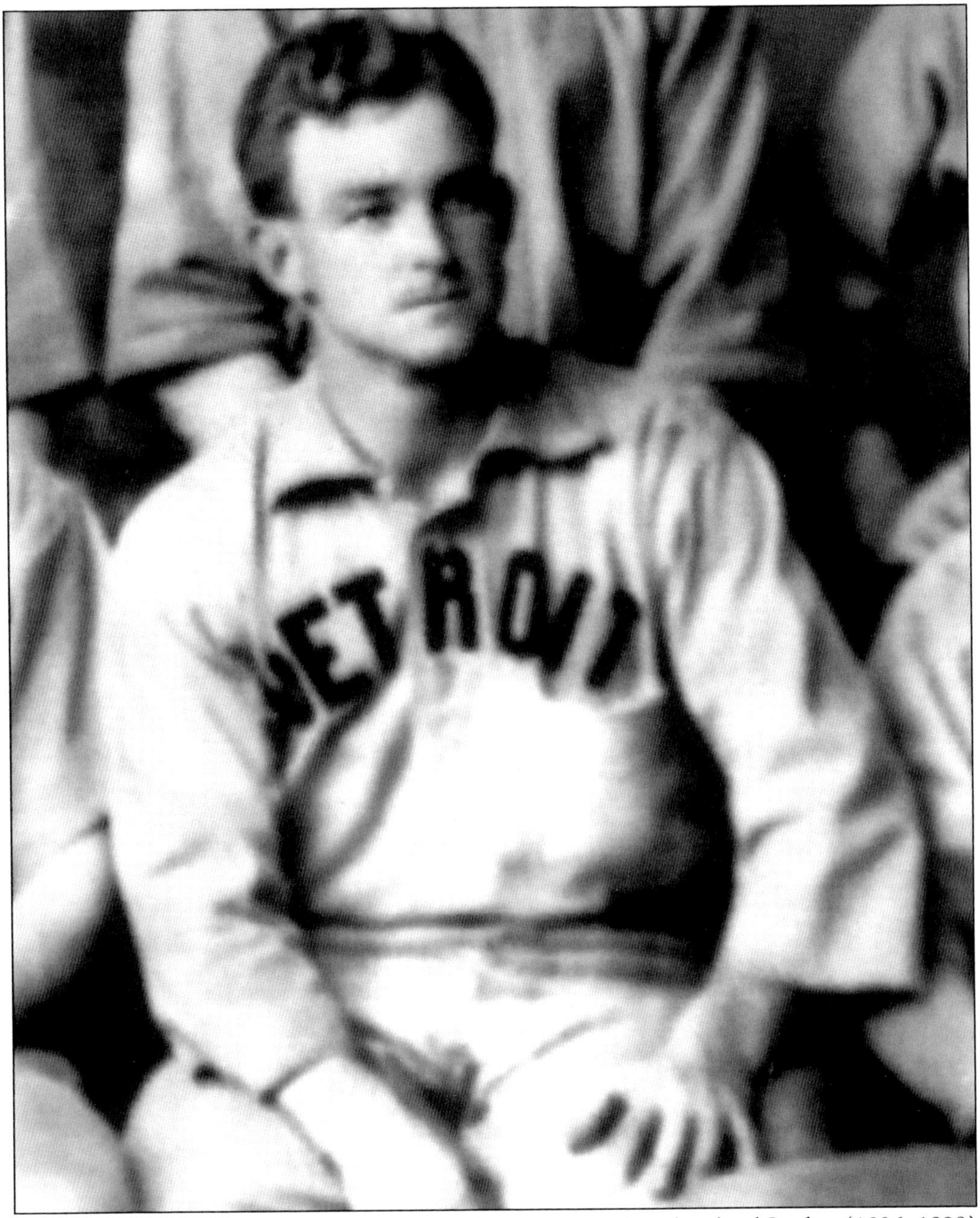

Lew "Sport" McAllister was a multipurpose utility player for the Cleveland Spiders (1896–1899) and Detroit Tigers (1901–1903). Though primarily a catcher and second baseman, McAllister at some time played every position on the diamond. In 1904, he served as assistant baseball coach at Michigan under Jerry Utley. Popular among the players, McAllister was hired as head coach for the 1905, 1906, 1908 and 1909 seasons at Michigan. McAllister continued to play in minor league cities such as Buffalo, Toronto, Newark, New Jersey and Lincoln, Nebraska until retiring from baseball. His later life was also spent as a part-time actor. In his last years, McAllister frequently criticized the current (*c.* 1960) players: "Nobody takes any chances any more. . . . It's just hit the ball and wait for the next guy to hit it."

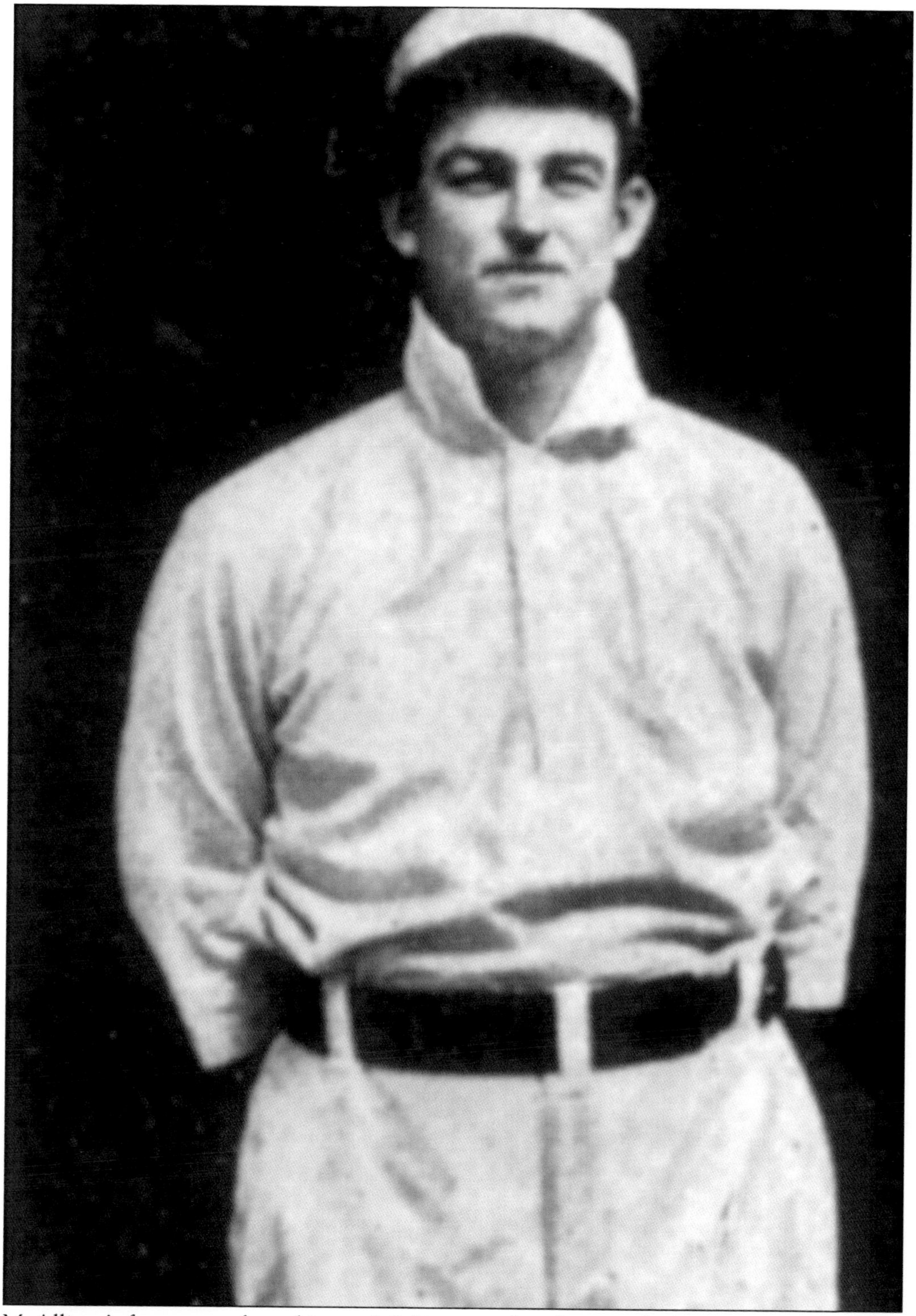

McAllister's four years of coaching at Michigan produced a record of 53-15-1, including one conference championship (1905). (Courtesy of the *Michiganensian*.)

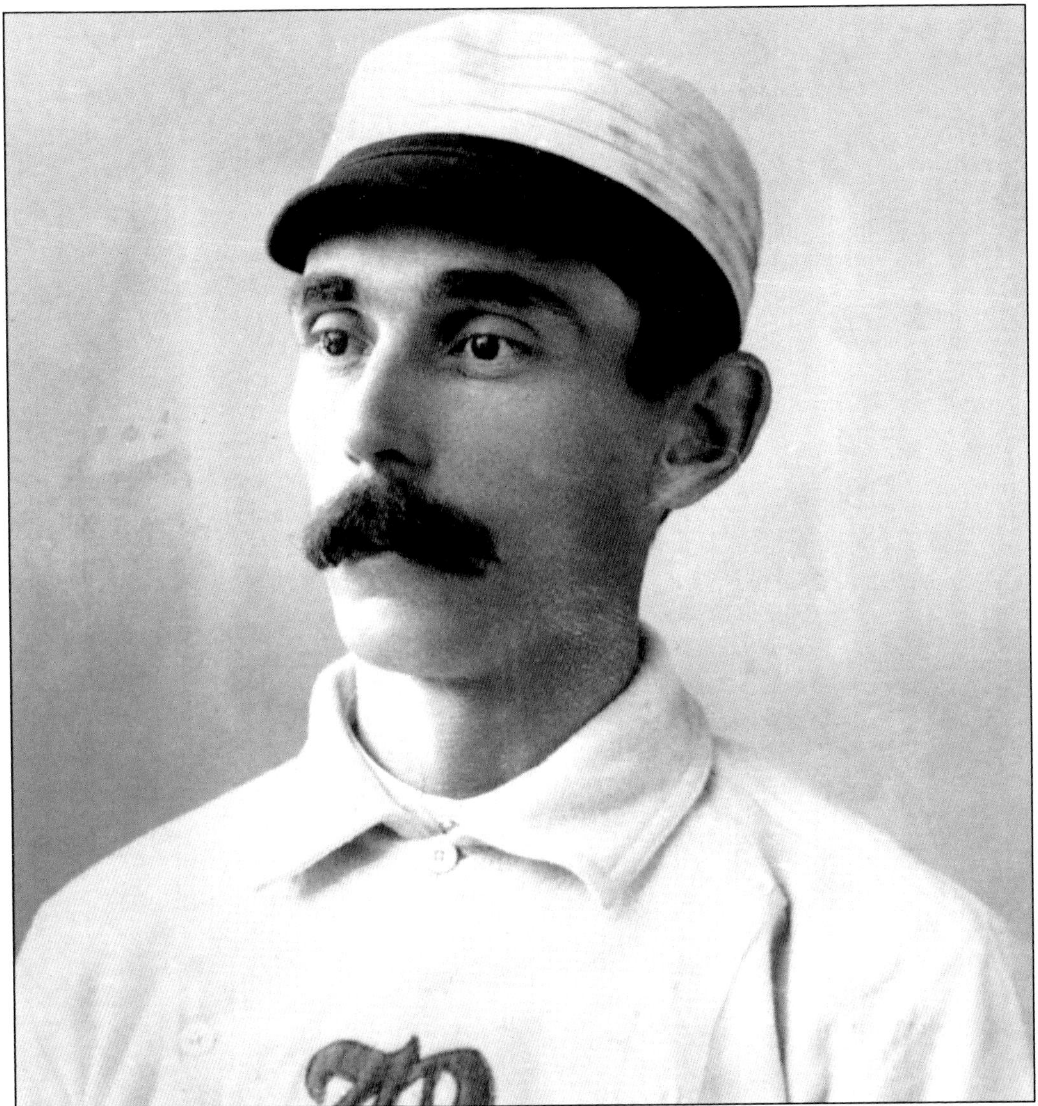

Bobby Lowe served as Michigan baseball coach for the 1907 season, finishing with a record of 11-4-1. At the time, he was a utility player with the Detroit Tigers, and was a reasonable choice to be interim coach given the proximity of Detroit. Lowe's principle claim to notoriety occurred May 30, 1894. As the second baseman for Boston of the National League in a contest with Cincinnati, he became the first player to hit four home runs in a single game. The performance would not be repeated until Lou Gehrig accomplished the same feat some 36 years later. By 1907, it was apparent that Lowe's major league career was approaching an end. Before the next season, he was released by Detroit and signed by Grand Rapids of the Central League as a playing-manager. 1908 was Lowe's last year as an active player, though he did spend time as a scout with the Tigers. An argument in favor of Lowe's induction into the National Baseball Hall of Fame can be made for reasons other than his day of glory. Lowe spent 18 years as a Major League player with Boston, Chicago and Detroit. He managed Detroit in 1904. His career average of .273 included over 1900 hits. Five times he hit over .300. On defense, Lowe was rated among the best of his time. His career fielding average of .953 was the highest for a second baseman at the time he retired. Lowe died in 1951. (Courtesy of the National Baseball Hall of Fame and Museum.)

THREE

The Conference Era

1896–1920

As schools increased the number of matches with other colleges, it was perhaps inevitable that athletic conferences would be established, in part for the purpose of determining a regional champion. During the 1880s, competition between the University of Michigan and other western schools, most notably Racine, Madison (Wisconsin), Chicago, and Northwestern, resulted in declaration of a regional champion. The earliest such reference, found in the student newspaper *The Chronicle*, followed the 1882 season; the "champion" was Michigan, having defeated each of the other schools twice. More formal such organizations, with officers and by-laws, appeared in New England, and involved what would later be referred to as the "Ivy League."

In April 1892, the Western Inter-Collegiate Athletic Association, an early precursor of the "Big Ten," was established. Consisting of Michigan, Minnesota, Wisconsin and Northwestern, the association was headquartered in Chicago, with Michigan's Ralph Stone as President. The championship could also be decided on the basis of a challenge: In 1895, Michigan and Chicago had split the two games in which they faced each other, and Coach Amos Alonzo Stagg of Chicago challenged Michigan Manager E.C. Weeks to a third game to decide the "championship of the West." Weeks declined.

The growing interest in inter-collegiate sports, accompanied by increasing abuse of the system, reflected the loss of control by faculty and administrators of the schools. "Ringers" would travel between schools, and under assumed names (Smith was a favorite) would compete in different sports for different schools. Some "professional" amateurs could be found competing over a period of five or more years.

In 1894, James Smart, President of Purdue, requested a meeting of college presidents for the purpose of establishing some form of regulatory body to eliminate the more blatant abuses. The meeting was held at the Palmer House in Chicago during January 1895. The Intercollegiate Conference of Faculty Representatives, also known as the Western Inter-Collegiate Conference Athletic Association (W.I.C.C.A.A.), was the result.

Initially, seven schools formed what was generally called the Western Conference: Michigan, Chicago, Illinois, Minnesota, Northwestern, Purdue, and Wisconsin. Indiana and Iowa were added in 1899, producing the nucleus of nine. Ohio State joined in 1912, replacing Michigan, the school having temporarily withdrawn from the conference in 1907. As a result, despite the loss of Michigan, the conference retained a total of nine schools. It was in 1912 that the media more informally dubbed the conference as the "Big Nine." Membership remained stable until 1946, when Chicago withdrew, temporarily reducing the membership once again to nine schools. Michigan State was added in 1949, and Penn State in 1990, completing the eleven colleges which currently constitute the "Big Ten."

Despite losing three players during the course of the 1896 season because of "professionalism," Michigan defeated other members of the conference in six of nine games. However, the three losses came at the hands of the University of Chicago, which won the first of three consecutive conference championships.

During the period between 1896 and 1906, Michigan would lead the conference three times (1899, 1901, 1905), and finish second four times (1896, 1898, 1903, 1906). The 1899 season was particularly satisfying. Michigan had more than held its own against non-conference competition from the east. A victory over Illinois would also clinch their first conference championship. In the

6th inning, Illinois had men on 2nd and 3rd base, nobody out, and Guy Miller was brought in to relieve. "Sox" Miller had already pitched the day before. But he managed two strikeouts, and held Illinois the remainder of the game. Michigan was victorious, 4-2.

The conference was formed in part to provide greater faculty control over athletics by establishing specific rules for practice and eligibility. Players had to be enrolled in the schools which they represented, and could not accept any form of gratuity to play. In 1897, for example, Michigan refused to play Northwestern because Sickles, the Northwestern pitcher, was a professional. Other games against Wittenburg and Detroit were considered practices as well, because of the participation of professionals. (An April 22 match with Illinois, won by Michigan 7-3, was played within the "Chicago rules," but for unknown reasons is not included among the records for the season.)

The definition of "gratuity" was sometimes open to debate:

"Henry and Kyer tailors on N. University have offered a suit of clothes to the man who makes the best average."

– Michigan Daily News, *April 23, 1902.*

On December 1, 1906, conference representatives met to discuss revision of existing rules. Some changes were accepted without controversy, though they appear "quaint" by today's standards. The football season was extended from five to seven games to allow athletics to be self-supporting. Football practice could not begin in the fall before September 20, rather than on the day school began. But the conference also refused to abolish a retroactive three-year rule for eligibility, which meant several Michigan athletes in different sports would not be eligible to participate in the upcoming season. When the conference representatives refused to change this decision at a meeting held the following January, Michigan withdrew from the conference. The student body supported the school's decision.

As a consequence, Michigan found it increasingly difficult to schedule games with western schools. The University continued to schedule football matches with Minnesota through 1910, a result of the storied "Little Brown Jug." But with adoption of the so-called "Non-Intercourse Rule," even these contests ended and Michigan was forced to participate in sports as an "independent" for a decade. The issue became moot as athletes graduated and students moved on; freshman ineligibility was the standard anyway. In 1916, the Board of Control of Athletics recommended that Michigan athletics was to be overseen by the University Senate, a stipulation for re-entry into the Western Conference. As a result, at its June, 1917 meeting the Conference participants formally invited Michigan to resume membership. The invitation was accepted, and became effective the following November. Ironically, the Michigan baseball team would be "Big Ten" champions from 1918 to 1920.

Two coaches of note led Michigan during this second decade of the century. In 1910, Branch Rickey enrolled in the University law school, and was hired at the same time to coach baseball. In addition, he served as a part-time scout for the St. Louis Browns American League team. Though he completed his law degree program in two years, Rickey remained as coach through 1913, compiling a record of 69-31-4. It was during Rickey's last two years as coach that a pitcher-first baseman first came to his attention: George Sisler. As a freshman in 1912, Sisler threw a one-hit shutout, striking out 20 against Rickey's varsity squad. The next season, Sisler joined the varsity.

After Rickey's departure following the 1913 season, Carl Lundgren was hired as Michigan coach. Lundgren remained through the 1920 season, compiling a record of 94-33-6, including three consecutive Big Ten titles after Michigan's reinstatement for the 1918 season.

Year	Won (overall)	Lost (overall)	Won (conference)	Lost (conference)	Position	Coach
1896	17	4 (1 Tie)	6	3	2nd	Sexton
1897	4	8	2	6	4th	Watkins
1898	15	6	7	3	2nd	Watkins
1899	14	5	5	2	1st	H.T. Clarke
1900	12	9 (1 Tie)	6	5 (1 Tie)	3rd	Watkins
1901	13	8	8	2	1st	Sexton
1902	8	10	1	7	5th	Sexton
1903	12	5	7	3	2nd	Roach
1904	10	5	4	5	4th	Utley
1905	16	3	9	3	1st	McAllister
1906	12	7	5	3	2nd	McAllister
1907	11	4 (1 Tie)	*			Lowe
1908	12	4				McAllister
1909	18	3 (1 Tie)				McAllister
1910	17	8				Rickey
1911	16	10 (1 Tie)				Rickey
1912	14	10 (2 Ties)				Rickey
1913	21	4 (1 Tie)				Rickey
1914	22	6				Lundgren
1915	16	7 (3 Ties)				Lundgren
1916	9	12 (2 Ties)				Lundgren
1917#						Lundgren
1918	16	1	9	1	1st	Lundgren
1919	13	1	9	0	1st	Lundgren
1920	17	6 (1 Tie)	9	1	1st	Lundgren

* Withdrew from conference: 1907–1916
\# No season due to war

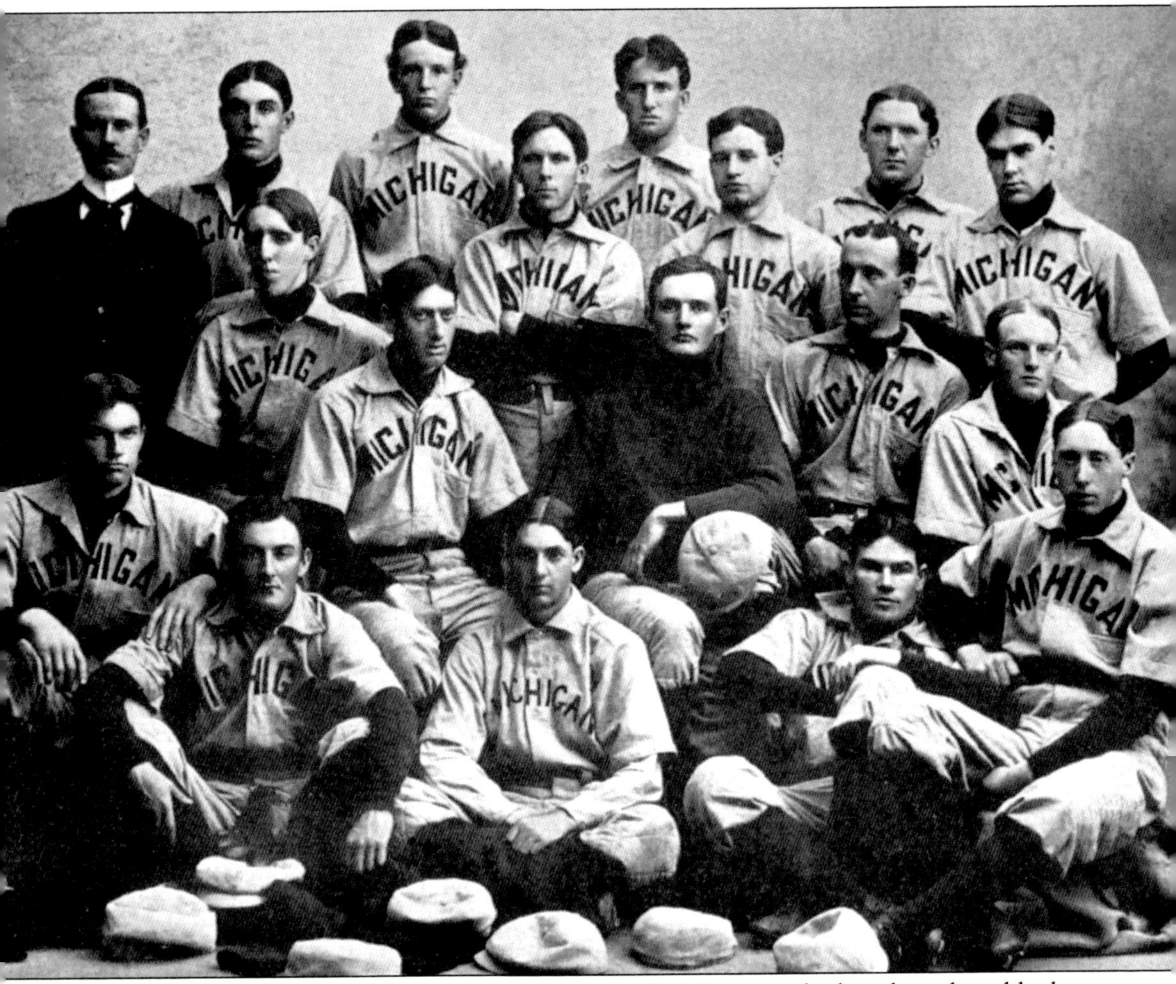

Many from the strong squad of 1896, which won 17 of 22 games, had graduated, and little was expected from the 1897 team. But strong pitching by (captain) Guy Miller (center, with turtle-neck) helped the team make a somewhat credible 4-8 showing, a record that does not include several early season practice matches. Charles Watkins (middle with folded hands) was in his first season as coach. He also took to the mound once more in a 6-0 loss to Detroit in an April 17 practice game. (Courtesy of the *Michiganensian*.)

Alatau Leonard Charles Atkinson, an 1898 Law graduate from the university, served as student manager for both the track and baseball squads as well as holding a position on the Board in Control of Athletics. Among the more distinguished of the University graduates, Atkinson entered law practice with Albert Judd, son of the Chief Justice of the Hawaiian Territory. Atkinson served as the assistant attorney general of the H.T., followed by the position of Secretary of Hawaii (1903–1907). He was President, Board of Agriculture and Forestry for the H.T. from 1921 until his death six years later. (Courtesy of the *Michiganensian*)

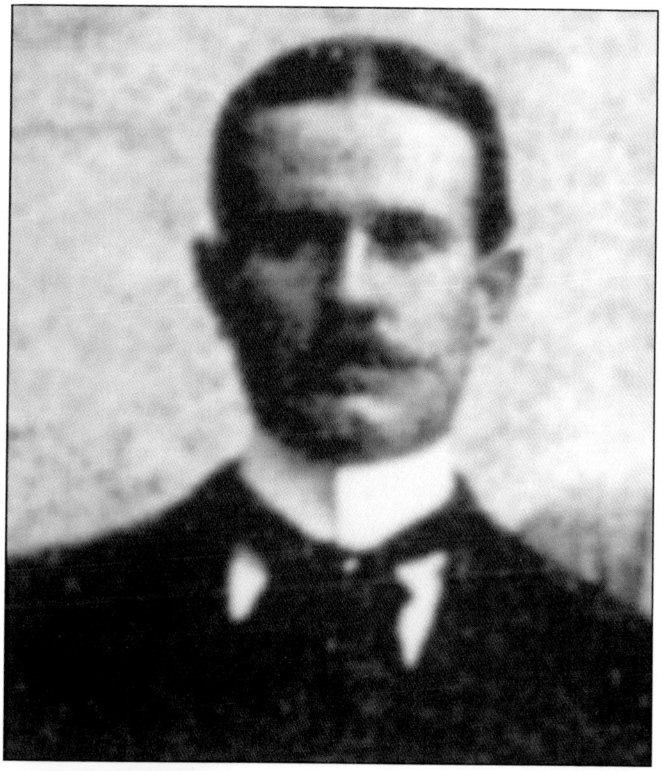

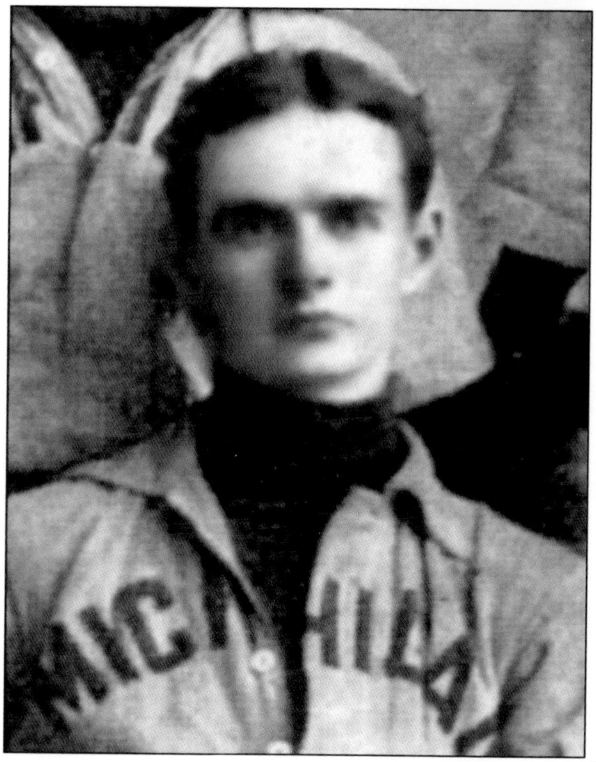

From 1896–1899, Guy Alonzo Miller developed into one of the stronger pitchers on the squad, "increasing in speed, and having a number of new ideas that will puzzle old batters" for the '97 season. Miller received degrees in Liberal Arts ('99) and Law ('00). He later became a Detroit Circuit Judge. (Courtesy of the *Michiganensian*.)

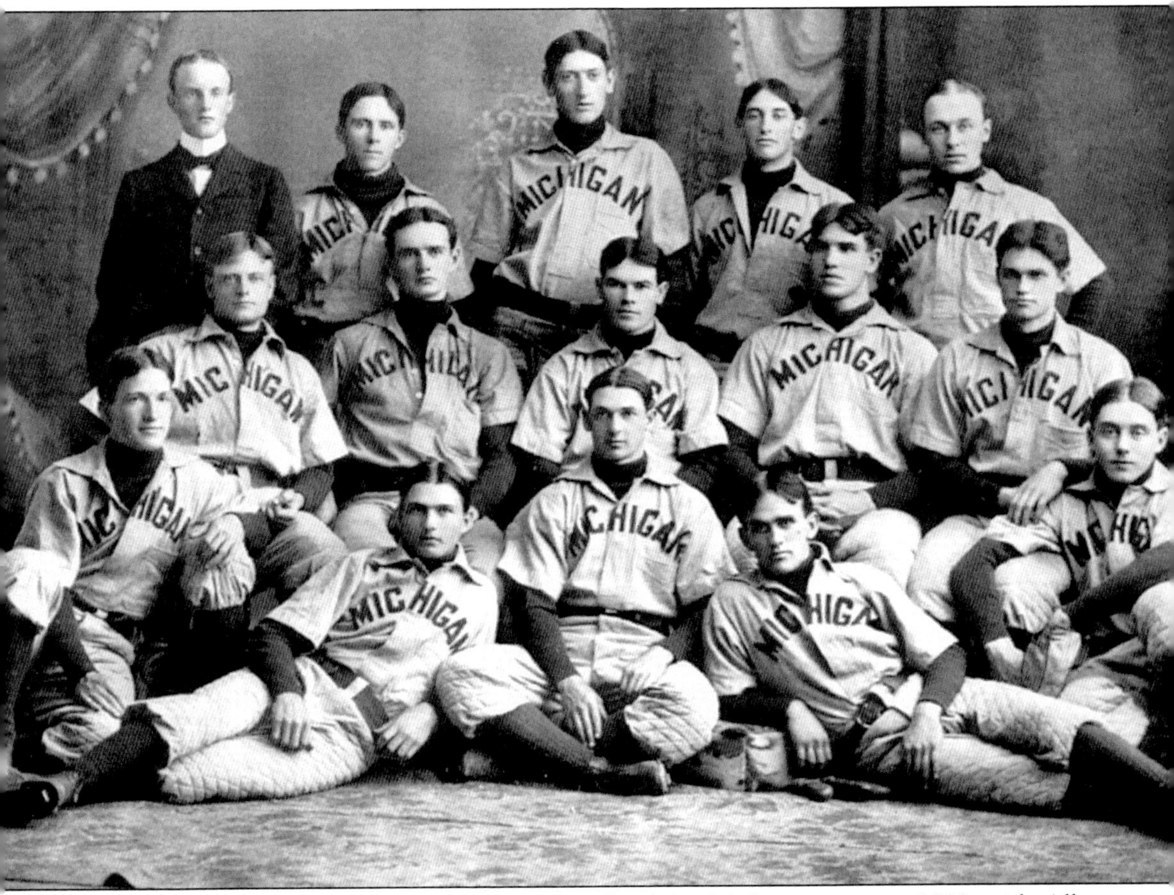

Charles Watkins began his second year as coach of the Michigan team in 1898, with Albert Keith (top left) as student manager. Rightfielder John Butler was elected captain. The team began the season with three losses in five games against western opposition, but finished strong while compiling an overall record of 15-6. With a 7-3 record in conference play, Michigan finished second behind Chicago for the second time in three years. In addition to Guy Miller (middle row, second from left) who became a circuit court judge in Detroit, Frank Condon (top row, middle) received a degree in Law, practicing in Hancock, Michigan. Edwin McGinnis (bottom row, right) was also the quarterback for the football team. (Courtesy of the *Michiganensian*.)

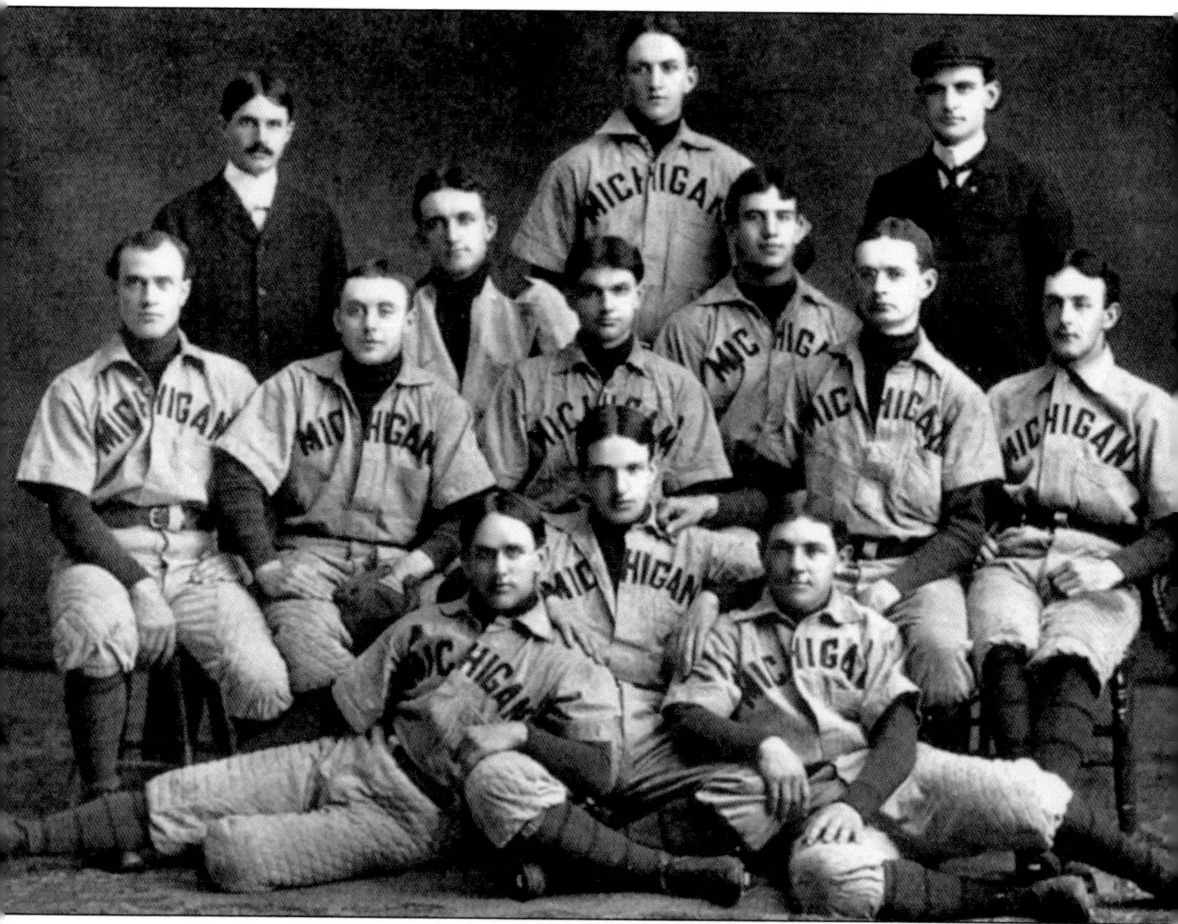

Led by outfielder Neil Snow (top center), and a strong pitching staff, the 1899 squad won the first of many conference titles. Their overall record was 14-5, with a record of 5-2 in conference play as they ended Chicago's three-year run as champion. Charles Baird (top row, left) served as graduate manager for the team, and would shortly be appointed Michigan's first athletic director. Henry T. Clarke, Jr. (next to Baird) would graduate that year with a degree in Law, and serve one year as interim coach. (Courtesy of the *Michiganensian*.)

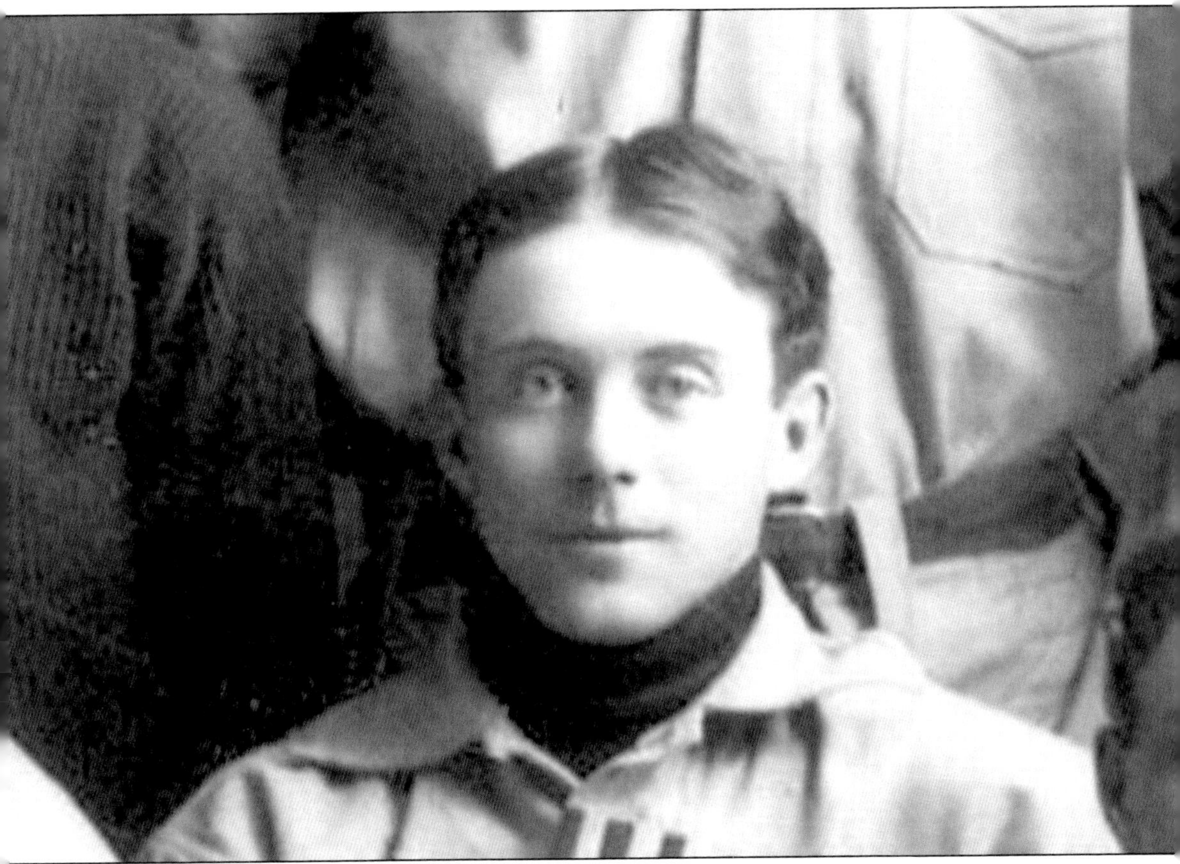

Edwin McGinnis played four seasons (1898–1901) and was captain of both the 1900 and 1901 Michigan teams. An all-around athlete, McGinnis also played quarterback for the football team. McGinnis later earned a medical degree from Northwestern. He practiced surgery in Illinois until his death in 1933. (Courtesy of the Bentley Historical Library.)

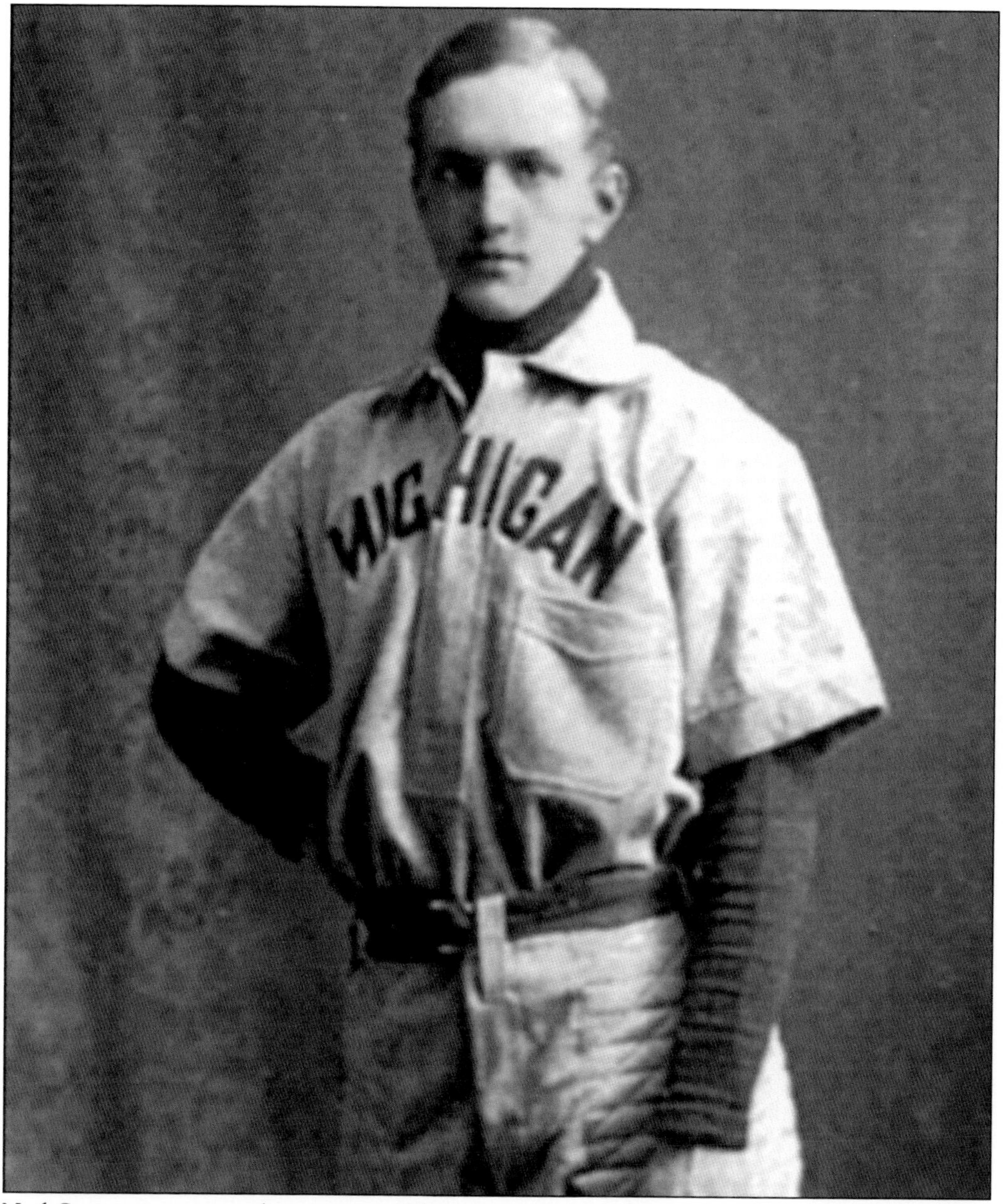

Neil Snow was among the greatest athletes to attend Michigan during the first years of the Twentieth Century. Between 1899 and 1902, he earned 11 letters in track, football and baseball. Better known among Michigan alumni for his football exploits, Snow scored five touchdowns in the inaugural Rose Bowl of 1902, while serving as captain of Coach Fielding H. Yost's first football team. As an outfielder on the baseball squad, Snow was a major contributor to two conference championships. In 1899, he batted over .380, following this up with an average over .320 in 1900. Snow finished his baseball career in grand style. In his final game, a 7-4 victory over Cornell, Snow was responsible for six of the runs. Three scored on his bases-loaded triple. Turning down several coaching offers following graduation, Snow worked his way to the presidency of the Detroit Drill Twist Company. In 1914, at the age of 34, Snow died suddenly from a heart attack at the Detroit Racquet Club. (Courtesy of the *Michiganensian*.)

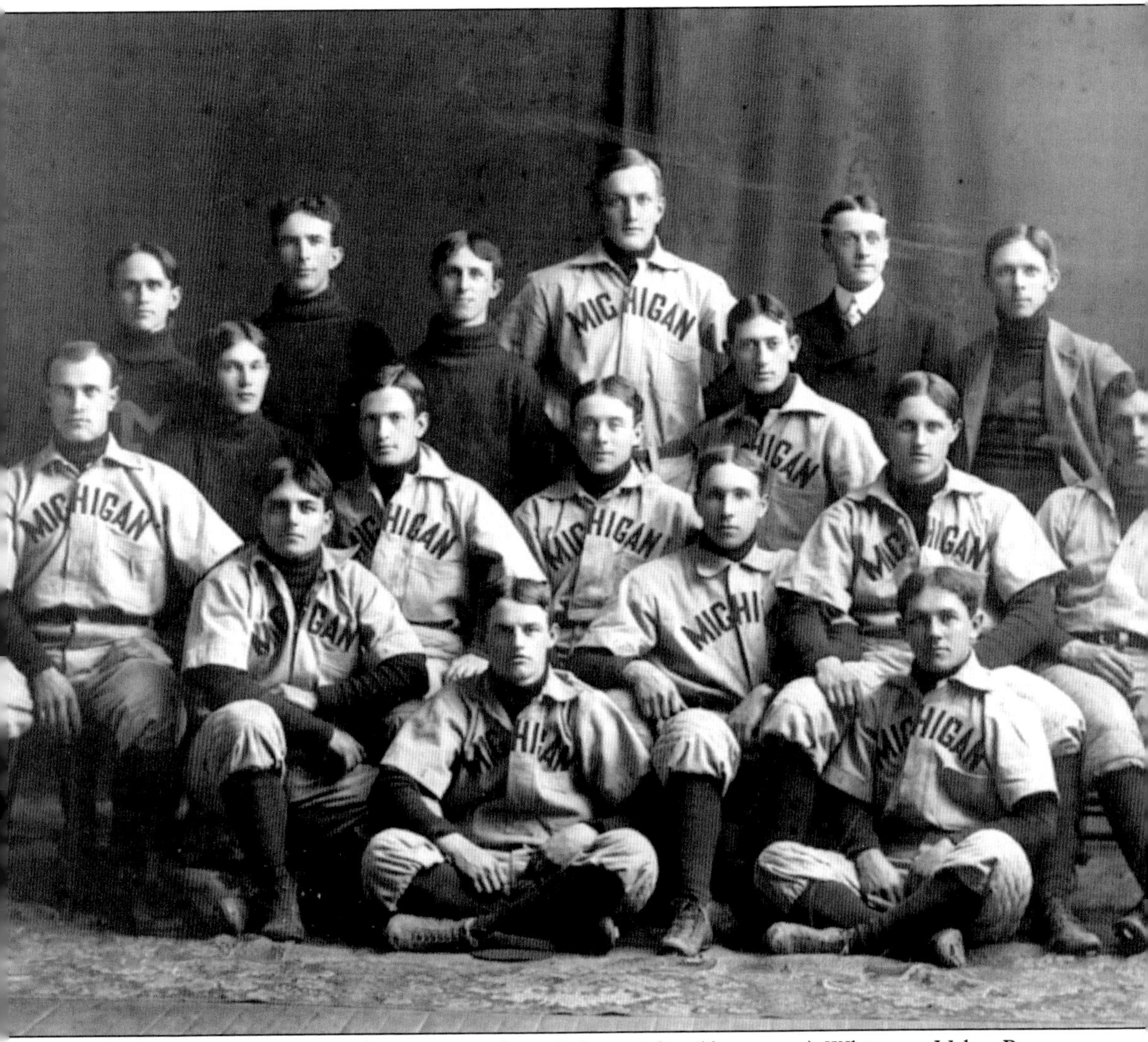

Pictured is the 1990 Michigan team, from left to right: (front row) Whitney, Utley Bennett, and Flesher; (middle row) Blencoe, Matteson, Davies, McGinnis (cap.), Condon, Beistle, and Cutting; (top row) unknown, unknown, unknown, Snow, Lancashire (stu. mgr.), and Watkins (coach). Descpite the strong hitting of outfielder Neil Snow, and sandwiched between two conference champions, the 1900 squad was mediocre at best. The team was able to defeat eastern rivals Cornell and Penn in three of four contests, as well as besting rival Chicago two of three times (with one tie). Overall, however, the team finished with a record of 12-9-1. In conference competition, Michigan finished in third place with a record of 6-5-1. (Courtesy of the Bentley Historical Library)

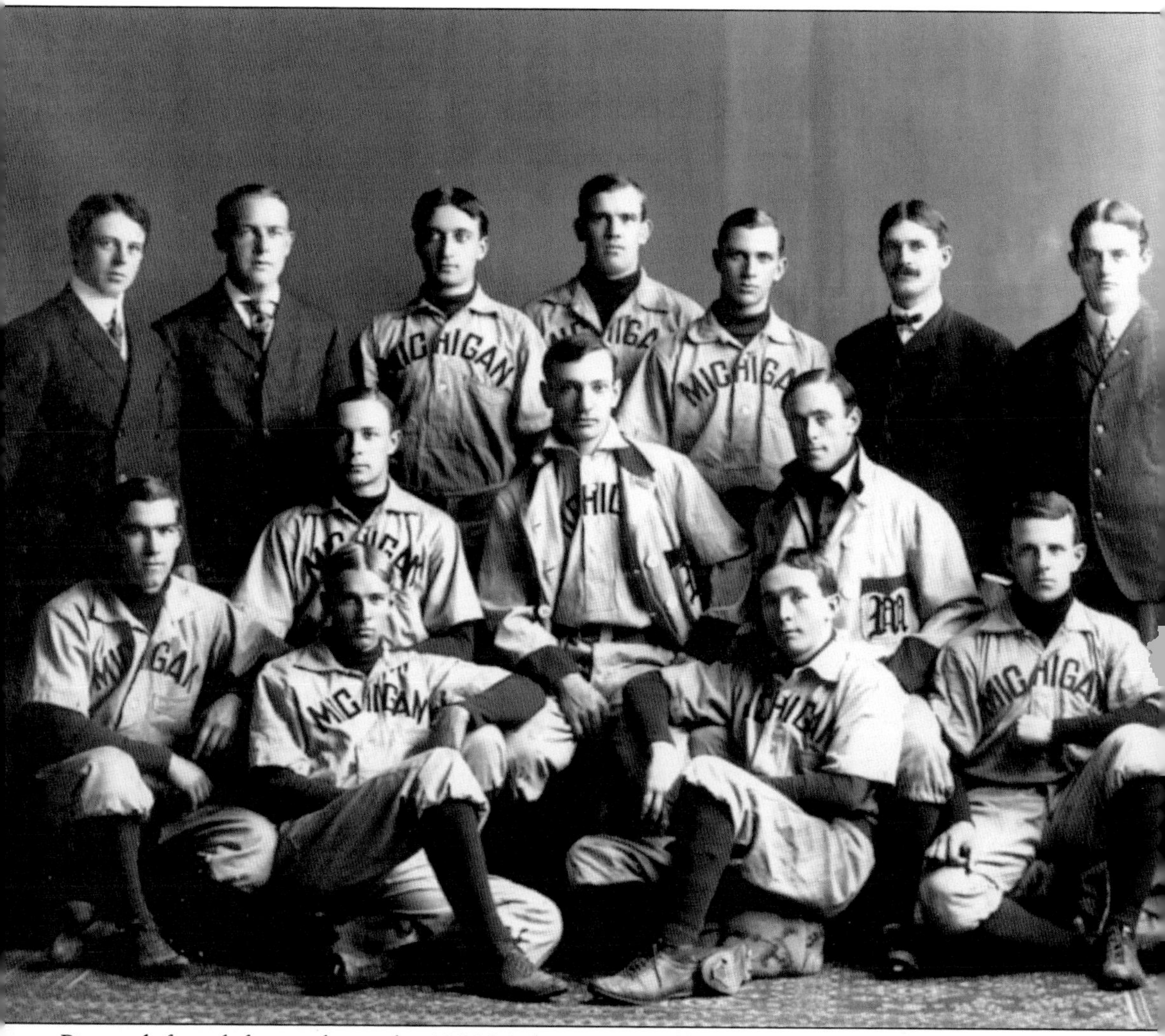

Pictured, from left to right, is the 1904 Michigan team: (front row) Nagle and Boyle; (middle row) Carrothers, Wendell, Redden (captain), Bird, and O'Brien; (top row) Johnson, Brennan, Depree, Turner, Campbell, Baird (ath. dir.), and Utley (coach). The 1904 team was depleted by the loss, through graduation, of pitcher (now coach) Jerry Utley and "Doc" Roche, along with other veterans. James DePree and Pat Boyle anchored a steady infield, but the team was hurt during conference play by an inability to produce timely hitting. Nevertheless, Michigan produced a respectable 10-5 record overall, though finishing fourth in the conference with a 4-5 record. Curtis Redden, (middle row, center), in addition to election as captain of the baseball team for the 1904 season, was also captain of the football squad that previous fall, while playing end on the team. Redden had been a veteran of the Spanish-American War prior to enrolling at Michigan. He later was appointed to the faculty of Knox College in Illinois, as an instructor in Physical Education. In 1919, Redden died of wounds suffered while serving with the American Expeditionary Force in World War I. (Courtesy of the Bentley Historical Library)

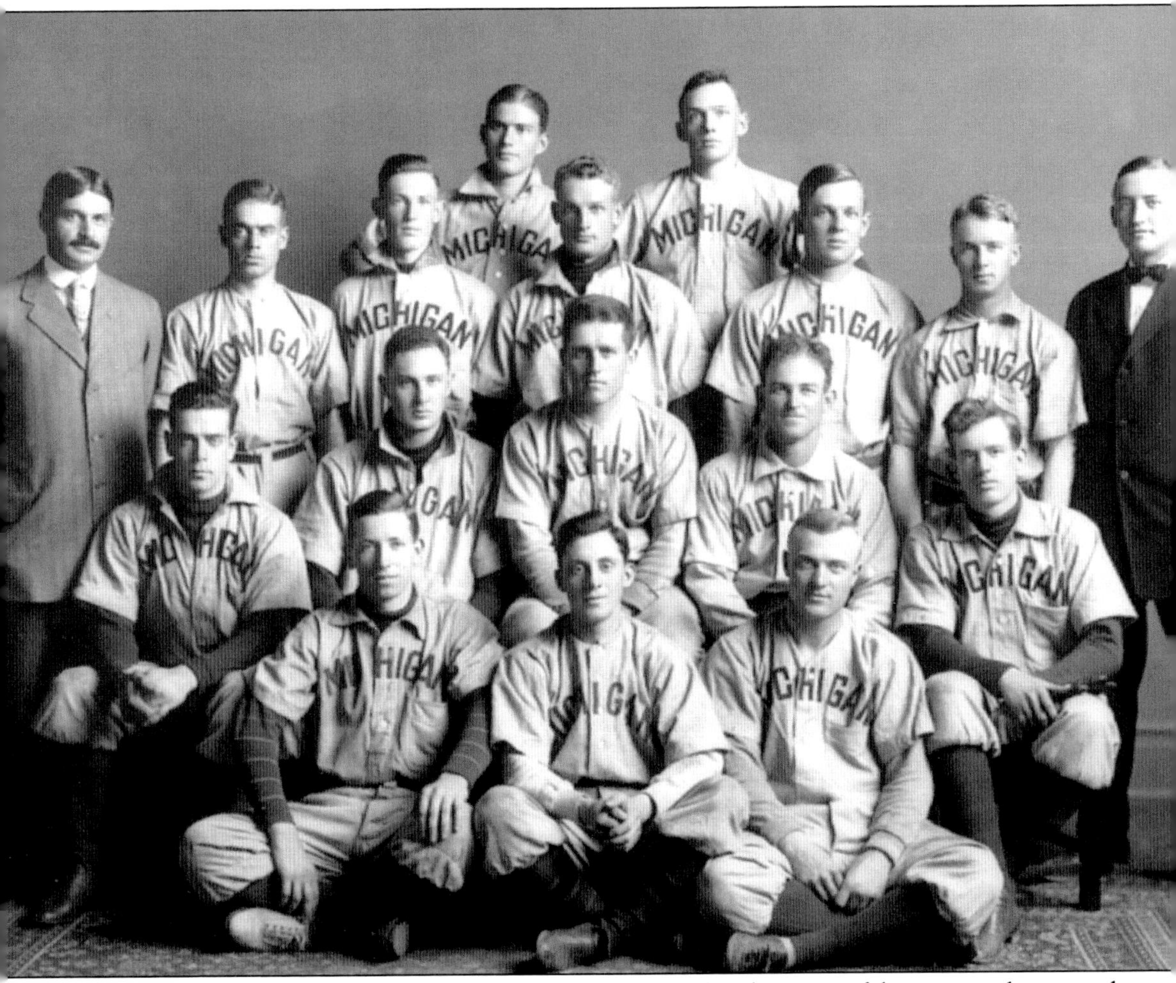

Playing its largest schedule to date, the 1909 team completed a successful season with a record of 18-3-1, while outscoring its opponents by 140-59. Strong pitching was the key. Staff ace Fred Blanding (third row, middle) struck out 64 in 13 games, while Dave Barr struck out 54 in 11 games, and Fred Dean had 15 in the three games in which he appeared. Third-baseman Charles "Chick" Lathers (fourth row, right) led the team with a batting average of .383, while John "Rabbit" Fountain finished with an average of .375. Blanding, Lathers, and Jack Enzenroth (front, right) would sign with Major League teams. (Courtesy of the Bentley Historical Library.)

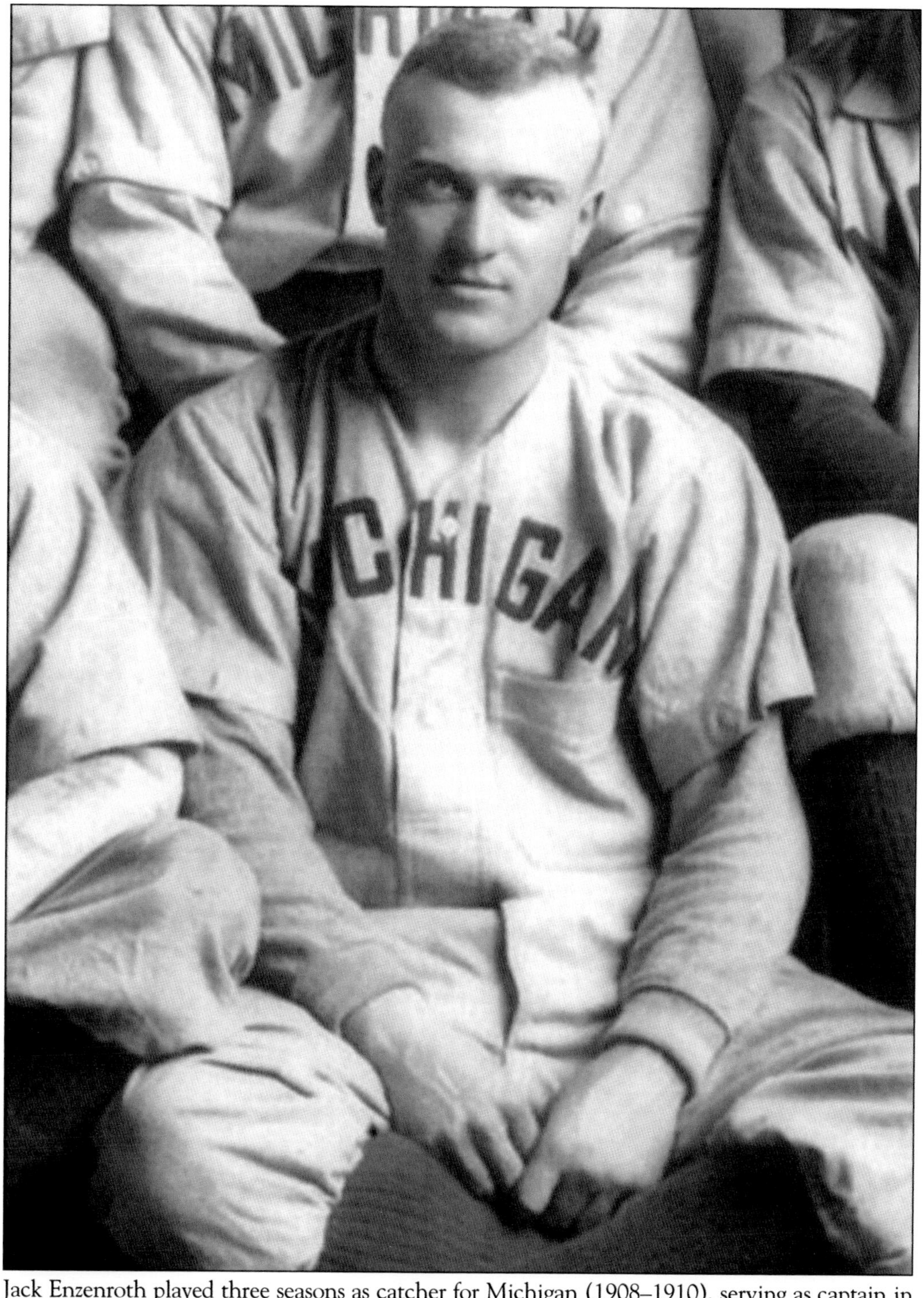

Jack Enzenroth played three seasons as catcher for Michigan (1908–1910), serving as captain in 1910. In 1909, he hit .266. Enzenroth briefly played in the majors, with the St. Louis Browns early in 1914, and the Kansas City Packers of the Federal League in 1914 and 1915. His lifetime average was .174. Enzenroth died at age 58 in 1944. (Courtesy of the Bentley Historical Library.)

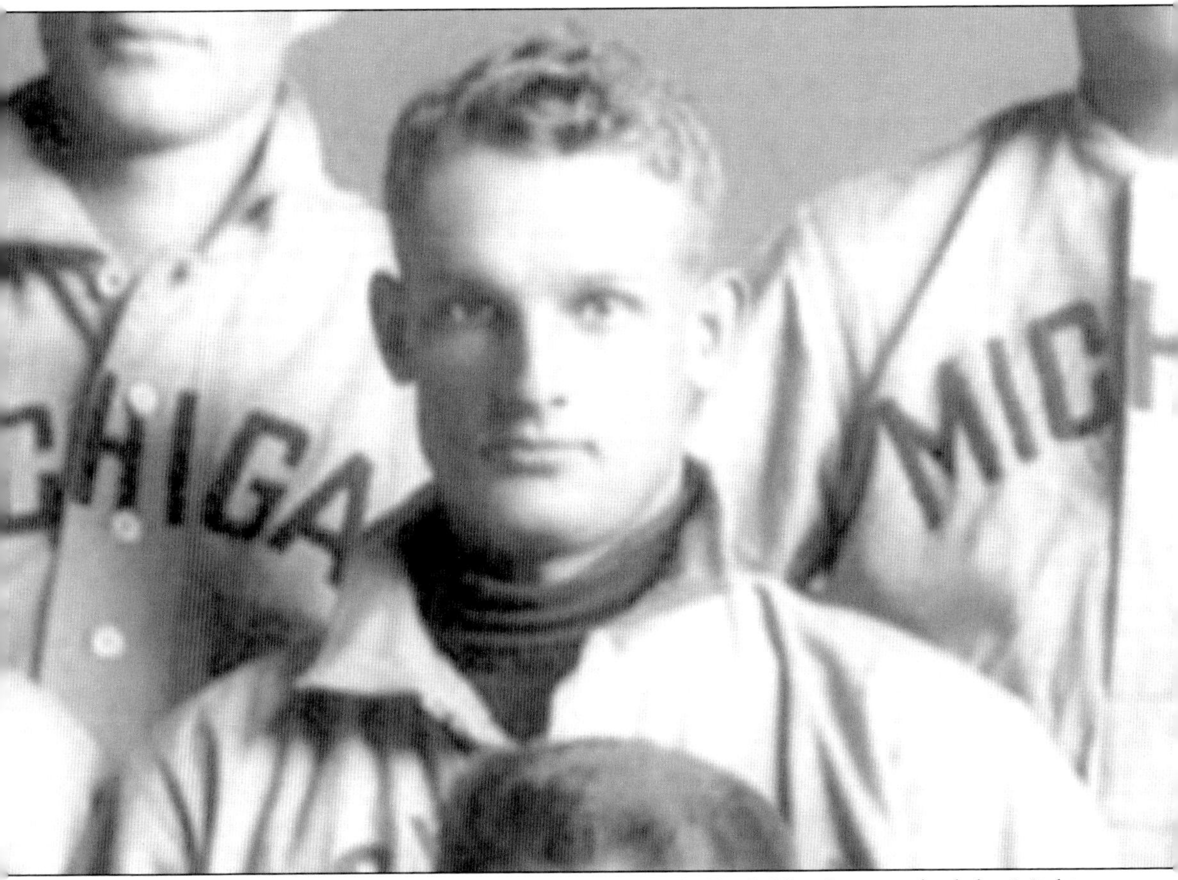

Enrolled in the College of Engineering (1907–1909), Fred Blanding pitched for Michigan during the 1909 and 1910 seasons. He left school early, signing with the Cleveland Naps of the American League. In his debut, September 15, 1910, he shut out the Washington Senators and Walter Johnson, 3-0. Blanding spent five years with Cleveland, composing a record of 45-46. His best year was 1912, when he finished with a record of 18-14. Blanding later owned one of the early Ford Motor dealerships in Lansing, Michigan. He died in 1950 at age 62. (Courtesy of the Bentley Historical Library.)

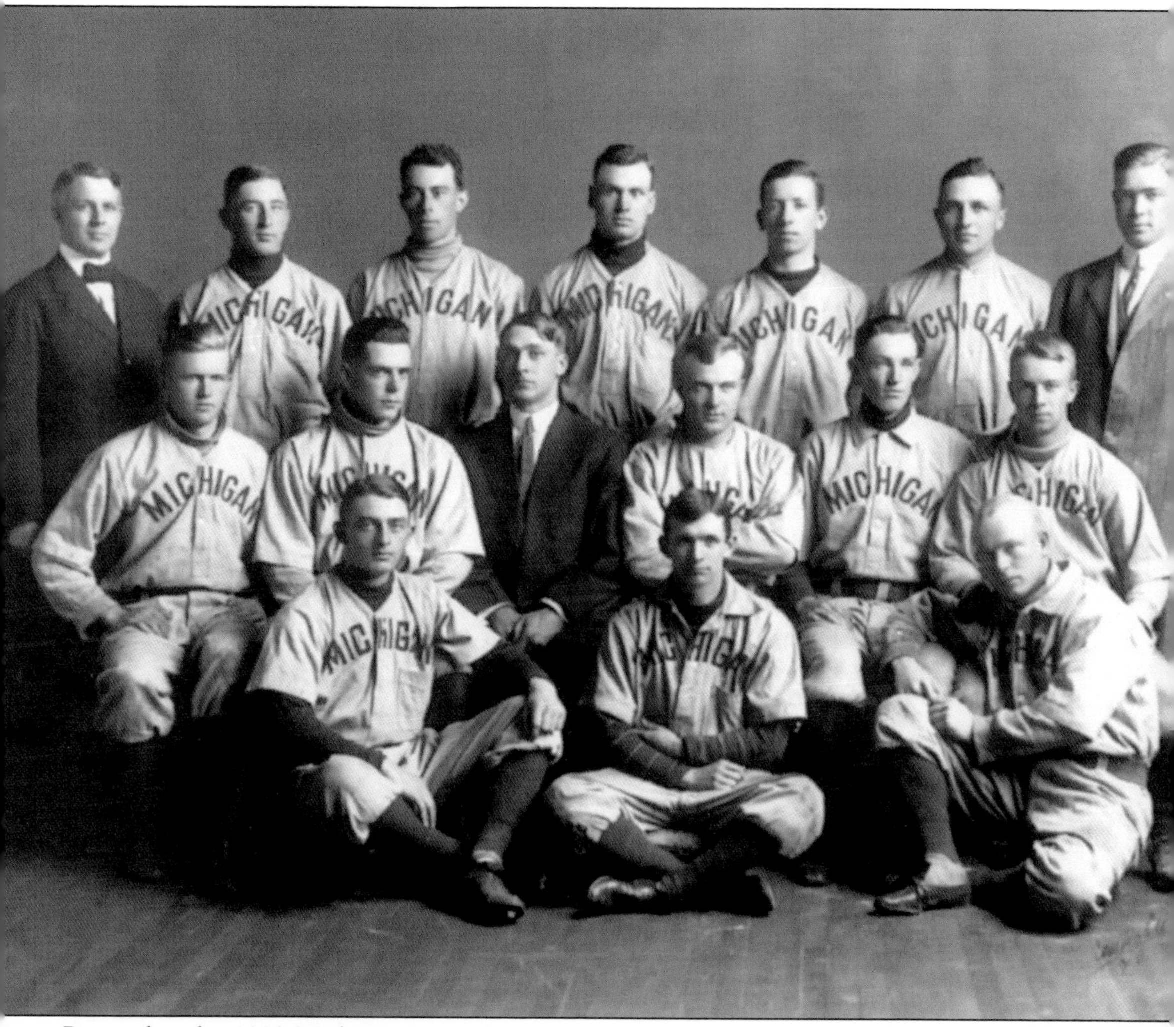

Pictured is the 1910 Michigan team, from left to right: (bottom row) Drake, Campbell, and Marlin; (middle row) Hayes, Hill, Rickey (coach), Enzenroth (cap.), Smith, and Lathrop; (top row) Bartelme (ath. dir.), Verheyen, Campbell, Mitchell, Walsh, Waltner, and Haskins (mgr.). The 1910 season began with the usual challenges. Coach Lew McAllister had departed, leaving only the nucleus of four veterans: Jack Enzenroth (c), Norman Hill (1B), John Walsh (c) and Thompson Lothrop to anchor the team. Branch Rickey, attending the University Law School, was hired as coach. Rickey had previously coached both baseball and football at Ohio Wesleyan, and therefore had previous experience in the position. Six weeks worth of practice in an indoor cage, as well as on the field at the old Fair Grounds in Ann Arbor, provided Rickey an accurate assessment for the team. The team began play with the traditional Southern trip, winning four of seven games. Once the home season began, the team pulled together, winning 13 of 18 games against admittedly weaker competition than they had encountered during conference play. They lost only twice at home, both losses being against Syracuse. At the end of May, Michigan twice defeated Syracuse at their home field in New York, the first defeats suffered by that team during the season. Rickey finished his Law program in two years at Michigan, but continued to coach through the 1913 season, while at the same time scouting part-time for the St. Louis Browns. He compiled a record of 68-32-4. (Courtesy of the Bentley Historical Library.)

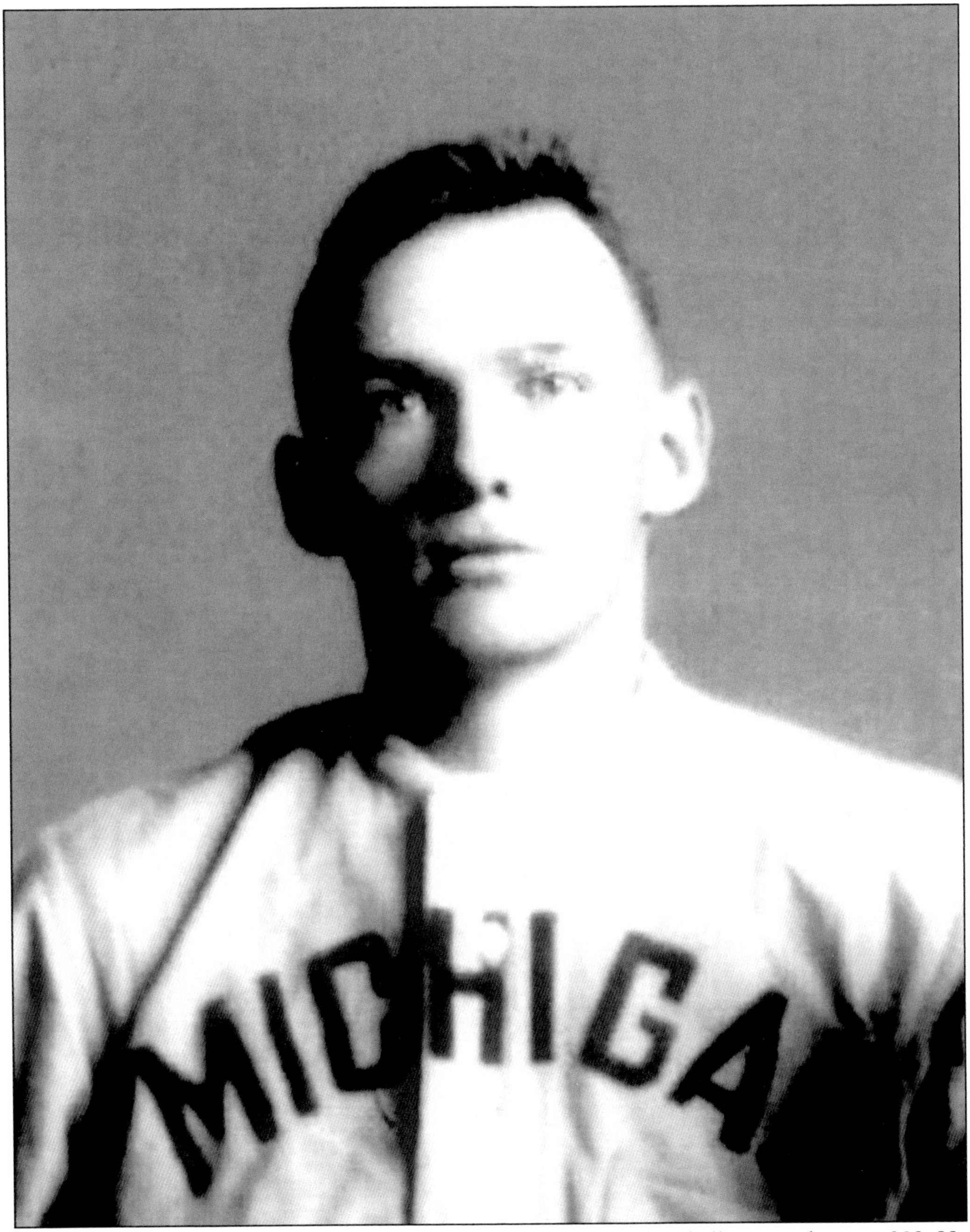

"Chick" Lathers was a major contributor to the successful 1909 baseball season, hitting .383. He was enrolled in the engineering program from 1907–1910. But instead of completing his degree requirements, Lathers signed with the Detroit Tigers. Playing two seasons with Detroit at various infield positions (1910–1911), he composed a lifetime batting average of .228 while appearing in 70 games. During World War I, Lathers served with the American army as an ordnance officer. Following the war, he became a branch manager with Ford Motor Company. From 1934 to 1962, Lathers managed a large dairy farm near Burt Lake, Michigan, while remaining active in community affairs. Lathers died in 1971 at age 82. (Courtesy of the Bentley Historical Library.)

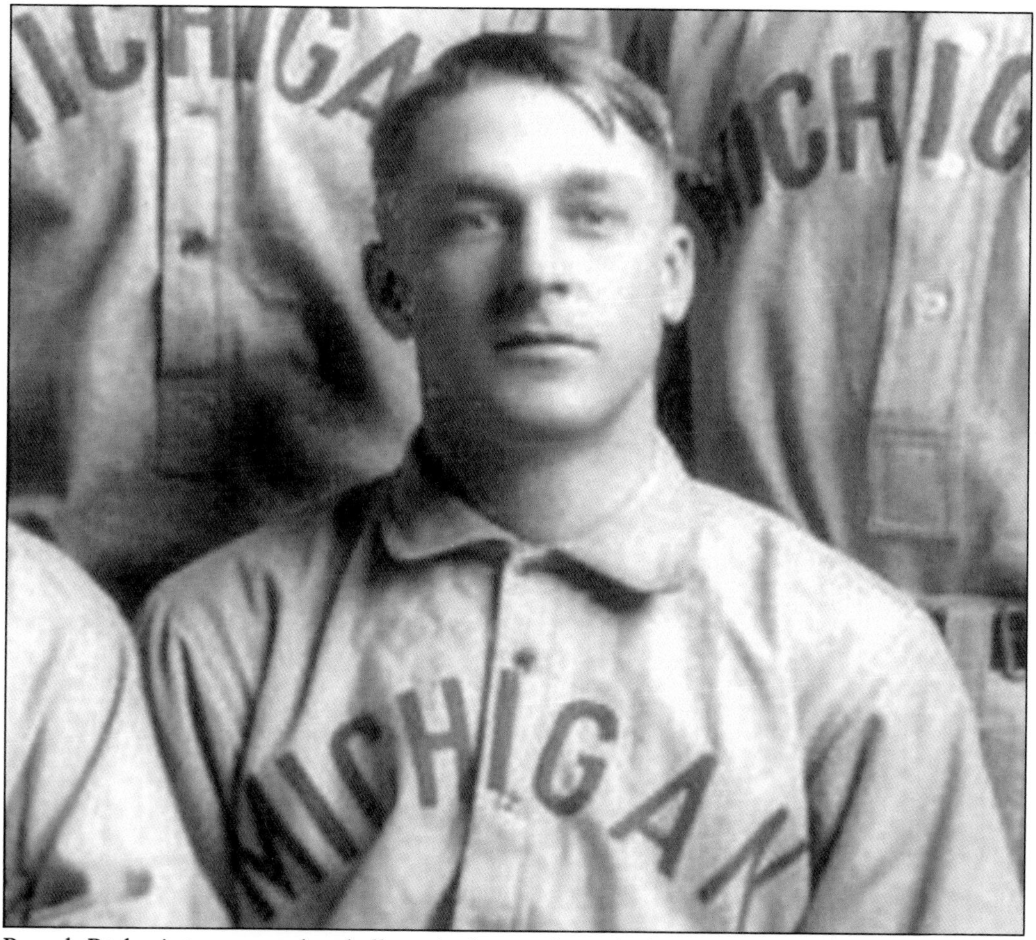

Branch Rickey's impact on baseball reached its nadir with the signing and promotion of Jackie Robinson for the Brooklyn Dodgers during the 1940s, breaking the color barrier, which had stood in the Major Leagues since the 19th century. Yet Rickey's influence was felt for generations prior to that point. His career in semi-professional football ended with a fractured leg in 1902. But the following year he signed his first baseball contract with the Laramie, Wyoming club. Released for refusing to play on Sundays, Rickey was hired as Athletic Director and baseball coach at Ohio Wesleyan. His team won 14 games, a record that would stand for 81 years. In 1905, Rickey's player contract was purchased by the St. Louis Browns. Playing primarily in the position of catcher, Rickey's defensive shortcomings were only too apparent. Appearing briefly with the New York Highlanders in 1907, he finished last in the league in fielding. The Washington Senators once stole 13 bases off him in a single game. In 1910, he was hired as baseball coach at the University of Michigan, where from 1910 to 1913 he compiled an overall record of 68-32-4 (not including a 1912 victory over an alumni team). During this period, he maintained his ties with the Browns as a part-time scout. His most important protégé during these years was George Sisler, and Rickey was instrumental in Sisler's signing with the Browns after graduation in 1915. Rickey managed the Browns from 1913 to 1915. In 1919, he moved to the St. Louis Cardinals, where as manager and general manager he began the first farm system. In 1945, Rickey moved to the Brooklyn Dodgers as general manager, where in addition to signing Robinson, he built the team that would dominate the National League for a decade. Among Rickey's other innovations were the use of batting cages, pitching machines and even batting helmets. He died in 1965. (Courtesy of the Bentley Historical Library.)

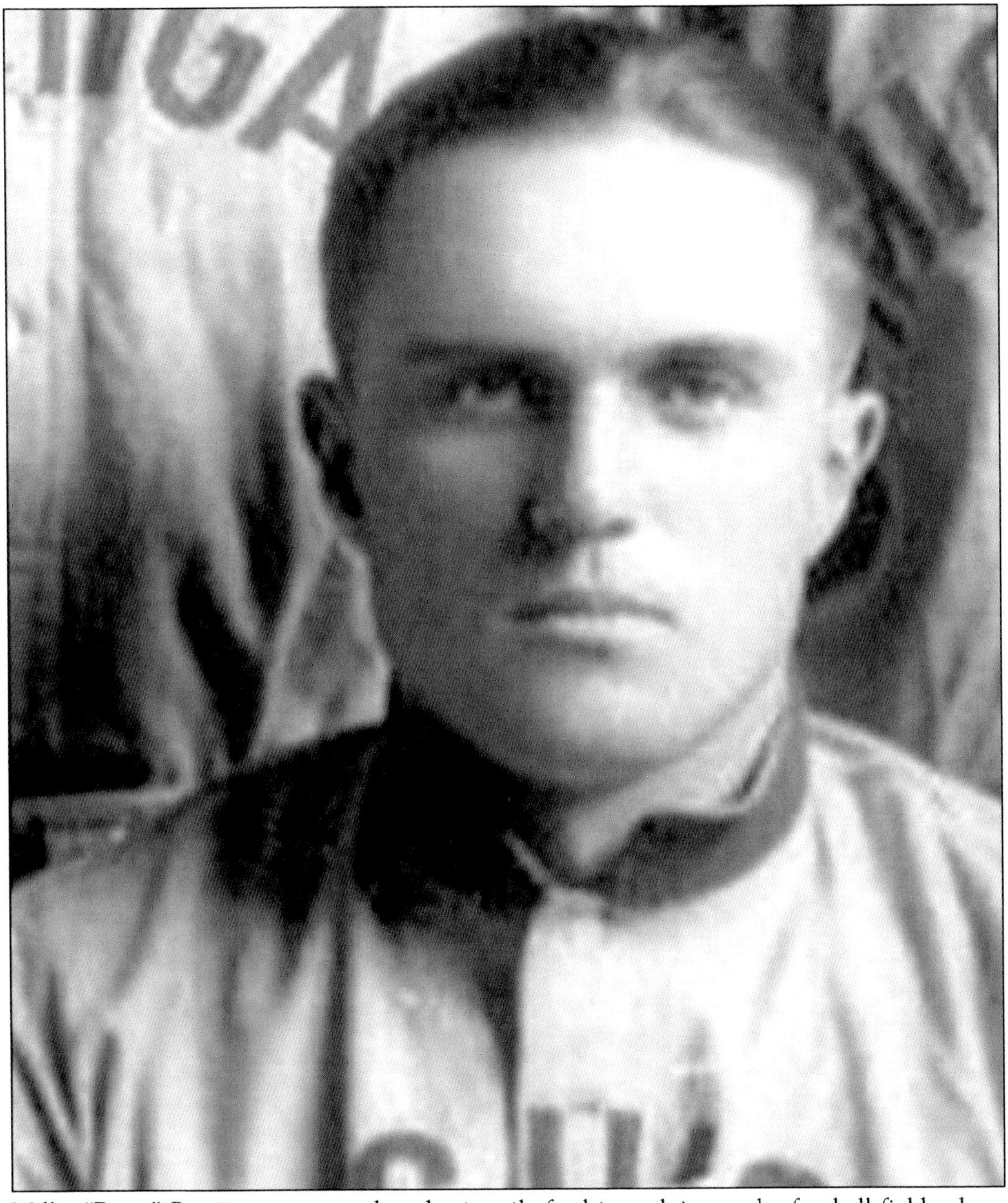

Miller "Brute" Pontius was remembered primarily for his exploits on the football field, where he was named to the All-Western team in 1912 at end, and was a consensus All-American the following year at tackle. As a first-baseman, Pontius earned two letters under Coach Branch Rickey (1912–1913). Following graduation with a degree in Liberal Arts, Pontius entered Michigan Law School, from which he was graduated in 1914. During World War I, he served as a field artillery officer with the American Expeditionary Force. Following the war, Pontius returned to college sports as an assistant football coach, first at Tennessee, and then under Fielding Yost at Michigan. In 1925, he began a long career in investment banking. At the time of his death in 1960 at age 69, Pontius was Vice-President of the Michigan Alumni Association as well as a governor of the Clements Library Association on the University campus. (Courtesy of the Bentley Historical Library.)

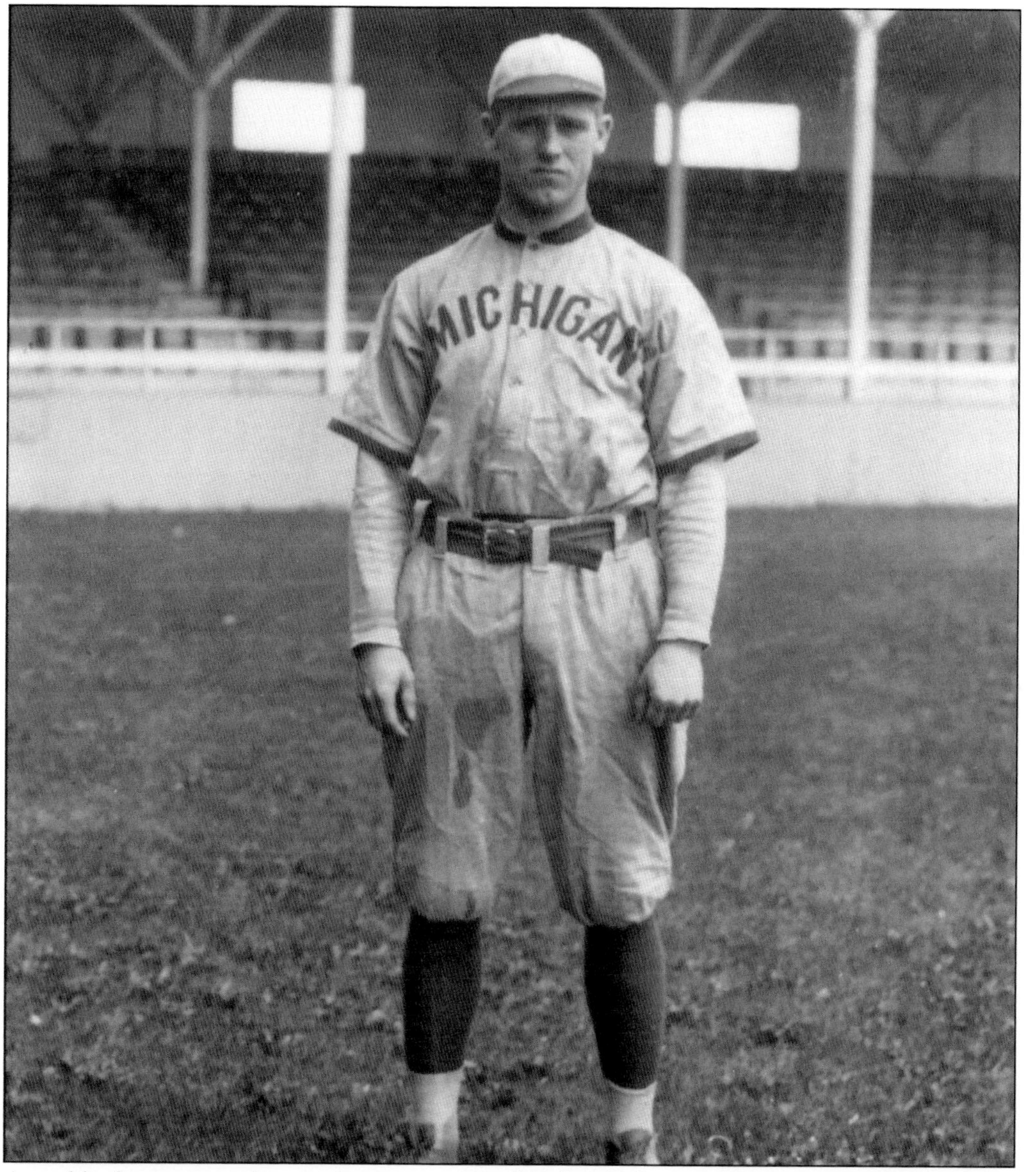

Arguably the greatest player to have participated in baseball at Michigan, George Sisler earned three varsity letters in the sport (1913–1915). Sisler first came to the attention of Coach Branch Rickey in 1912, when as a pitcher for the freshman team he tossed a one-hitter against the varsity while striking out 20. Playing three positions at various times during his career: pitcher, first base and outfield, Sisler produced a career batting average of .404. During his first year with the varsity (1913) he led the team with a .449 average, while in 1915, he batted .420. His career offensive statistics included 10 home runs and 48 stolen bases. Many of Sisler's statistics would be Michigan records if such totals were included along with those of more recent players. Were it not for chronic problems with a sore arm, Sisler might have made his mark as a pitcher. In 26 games over the course of his varsity career, he compiled a record of 20-3. In 189 innings, Sisler struck out 264 batters, an average of over 12 per game. One week after graduating with a degree in mechanical engineering, Sisler was pitching in the major leagues for the St. Louis Browns and Manager Branch Rickey. (Courtesy of the Bentley Historical Library.)

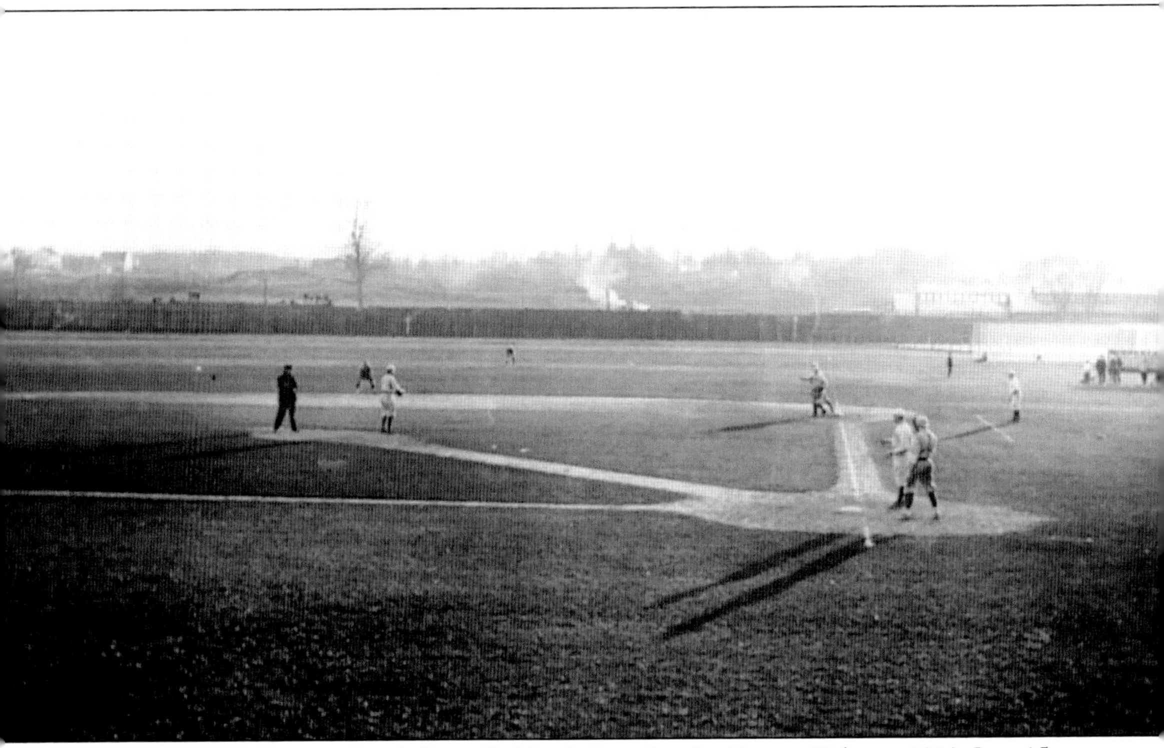

The batter seen here at South Ferry Field is believed to be George Sisler, *c.* 1912. In a 15-year Major League career, Sisler compiled a lifetime batting average of .340. Twice he batted over .400. In 1920, he set a record with 257 hits. A severe sinus infection in 1923 cost him that season, and undoubtedly limited his impact in subsequent years. Sisler was elected to the National Baseball Hall of Fame in 1939, among the first of the inductees. He died in 1973.

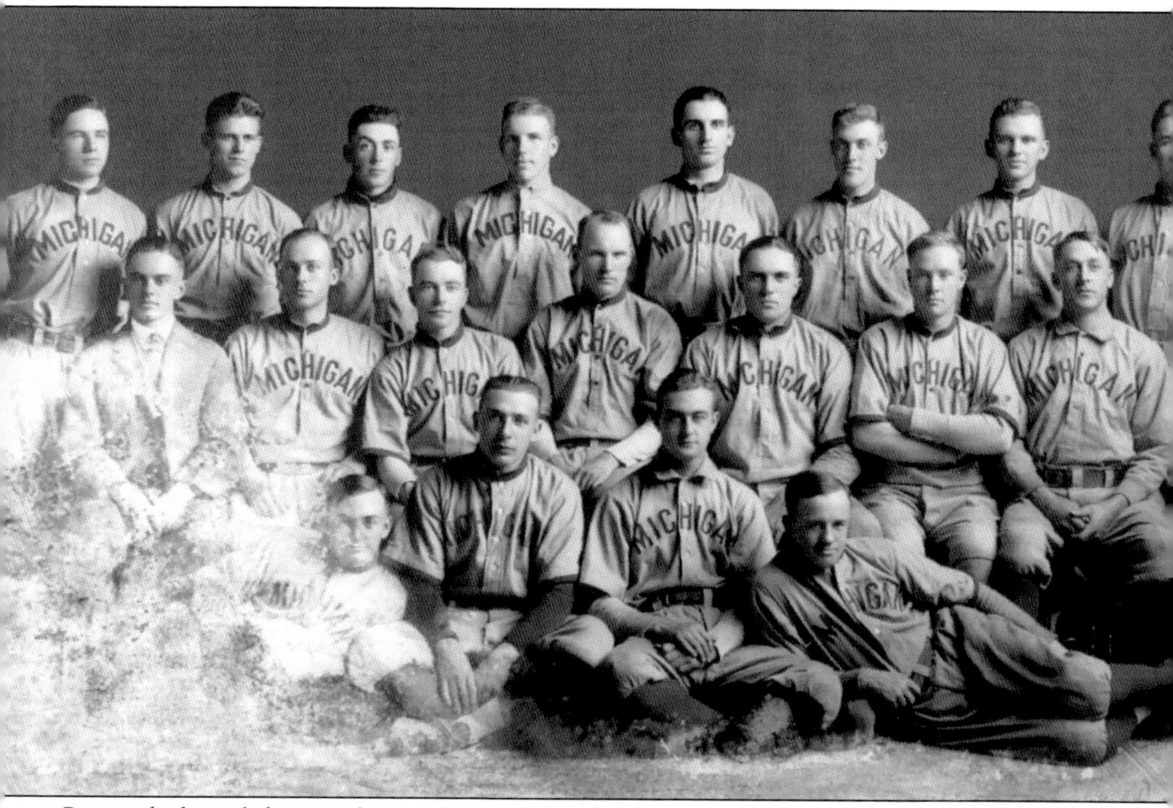

Pictured, from left to right, is the 1913 Michigan team: (front row) Sheehy, Stewart, Davidson, and Hughitt; (middle row) Ford, Baribeau, Dunagan, Bell, Pontius, Howard, and Rickey (coach); (back row) Webber, Sisler, Baker, Rodgers, McQueen, Cory, Baier, and Quaintance. The 1913 team proved to be the strongest squad during Branch Rickey's four years as coach. Starting with a 5-2 record during the annual Southern tour, the team finished with a record of 27-4-1. Pitcher/outfielder George Sisler batted .464 during the Southern trip, as well as winning two of the five games from the mound. Sisler finished the season, his first with the varsity, with an average of .449, including four home runs and 20 stolen bases. On the mound, Sisler was the leading hurler with a record of 8-1, including 104 strikeouts in his 72 innings pitched. Other contributors to the outstanding season included pitchers Roy Baribeau and Cregar Quaintance. (Bentley Historical Library.)

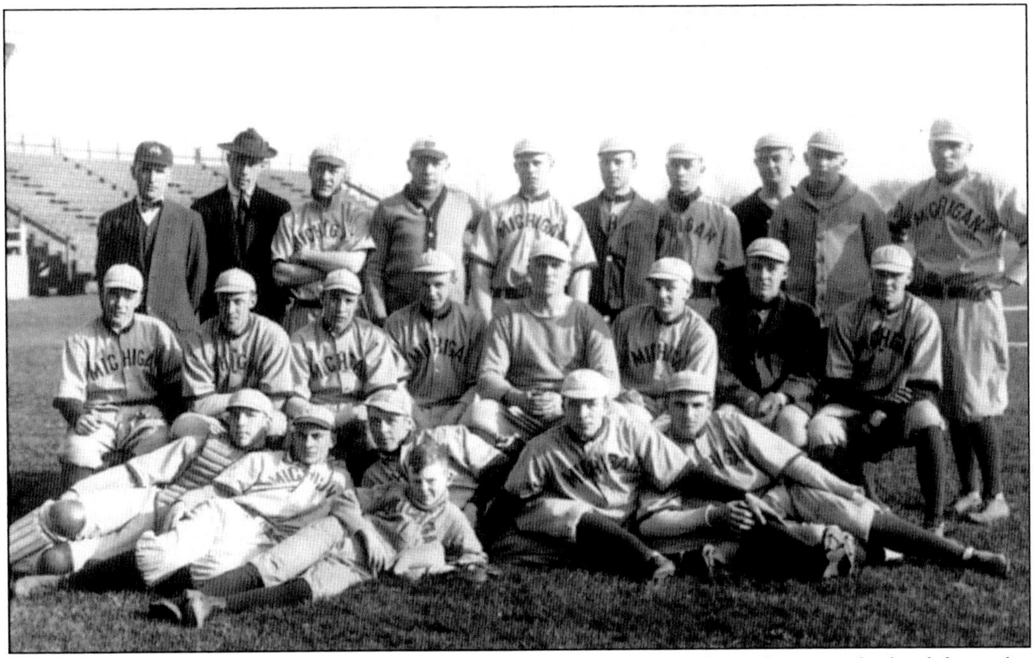

Photo of the 1913 team taken on South Ferry Field. Coach Branch Rickey stands third from the left, back row. George Sisler is fifth from the left. (Courtesy of the Bentley Historical Library.)

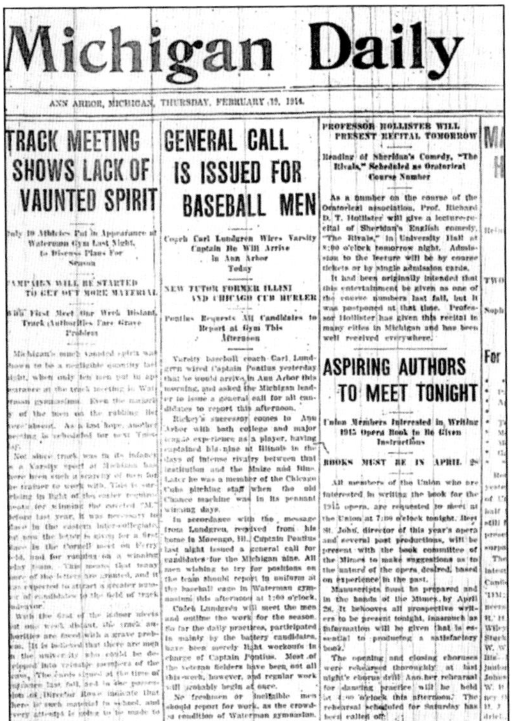

Michigan Daily

ANN ARBOR, MICHIGAN, THURSDAY, FEBRUARY 19, 1914.

TRACK MEETING SHOWS LACK OF VAUNTED SPIRIT

Only 10 Athletes Put in Appearance at Waterman Gym Last Night, to Discuss Plans For Season

CAMPAIGN WILL BE STARTED TO GET OUT MORE MATERIAL

With First Meet One Week Distant, Track Authorities Face Grave Problem

GENERAL CALL IS ISSUED FOR BASEBALL MEN

Coach Carl Lundgren Wires Varsity Captain He Will Arrive in Ann Arbor Today

NEW TUTOR FORMER ILLINI AND CHICAGO CUB HURLER

Pontius Requests All Candidates to Report at Gym This Afternoon

Varsity baseball coach Carl Lundgren wired Captain Pontius yesterday that he would arrive in Ann Arbor this morning, and asked the Michigan leader to issue a general call for all candidates to report this afternoon.

Rickey's successor comes to Ann Arbor with both college and major league experience as a player, having captained his nine at Illinois in the days of intense rivalry between that institution and the Maize and Blue. Later he was a member of the Chicago Cubs pitching staff when the old Chance machine was in its pennant winning days.

In accordance with the message from Lundgren, received from his home in Marengo, Ill., Captain Pontius last night issued a general call for candidates for the Michigan nine. All men wishing to try for positions on the team should report in uniform at the baseball cage in Waterman gymnasium this afternoon at 1:00 o'clock. Coach Lundgren will meet the men and outline the work for the season. So far the daily practices, participated in mainly by the battery candidates, have been merely light workouts in charge of Captain Pontius. Most of the veteran fielders have been out all this week, however, and regular work will probably begin at once.

No freshmen or ineligible men should report for work, as the crowded condition of Waterman gymnasium makes it impossible to accommodate suitably the regular candidates.

PROFESSOR HOLLISTER WILL PRESENT RECITAL TOMORROW

Reading of Sheridan's Comedy, "The Rivals," Scheduled as Oratorical Course Number

As a number on the course of the Oratorical association, Prof. Richard D. T. Hollister will give a lecture-recital of Sheridan's English comedy, "The Rivals," in University Hall at 8:00 o'clock tomorrow night. Admission to the lecture will be by course tickets or by single admission cards.

It had been originally intended that this entertainment be given as one of the course numbers last fall, but it was postponed at that time. Professor Hollister has given this recital in many cities in Michigan and has been well received everywhere.

ASPIRING AUTHORS TO MEET TONIGHT

Union Members Interested in Writing 1915 Opera Book to Be Given Instructions

BOOKS MUST BE IN APRIL 28

All members of the Union who are interested in writing the book for the 1915 opera, are requested to meet at the Union at 7:00 o'clock tonight. Bert St. John, director of this year's opera and several past productions, will be present with the book committee of the Mimes to make suggestions as to the nature of the opera desired, based on experience in the past.

Manuscripts must be prepared and in the hands of the Mimes by April 28. It behooves all prospective writers to be present tonight, inasmuch as information will be given that is essential to producing a satisfactory book.

The opening and closing choruses were rehearsed thoroughly at last night's chorus drill. Another rehearsal for dancing practice will be held at 4:00 o'clock this afternoon. The rehearsal scheduled for Saturday has been called off.

"SCARECROW" TO BE PLAYED IN PORT HURON SATURDAY

Former Chicago Cub hurler Carl Lundgren replaced Branch Rickey as Michigan coach following Rickey's resignation after the 1913 season. Lundgren would remain as Michigan coach through 1920, winning three consecutive conference championships. (Courtesy of the *Michigan Daily*.)

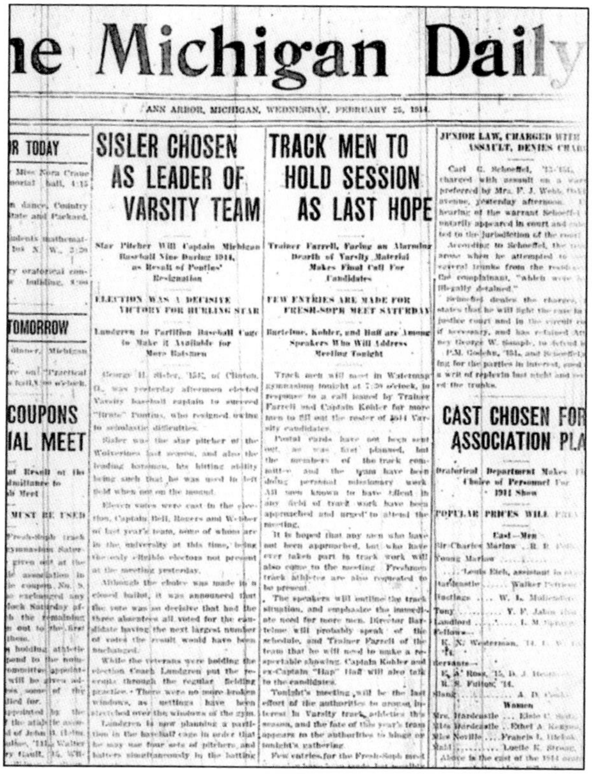

e Michigan Dail

ANN ARBOR, MICHIGAN, WEDNESDAY, FEBRUARY 25, 1914.

SISLER CHOSEN AS LEADER OF VARSITY TEAM

Star Pitcher Will Captain Michigan Baseball Nine During 1914, as Result of Pontius' Resignation

ELECTION WAS A DECISIVE VICTORY FOR HURLING STAR

Lundgren to Partition Baseball Cage to Make it Available for More Batsmen

TRACK MEN TO HOLD SESSION AS LAST HOPE

Trainer Farrell, Facing an Alarming Dearth of Varsity Material Makes Final Call For Candidates

FEW ENTRIES ARE MADE FOR FRESH-SOPH MEET SATURDAY

Bartelme, Kohler, and Huff are Among Speakers Who Will Address Meeting Tonight

CAST CHOSEN FOR ASSOCIATION PLA

George Sisler was arguably the greatest ball player to grace a Michigan diamond. The initiation of Sisler's major league career began with a strong element of controversy. In 1911, at the age of 17 and just out of Central High School, Sisler signed with Akron of the Ohio-Pennsylvania League. A year later, his contract was purchased by the Pittsburgh Pirates. Pittsburgh, perhaps not unreasonably, expected the former Michigan star to join the team after his graduation. But Branch Rickey, now a lawyer, pointed out that Sisler was underage at the time of his signing, and permission to sign had not been granted by his father. Judge George Codd, himself a former University of Michigan pitcher, ruled in favor of Rickey. The result was that the National Commission, which ruled baseball at the time, had no choice but to declare the original contract void and Sisler a free agent. Sisler then signed with Rickey. (Courtesy of the *Michigan Daily*.)

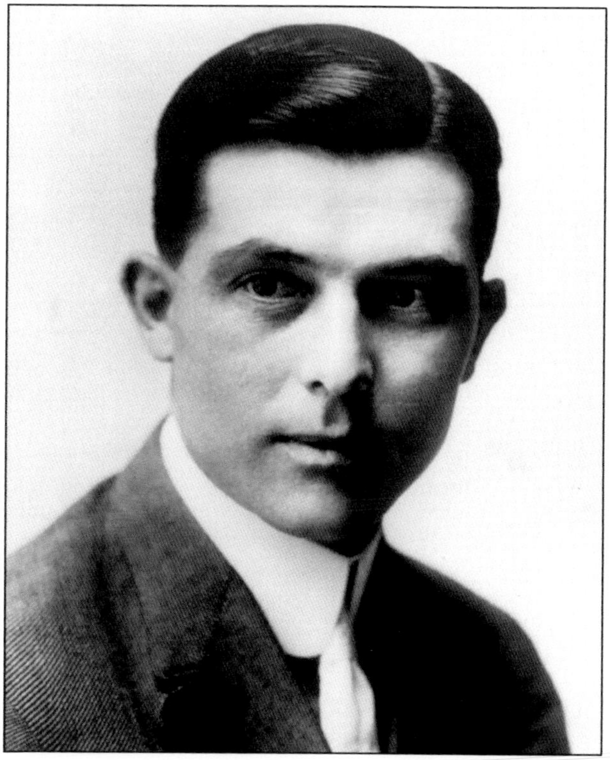

Carl Lundgren coached Michigan baseball from 1914–1920, finishing with a record of 94-33-6, and directing the team to three consecutive conference championships. While a student at the University of Illinois, Lundgren lettered in both football and baseball. Twice Illinois won the conference title (1900, 1902), in large part as a result of Lundgren's pitching. He was honored by election to captain his senior year of 1902. Following graduation, Lundgren signed with the Chicago Cubs. In eight seasons, he compiled a lifetime record of 91-55. After leaving Michigan following the 1920 season, Lundgren returned to Illinois where he served as baseball coach and assistant athletic director until his death in 1934. During his tenure at Illinois, Lundgren's squads won five "Big Ten" Conference titles. (Bentley Historical Library.)

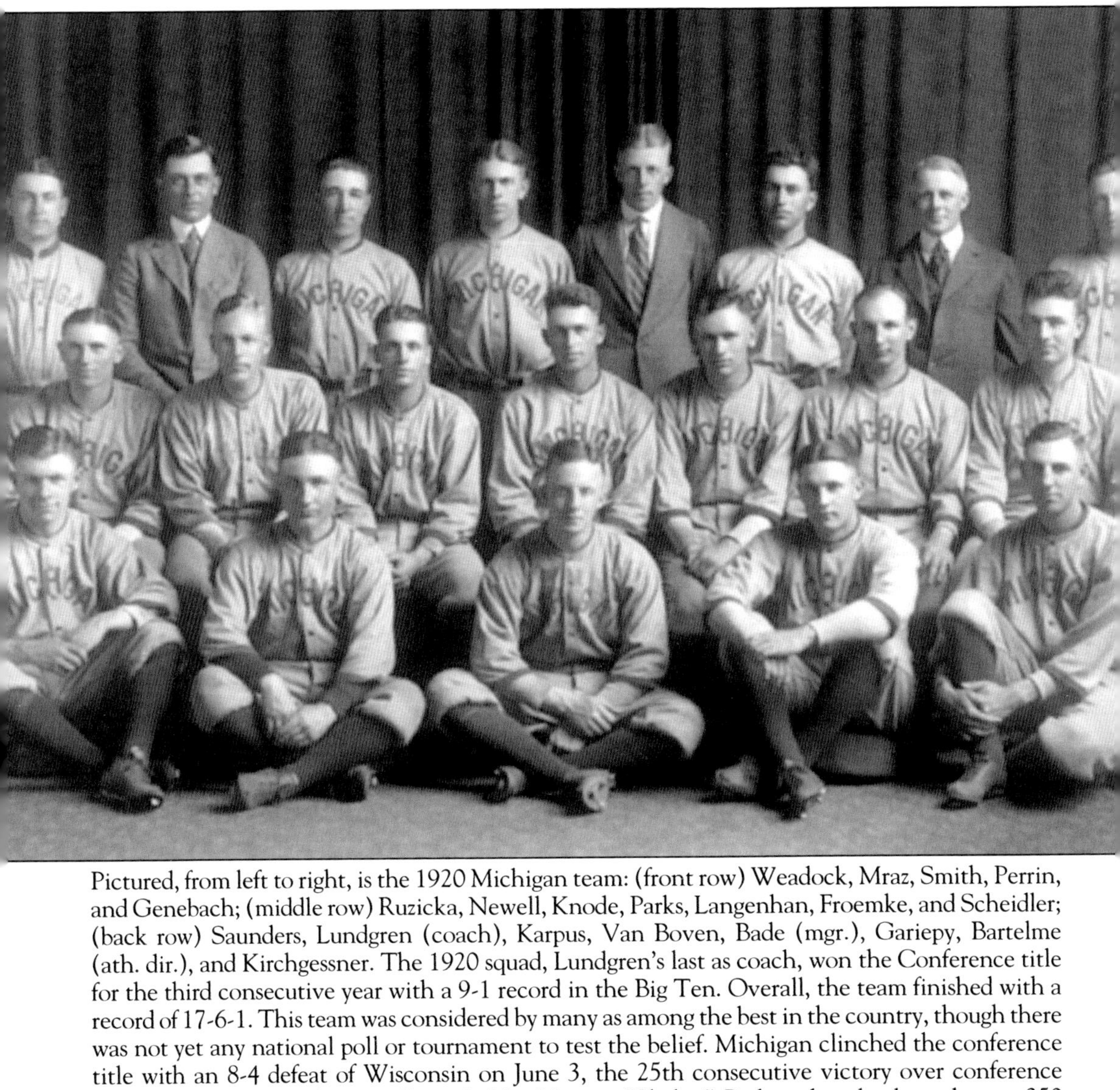

Pictured, from left to right, is the 1920 Michigan team: (front row) Weadock, Mraz, Smith, Perrin, and Genebach; (middle row) Ruzicka, Newell, Knode, Parks, Langenhan, Froemke, and Scheidler; (back row) Saunders, Lundgren (coach), Karpus, Van Boven, Bade (mgr.), Gariepy, Bartelme (ath. dir.), and Kirchgessner. The 1920 squad, Lundgren's last as coach, won the Conference title for the third consecutive year with a 9-1 record in the Big Ten. Overall, the team finished with a record of 17-6-1. This team was considered by many as among the best in the country, though there was not yet any national poll or tournament to test the belief. Michigan clinched the conference title with an 8-4 defeat of Wisconsin on June 3, the 25th consecutive victory over conference competition. The pitching staff was led by Vernon "Slicker" Parks, who also batted over .350 for the season. In his two years as pitcher (1919–1920), Parks never lost a conference game. He served as team captain for the season, and was re-elected to the position for the following year. Only John Hibbard ('87) had previously been so honored to that point. However, that summer of 1920, Parks played professionally for the minor league team in Portland, and was subsequently dismissed from the squad. In July, Carl Lundgren announced he was resigning as coach to return to his alma mater Illinois, replacing the equally legendary George Huff. Lundgren had graduated from Illinois some fifteen years earlier, and where he had also been captain of the baseball team. Following a career with the Chicago Cubs, Lundgren came to Michigan in 1914, replacing Branch Rickey. (Courtesy of the Bentley Historical Library.)

FOUR

The Ray Fisher Era

1921–1958

Following the resignation of Carl Lundgren in July 1920, Philip Bartelme, Athletic Director at the University, contacted former coach Branch Rickey for advice on Lundgren's successor. Rickey suggested Derrill Pratt, second baseman on Rickey's St. Louis Browns between 1912 and 1917, with the result that Pratt signed a three-year contract to serve as the new coach. In the meantime, Ray Fisher had also heard the coaching position at Michigan had become vacant, and he too let his interests be known to Bartelme. Fisher applied too late, as the contract with Pratt had already been signed.

But other opportunities intervened. Harry Frazee, owner of the Boston Red Sox, was in need of a hard hitting second baseman, and Pratt seemed the man for the job. Following extended negotiations between Frazee and Pratt, a contract rumored to be $25,000 for two years was offered by the Red Sox and tentatively accepted, dependent on the Board in Control of Athletics granting permission for Pratt to leave. On April 6, 1920, the Board agreed to release Pratt from his contract, and on April 8, Fisher was signed as the new baseball coach at a salary of $5,000 per year. Fisher's duties also included roles as assistant coach for the football team, and coach of freshman basketball.

There remained a problem, however. Fisher was still under contract to the Cincinnati Reds, and Owner Garry Hermann refused to approve any release. Fisher joined the Michigan team during its southern tour, turning his back on Cincinnati. In consequence, Hermann placed him on the ineligible list, a move later supported by Baseball Commissioner Kenesaw Mountain Landis. Fisher would spend most of the rest of his long life banned from Major League baseball.[1]

Fisher's 1921 team contained as a nucleus many of the same players who had led the team to three consecutive Big Ten championships under Carl Lundgren. But before the season began, star pitcher Vernon "Slicker" Parks was accused, correctly, of having played professionally for Portland under the name of Harold Brooks. The loss of Parks left Fisher with few veteran pitchers. Nevertheless, the season came down to the final game, with Michigan in a tie for the championship. A 7-6 loss to Wisconsin in the final conference match cost Michigan the title.

Fisher had helped arrange for two games to be played with a touring club from Waseda University in Japan, and so at the end of June 1921, Michigan defeated the Japanese club by scores of 2-1 and 1-0. The second game was won on a ninth inning home run by shortstop and team captain Pete Van Boven, on Van Boven's last swing in a Michigan uniform.

Michigan again placed second in the "Big Ten" the following year, but by 1923, the team was ready to challenge strong Ohio State and Illinois squads for the title. Despite the loss of hard hitting first baseman Bob Knobe, declared ineligible midway through the season, the "Big Ten" season came down to the final two games. A home run by Knobe's replacement, John Shackleford, into the right field tennis courts provided the difference for Howard Liverance in an 11-7 victory over Illinois. Liverance then pitched Michigan to a 5-2 victory over Ohio State to clinch Fisher's first of fifteen conference championships.

During the 1920s and 1930s, Fisher was instrumental in arranging a series of baseball exchanges between teams from Japan and the University of Michigan. Ann Arbor had been host to a team from Keio in 1911, and the goodwill exchange was repeated in 1921, when a touring squad from Waseda University visited in 1921. In 1924, Ann Arbor was host to a team from Meiji in 1924, and Osaka Mainichi in 1925.

In 1929, Coach George Otsuki invited Fisher and the Michigan team to tour Japan, and on July 31st of that year, fourteen players from the 1928 "Big Ten" champion, as well as Fisher and his family, left Ann Arbor for a month-long tour of California, Hawaii and Japan. After defeating the Honolulu Giants, Michigan proceeded to Japan. The Michigan squad won eleven of thirteen games, losing once each to Meiji and Waseda Universities. In 1932, Fisher and the Michigan team again toured Japan, winning eleven of fifteen games.[2]

During the ten-year period from 1941 to 1950, Fisher's teams won seven conference championships, representing the longest string of victories in his career. Future Tiger Dick Wakefield, who played for Fisher in 1941, was among the powerful hitters during this period. Approaching retirement over a decade later, Fisher would still consider Wakefield among his most outstanding players,

The war years were particularly difficult, with travel restrictions and movement of players within the armed services. Between 1943 and 1946, Michigan defeated "Big Ten" opponents twenty-one consecutive times; between 1945 and 1946, Michigan won twenty-seven consecutive games. The 1944 squad was led by pitcher Elroy "Crazy Legs" Hirsch, more noted for his football exploits at Wisconsin, but who was a Marine trainee at Michigan that year. Hirsch led the staff with a 6-1 mark, as well as hitting .355 in nine games. Lefthander Bo Bowman finished with a record of 6-2, helping lead Michigan to an undefeated season in the conference.

Fisher retired following the 1958 season, leaving with a coaching record of 637-294-8, including 15 conference championships and 1 NCAA Championship in the 1953 College World Series. Fisher continued as an adviser for his replacement, Don Lund, as well as serving as spring training pitching coach in later years for both the Braves and Tigers. In 1980, Fisher was reinstated by baseball Commissioner Bowie Kuhn. Fisher died two years later at the age of 95.

[1] An excellent account of the political machinations related to the banning of Fisher can be found in the article by Donald Proctor: "The Blacklisting of Baseball's Ray Fisher." (See Bibliography.)

[2] Yoshimura, Valerie. "Samarais of Summer." *Michigan Today*, vol. 30, #2, 1998. p.24.

Year	Won(overall)	Lost(overall)	Won(conference)	Lost(conference)	Position
1921	21	4	10	2	2nd
1922	21	6	9	3	2nd
1923	22	4	10	0	1st
1924	13	3	8	2	1st
1925	17	8	7	4	4th
1926	16	7	9	2	1st
1927	16	8	8	4	3rd
1928	22	5	11	1	1st
1929 [3]	15	6	7	2	1st
1930	9	15 (1 Tie)	3	6	7th
1931	11	7	5	4	5th
1932 [4]	19	15 (1 Tie)	4	5	7th
1933	12	4	8	2	2nd
1934	15	9	6	6	3rd
1935	11	11	6	5	5th
1936	20	5	9	1	1st
1937	16	8	5	6	6th
1938	14	12	4	6	8th
1939	18	9 (2 Ties)	8	4	3rd
1940	10	12	7	5	5th
1941	24	8	10	2	1st
1942	17	9	10	2	1st (Tie)
1943	8	4	3	2	6th
1944	15	4 (1 Tie)	8	0	1st
1945	20	1	8	0	1st
1946 [5]	18	3	6	2	2nd
1947	18	10	7	4	3rd
1948	21	6	10	2	1st
1949	18	9 (2 Ties)	8	4	1st
1950	18	9	9	3	1st
1951	13	10	4	8	8th
1952	16	7	8	4	1st (Tie)
1953	21	9	10	3	1st [6]
1954	22	9	10	5	3rd
1955	17	11 (1 Tie)	8	7	5th
1956	17	9	6	5	4th
1957	17	7	7	4	3rd
1958	18	12	7	8	6th

[3] Record does not include four victories during tour of western United States in August, 1929, and victories in eleven of thirteen games during tour of Japan during August and September.
[4] Record includes victories in eleven of fifteen games during tour of Japan in August and September, 1932. In Pack's early history of Michigan sports, *100 Years of Athletics*, the author does not include results of the tour in Fisher's won and lost total.
[5] Record includes 6-1 loss in exhibition against Detroit Tigers.
[6] NCAA Champion

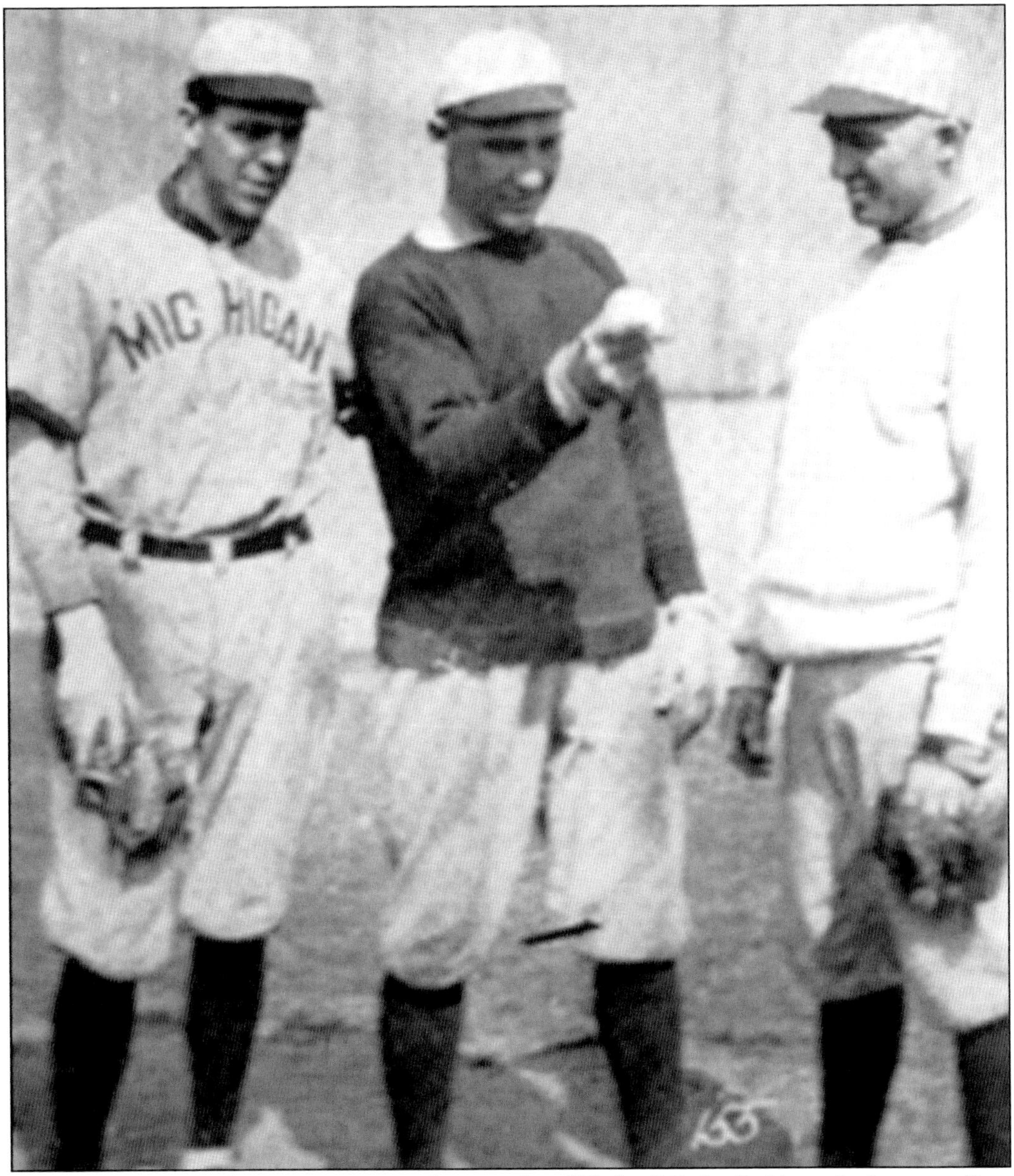

Coach Derrill Pratt demonstrates a pitch to pitcher "Slicker" Parks (left), with shortstop Pete Van Boven (right) looking on. Pratt was initially signed to replace Carl Lundgren as coach following the 1920 season. However, he found an offer from the Boston Red Sox too good to refuse. Pratt was replaced by Ray Fisher. Vernon "Slicker" Parks played on the conference champions of 1919 and 1920, hitting over .350 that second year in addition to having never lost a conference game in which he pitched. He was elected captain of both the 1920 and 1921 teams. However, it was disclosed that during the summer of 1920, he pitched for Portland under the name of Harold Brooks, and was dismissed from the Michigan team. Parks spent 1921 pitching for the Detroit Tigers, producing a record of 3-2 in his sole major league season. With the dismissal of Parks, Van Boven was elected captain of the 1921 team. Van Boven finished his senior season in style. In his final at bat, his home run produced the sole tally in a 1-0 victory over Waseda University of Japan. (Courtesy of the *Michiganensian*.)

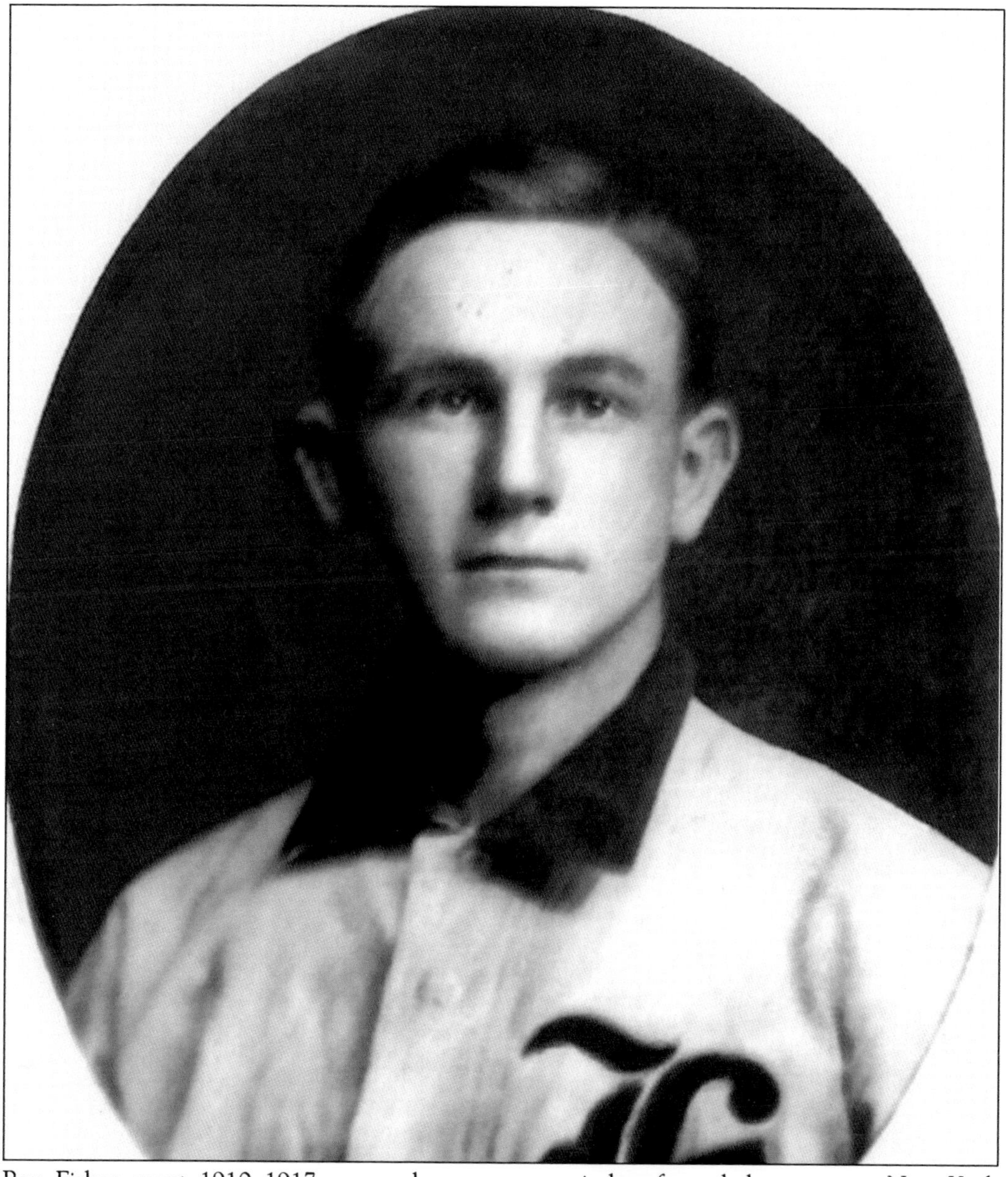

Ray Fisher spent 1910–1917 as an above average pitcher for a below average New York Highlanders/Yankees team, posting a record of 73-77. Both Ty Cobb and Nap Lajoie considered Fisher among the toughest dozen pitchers in the American League. Following service during the First World War, Fisher was traded to Cincinnati, where he immediately clashed with owner August "Garry" Herrmann over his salary. Fisher was a major factor in bringing the first modern pennant to Cincinnati in 1919, winning fourteen games. The World Series that year against the White Sox became notorious, as members of the Sox accepted bribes to "throw" the series. Despite such efforts, the Sox did manage to win three (of the best of nine) games, Fisher being the losing pitcher in one of them. "Even when they were throwing the game, you couldn't beat them!" – Don Lund, once snapped in anger at Fisher. Fisher played one more year at Cincinnati, finishing with a career record of 100-94 and an ERA of 2.82, before accepting the coaching position at Michigan. (Courtesy of the National Baseball Hall of Fame and Museum.)

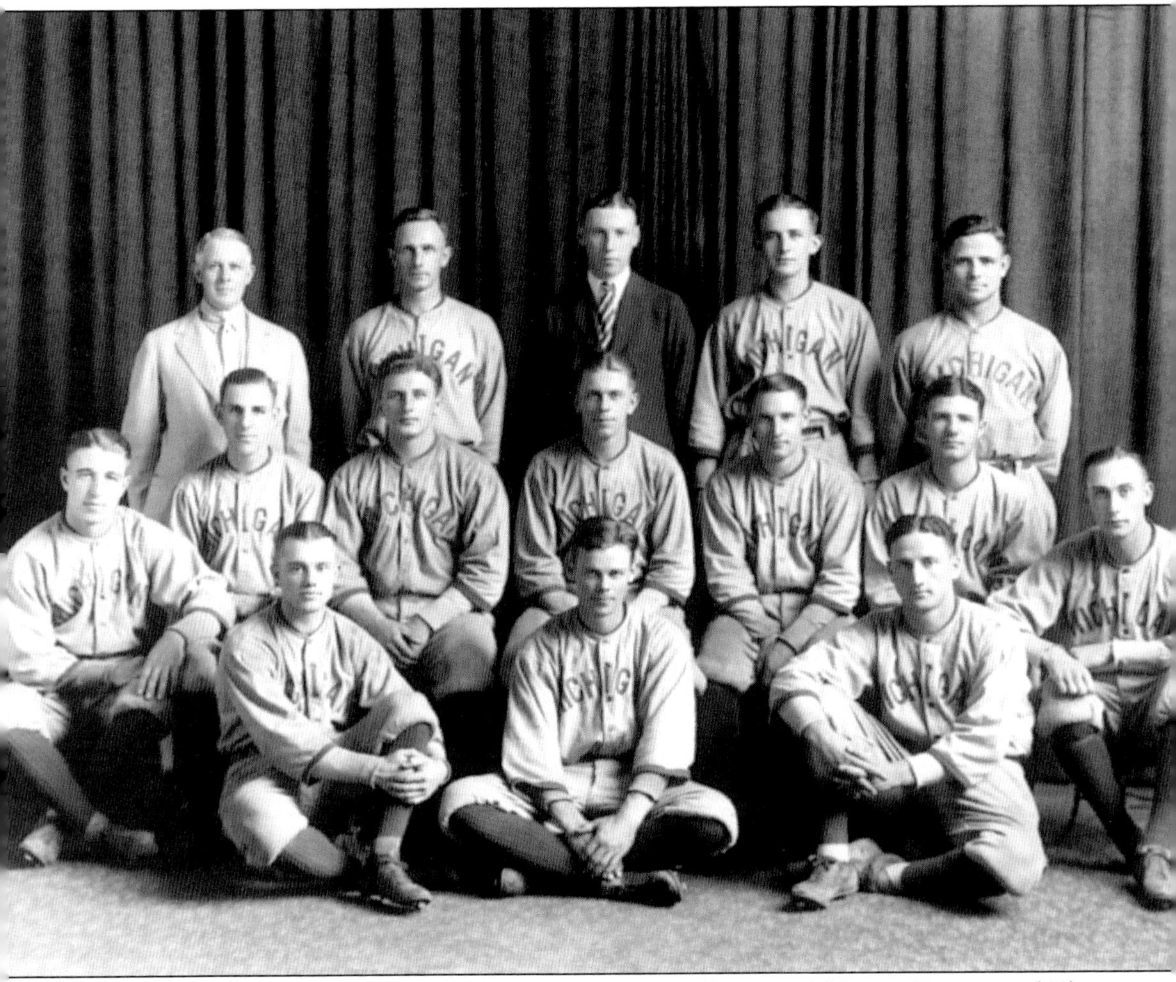

Pictured, from left to right, is the 1921 Michigan team: (front row) Uteritz, Ronan, and Klein; (middle row) Karpus, Genebach, Vick, Van Boven, Perrin, Johnson, and Liverance; (back row) Bartelme (ath. dir.), Fisher (coach), Porter (mgr.), Dixon, and Roby. 1921 was the first year as coach at Michigan for Ray Fisher. He had a tough act to follow. Carl Lundgren had led the team to three consecutive Big Ten championships. Ken Knode, backbone of the infield for the three championship years, had graduated. "Slicker" Parks, 1920 captain and star pitcher, was dismissed from the team for having played professionally. In addition, the question as to whether Lundgren's replacement would be Del Pratt or Fisher had created a significant amount of confusion. Pratt was in charge of the indoor practice early during the training season, while Fisher officially became the coach as the team returned from their spring trip on April 8. Under Fisher, the team won fourteen consecutive games until a 3-2 defeat at the hands of Illinois and their coach, Carl Lundgren. Michigan later defeated Illinois 10-4, and remained in the fight for the conference championship until the end of the season. But Wisconsin pushed through a run in the last inning of the last conference game on June 6, defeating Michigan 7-6 and dropping the team to second place behind Illinois. Pitcher Milt Dixon, pitching on only one day's rest, was unable to hold Wisconsin. (Courtesy of the Bentley Historical Library.)

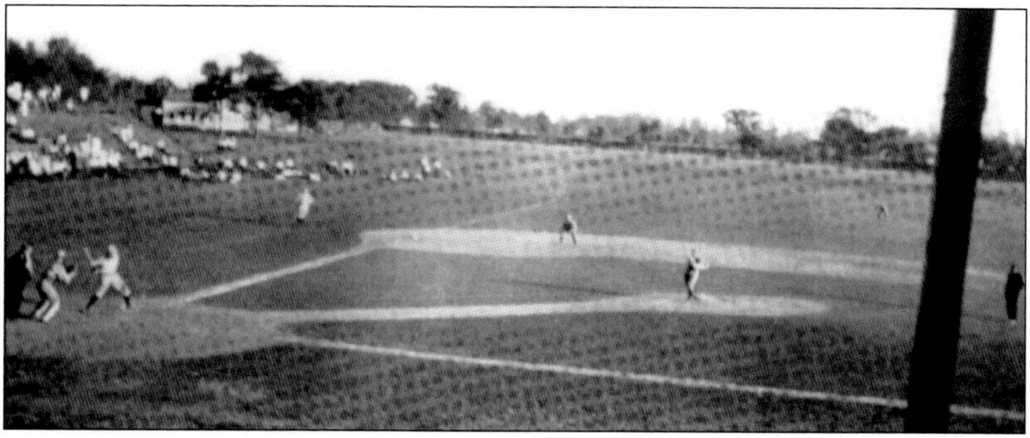

In the 15th inning of this May 30, 1921 ballgame, captain and shortstop Pete Van Boven slams the ball over the Wisconsin center fielder's head, and circles the bases for an inside the park home run. Michigan wins in the 18th, 9-8. Michigan was still playing on old Ferry Field at the time, approximately the site today of Yost arena. Note the absence of an outfield fence. (Courtesy of the *Michiganensian*.)

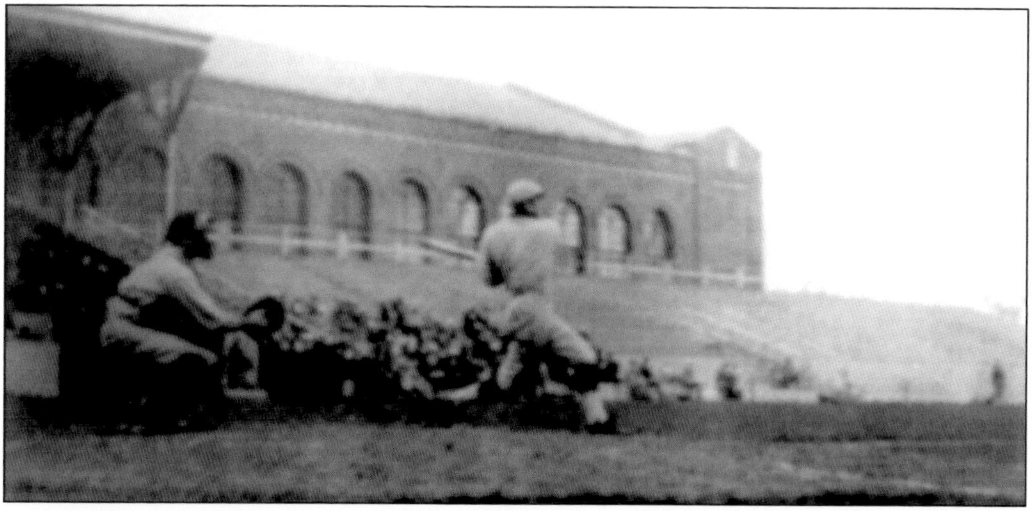

On May 31, 1924, Harry Kipke slammed a home run vs. Wisconsin. Michigan won 9-0, and clinched a tie for the Big Ten title. Harry Kipke ranks among the greatest student-athletes to attend the University of Michigan. Between 1921 and 1923, Kipke won nine letters in football, basketball and baseball. Following graduation, he was hired as baseball coach and assistant football coach at the University of Missouri. After four years at Missouri, Kipke spent one year as football coach at Michigan State College (1928) and then returned to his *alma mater*. As football coach at Michigan from 1929 to 1937, he led the team to four Big Ten titles. He was later honored with election to the National Football Hall of Fame. A University Regent in his later years, Kipke died in 1972. (Courtesy of the *Michiganensian*.)

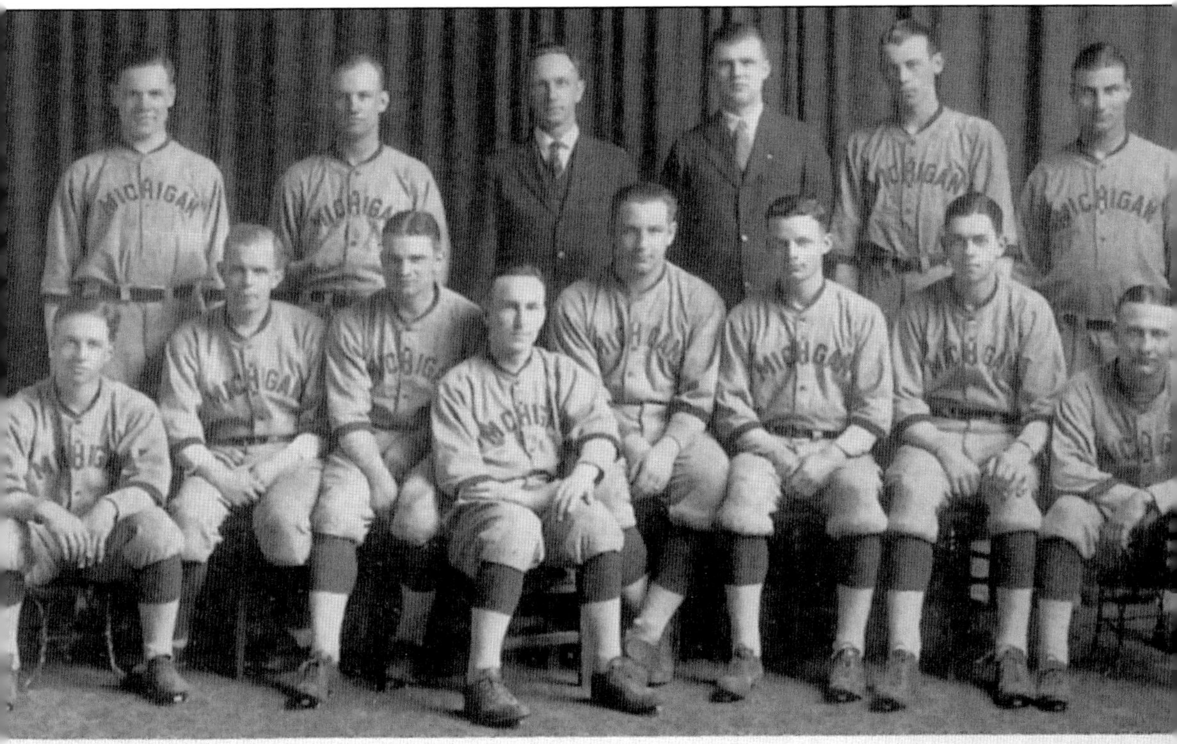

JABLONOWSKI STRYKER FISHER WHITE WILSON STEGER
GILES BENSON KIPKE DEVIEW BLOTT HAGGARTY DILLMAN BACHMA

The 1924 version of the team, conference champions the previous year, opened with only three returning lettermen: Jack Blott (C), George Haggarty (3B) and Harry Kipke (CF). Conference play began April 26 with a 6-5 victory over Ohio State, as Blott scored the winning run in the 11th inning. Blott, as well as Kipke, would provide much of the offense during the season. In a 7-3 victory against Minnesota, Blott led the team with three hits including a home run. Following graduation, Blott signed with Cincinnati of the National League, where he would have a brief career before returning to Ann Arbor.Pete Jablonowski wrapped up the Big Ten title for Michigan with a 9-0 shutout of Wisconsin, while striking out 11. Harry Kipke "iced" the victory with a home run in the 8th inning, his last appearance in a conference game. Jablonowski signed with Cincinnati following his graduation in 1926. Playing primarily under the name of Appleton, he composed a record of 57-66 for 7 teams between 1927 and 1945. In 1936, he posted a 14-9 record with the Washington Senators. (Courtesy of the *Michiganensian*.)

Robert "Ray" Knode was both a quarterback on the football team, and first baseman for Ray Fisher's 1922 baseball squad. Midway through the 1923 season, Knode was declared ineligible, and in June signed with the Cleveland Indians. Knode played four seasons with the Indians (1923–1926), compiling a lifetime average of .266 in 109 games. Knode later coached a variety of sports both in Battle Creek, Michigan and in Findlay, Ohio, as well as serving as an auditor for various companies. Knode died in 1982 at age 81. (Courtesy of the Bentley Historical Library.)

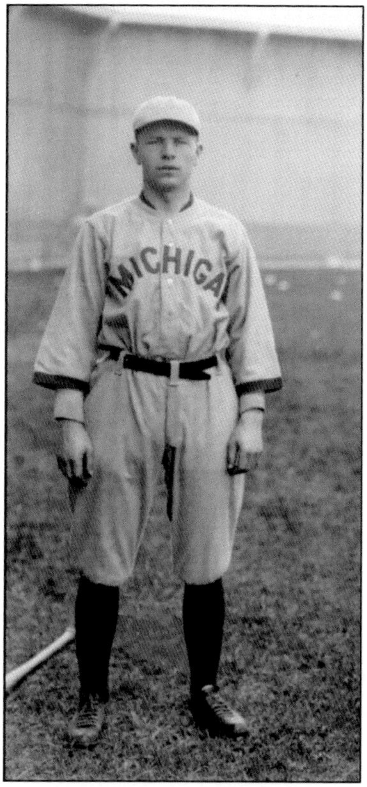

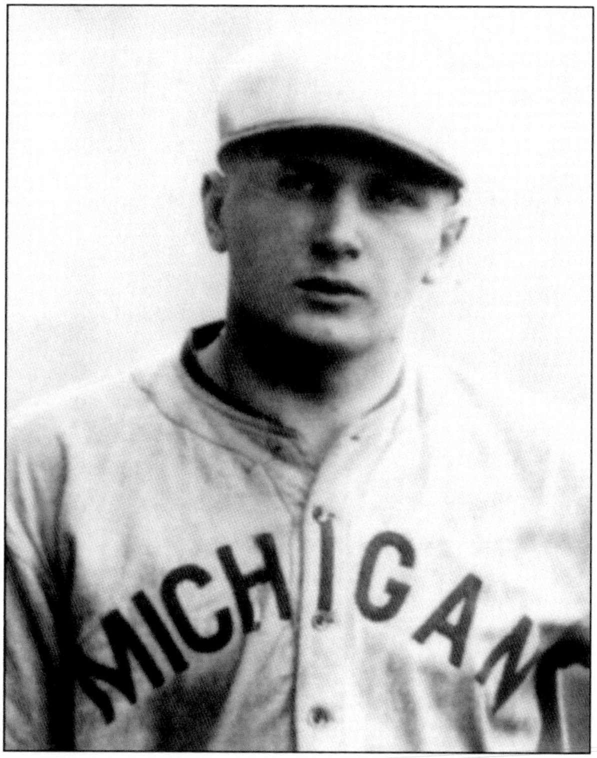

Henry "Ernie" Vick was the Michigan catcher in 1921–1922, as well as being elected captain for the latter season. Also playing center on the football team, Vick was named to the All-American team in 1921. Football coach Fielding H. Yost later hired Vick as an assistant line coach for the team. Following the 1922 season, the stocky (5'10", 185 lbs.) Vick signed with the St. Louis Cardinals. Vick played four seasons in St. Louis, primarily as a substitute catcher and compiling a lifetime batting average of .232. He did catch several games for Hall of Fame pitcher Grover Cleveland Alexander in 1926. Vick returned to football, playing briefly with the Chicago Bears. For 21 years, he was a Big Ten line judge before retiring in 1952. At the time of his death in 1980, Vick was the oldest living former All-American from Michigan. (Courtesy of the Bentley Historical Library.)

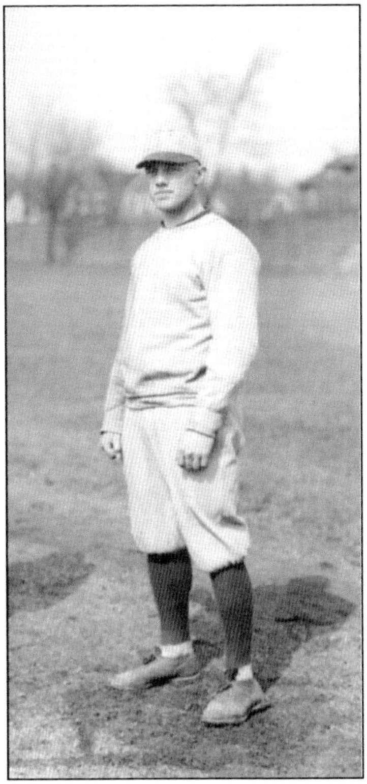

Irwin Uteritz was a mainstay in the infield for three years (1921–1923), primarily at shortstop, as well as being elected captain in 1923. He was considered one of the fastest on the team during his time. The 1923 team was undefeated in conference play, in no small measure due to Uteritz. His home run contributed to an 11-3 victory over Wisconsin, as well as his three hits in a 5-2 win against Ohio State. Uteritz was also a quarterback on the football team during his years at Michigan. Later that decade, Uteritz was hired as an assistant football coach at Wisconsin. In 1930, he was promoted to athletic director, but resigned after four months because of the pressure. Uteritz died in 1963. (Courtesy of the Bentley Historical Library.)

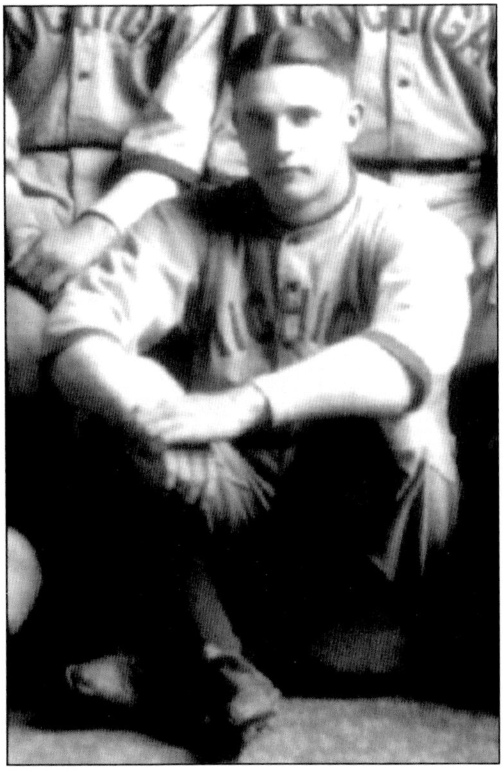

John Perrin was an outfielder for two seasons at Michigan (1920–1921). Following the 1921 season, he briefly played with the Boston Red Sox, hitting .231 his only season with the team. (Bentley Historical Library.)

William "Buck" Giles was the second baseman and leadoff hitter for Michigan during the 1924–1925 seasons. His ability to reach base was a critical factor in Michigan's conference championship in 1924. (Courtesy of the Bentley Historical Library.)

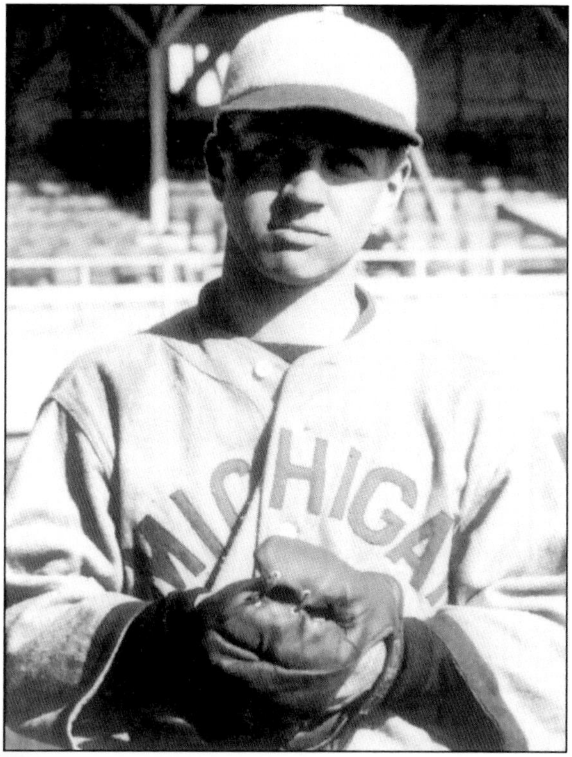

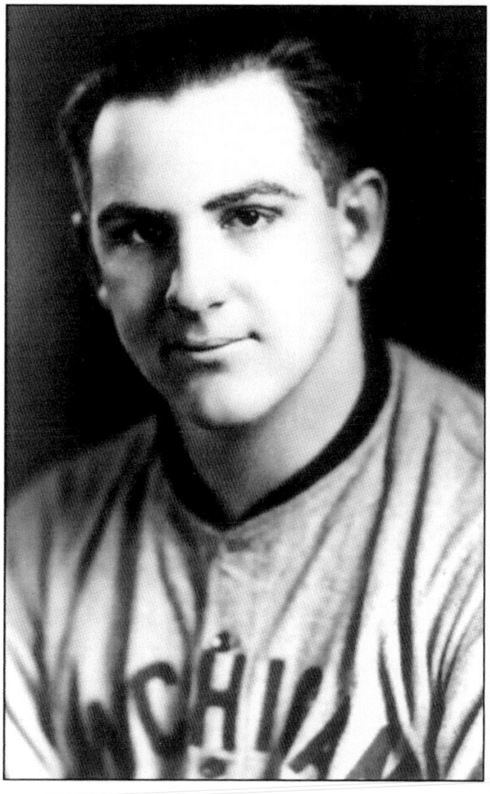

An All-American at center for the 1923 football team, Jack Blott played three seasons as catcher for Ray Fisher (1922–1924). In 1924, he was elected captain. Blott briefly appeared with the Cincinnati Reds in two games during the 1924 season. But he was better known for his football contributions at Michigan. In addition to lettering three years in that sport, Blott was an assistant coach for 23 years. He later managed the ice rink and golf course at the University. Blott died of a heart attack at age 61 in 1964. (Courtesy of the Bentley Historical Library.)

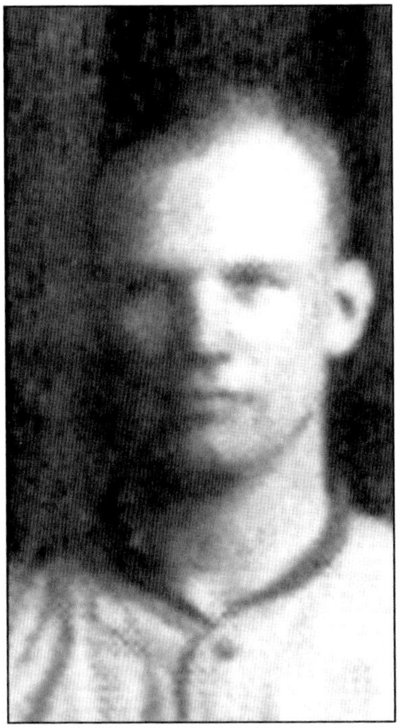

A pitcher on the 1924 Michigan squad, Homer Stryker became better known for his extensive civic contributions in Kalamazoo. Born in 1894, in Athens, Michigan, Stryker attended the University of Michigan, receiving his medical degree there in 1925. He also pitched with the semi-professional Grand Ledge team, as well as coaching baseball at the local high school. Stryker completed a degree program in orthopedic surgery at the University during the 1930s, while simultaneously inventing a walking heel and hospital turning frame. He set up practice in Kalamazoo, where in addition to his medical practice he began selling his orthopedic inventions. The Orthopedic Frame Company was the result. At the same time, Stryker maintained his interest in amateur baseball by coaching the Maroons, a Kalamazoo Legion team. In 1964, the company name was changed to the Stryker Corporation, with his son Lee as President. Lee Stryker died in a plane crash in 1976, and Homer Stryker died four years later at age 85. The company remains a major employer in the Kalamazoo area. In honor of Stryker, the home ballpark of the Kalamazoo Kings, a professional independent league team, was named Homer Stryker Field. (Courtesy of the *Michiganensian*.)

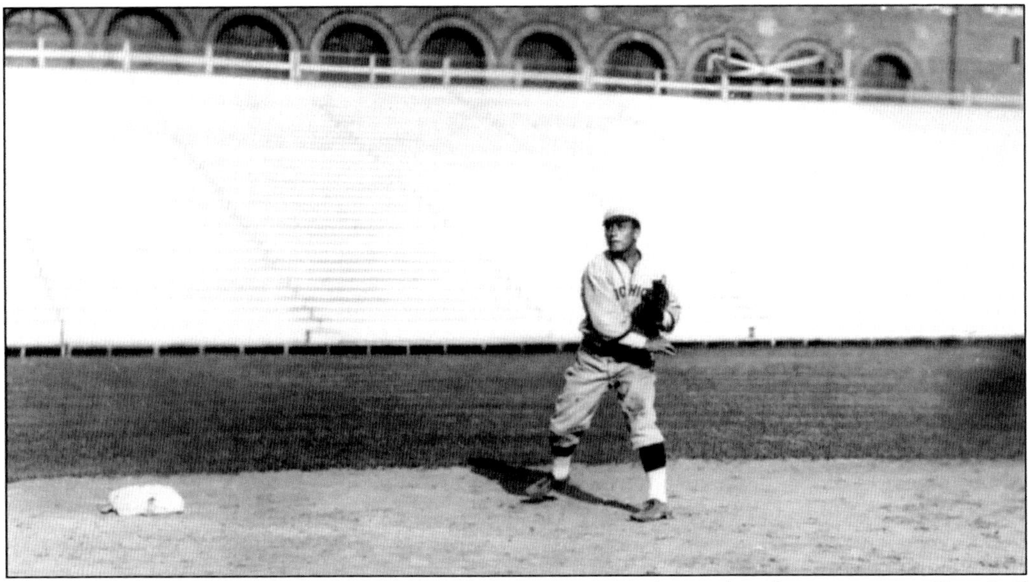

Noted more for his exploits on the football field, Bennie Friedman played two seasons of baseball at Michigan, primarily as a substitute outfielder. In 1925, he went 0-1 at bat, appearing in three games. In 1926, he batted .121. Though only about 5'8", 175 lbs, Friedman was twice named an All-American quarterback (1925, 1926), and was considered one of the greatest at that position for his time. Teamed with Bennie Oosterbaan at end, the two "Bennies" were a dominant force in Big Ten football. Friedman was also elected captain of the 1926 football team, the first Jewish athlete at Michigan to be honored in such a manner. After several years in professional football, Friedman became head coach at City College of New York, and then athletic director and football coach at Brandeis University. He died in 1982 at age 77. (Bentley Historical Library.)

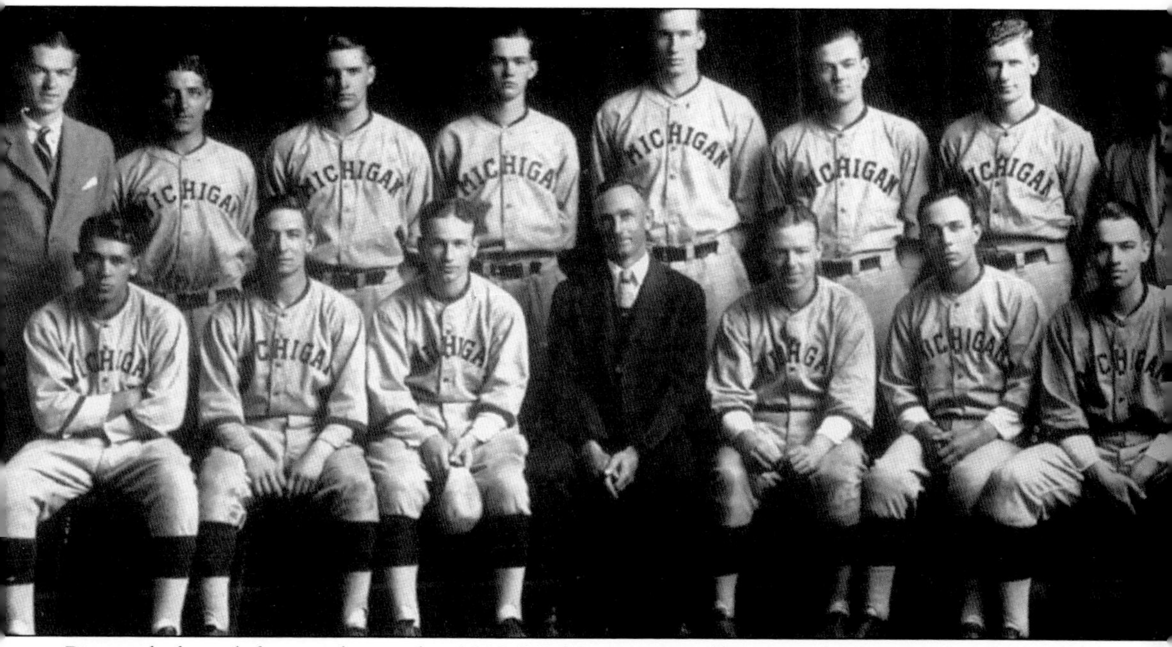

Pictured, from left to right, is the 1928 Michigan team: (front row) Weintraub, Nebelung, Loos (cap.), Fisher (coach), Coriden, Straub, and Slagle; (back row) McKillen, Reichman, Oosterbaan, Gawne, Asbeck, McAfee, McCoy, and Blott (asst. coach). The 1928 team was conference champion for the fourth time since Ray Fisher became coach seven years earlier. The season opened with a southern trip and a 7-3 loss to Cincinnati, as Fred Asbeck allowed nine hits, including two home runs. But Bill McAfee set Michigan back on a winning track, as he held Vanderbilt to one hit behind a 10-1 victory. McAfee (top, third from right) later briefly pitched with several Major League teams, compiling a lifetime record of 10-4. His best year was 1932 with Washington, winning 6 of 7 decisions. Big Ten action began against Northwestern, held to two hits by Asbeck after eight innings of perfect pitching. McAfee shut out Purdue, winning an easy 17-0 game. McAfee could also hit, attested by his home run in a 6-1 victory over Iowa. His record of 10-1 for the season ranks as the sixth highest season victory total among Michigan pitchers. First baseman Bennie Oosterbaan (top, third from left) contributed a home run and triple among his four hits against Ohio State in a game again won by Michigan, 13-9. By the end of the season, Michigan had won 11 of 12 Big Ten matches, achieving an overall record of 22-5. (Courtesy of the *Michiganensian*.)

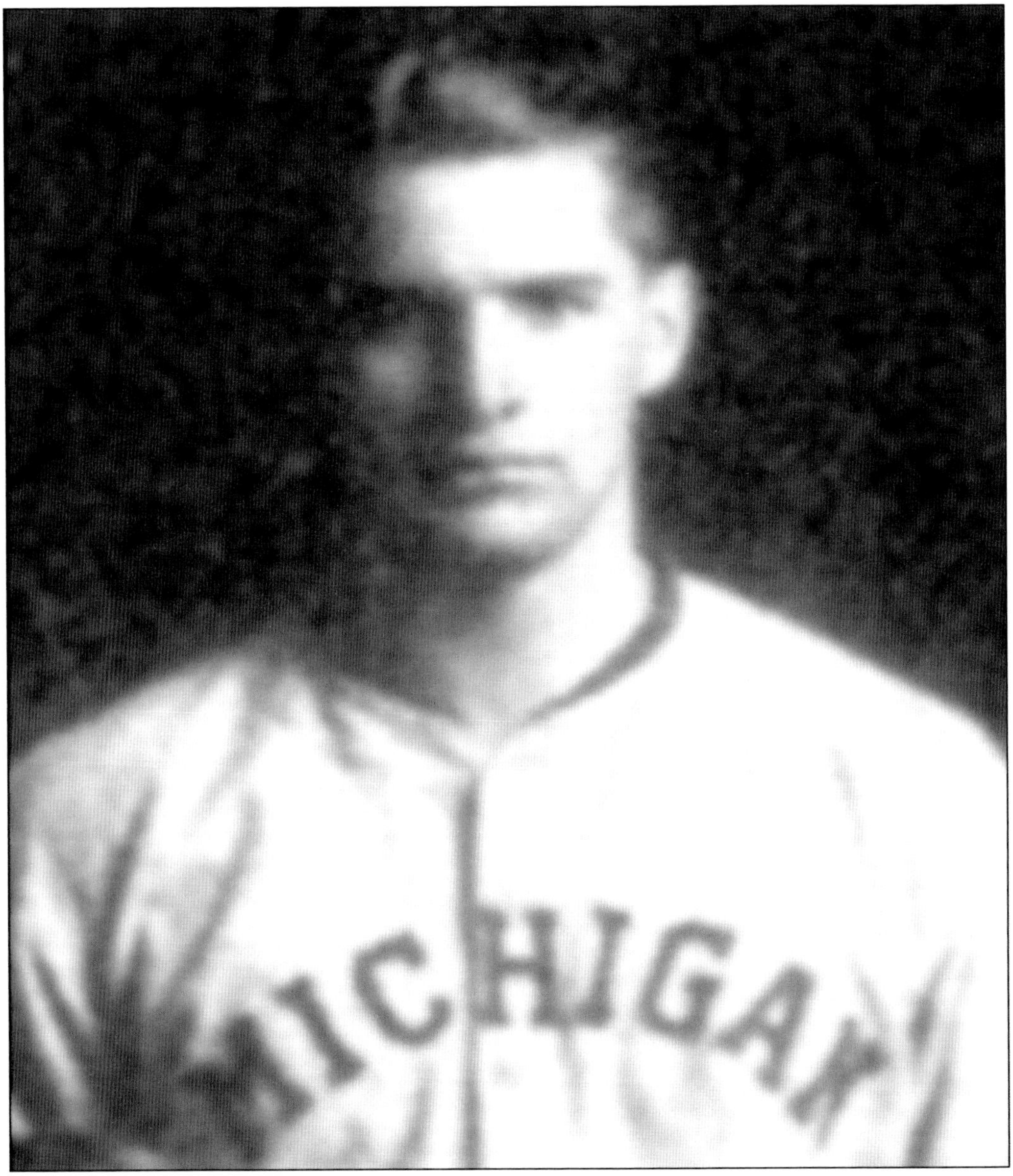

Bennie Oosterbaan is still considered one of the greatest athletes to come from the Big Ten, earning nine letters in basketball, football and baseball. Playing end on the football team, Oosterbaan was Michigan's first three-time All-American (1925–1927). Teamed with quarterback Bennie Friedman, Oosterbaan was part of a potent offensive attack considered one of the strongest in college football. After graduation, Oosterbaan turned down professional offers because he refused to play on Sundays for religious reasons. In 1948, he became head football coach at Michigan, that year becoming the first rookie coach to win a national title. Oosterbaan played first base under Coach Fisher from 1926–1928. His senior year he hit .361 (.489 in Big Ten play), his third consecutive season over .300 and a major factor in Michigan winning the conference title. Oosterbaan had become synonymous with Michigan sports by the 1960s. Upon Oosterbaan's death in 1990, fellow alum and football star Ron Kramer sprinkled his ashes around campus. (Courtesy of the Bentley Historical Library.)

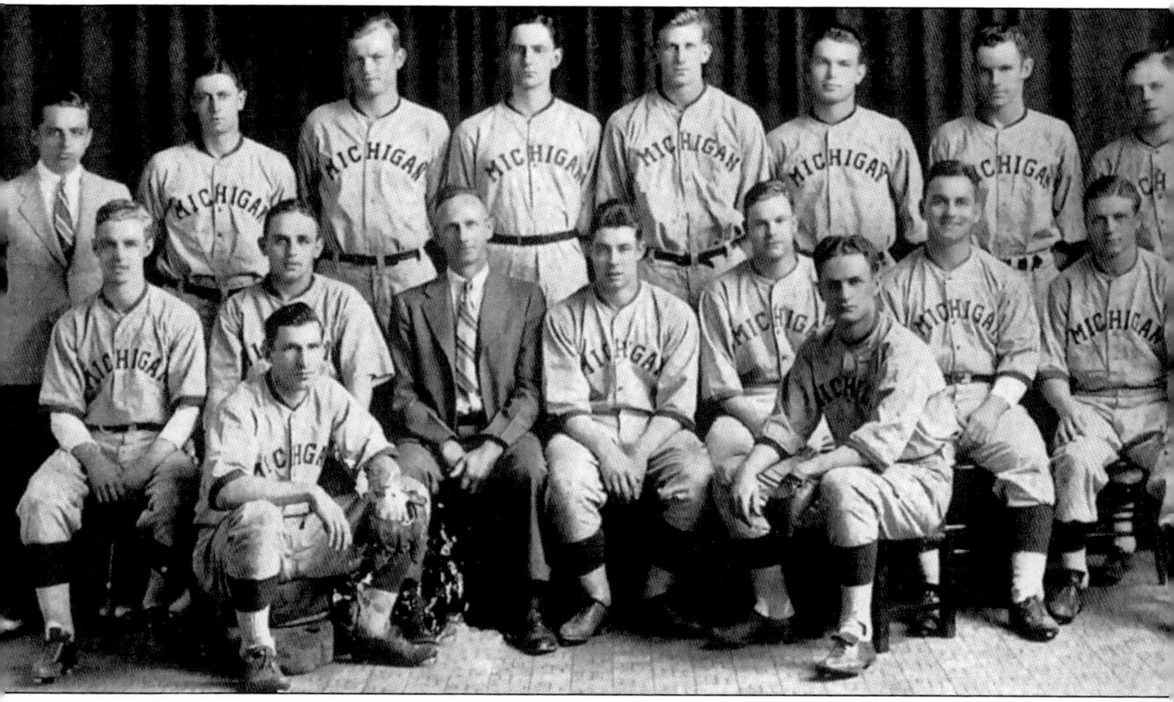

The 1938 squad was one of the weaker teams from the Fisher era, finishing eighth in the conference with a record of 4-6, while compiling an overall record of 14-12. In the final game of the season, Michigan defeated a strong California team, 8-6. California had a record of 26-4, including ten straight victories, prior to the contest. The team did include some "notables." Captain and left fielder Merle Kremer (middle row, fourth from left) batted .356 in conference play (.272 overall), and was considered by Coach Fisher to be one of his greatest hitters. Right fielder Dan Smick (third from left, back) led the team with an overall average of .345, which included five home runs. Smick would earn nine letters in baseball, football and basketball during his time at Michigan. First baseman Elmer Gedeon hit .285, with five home runs. He would later play with the Washington senators. Serving in the Army Air Force during World War II, Gedeon was killed in action. Charley Pink (back, right) stole 17 bases that season; he would bat .377 the following year. Fisher considered Pink to be one of his greatest leadoff hitters. Though Pink is not listed in Michigan records as part of the "modern era," both his season and career stolen base records rank among the team's highest. Forest Evashevski (back, third from right), a weak hitting backup catcher (.250 the following season), would earn greater fame for his football exploits. All-Big Ten at quarterback three times (1938–1940), Evashevski was better known as the blocking back for Tom Harmon. Following service during the war, Evashevski turned to the ranks of coaching, serving as football coach at Iowa for nine seasons, and then athletic director at that school. (Courtesy of the Michiganensian.)

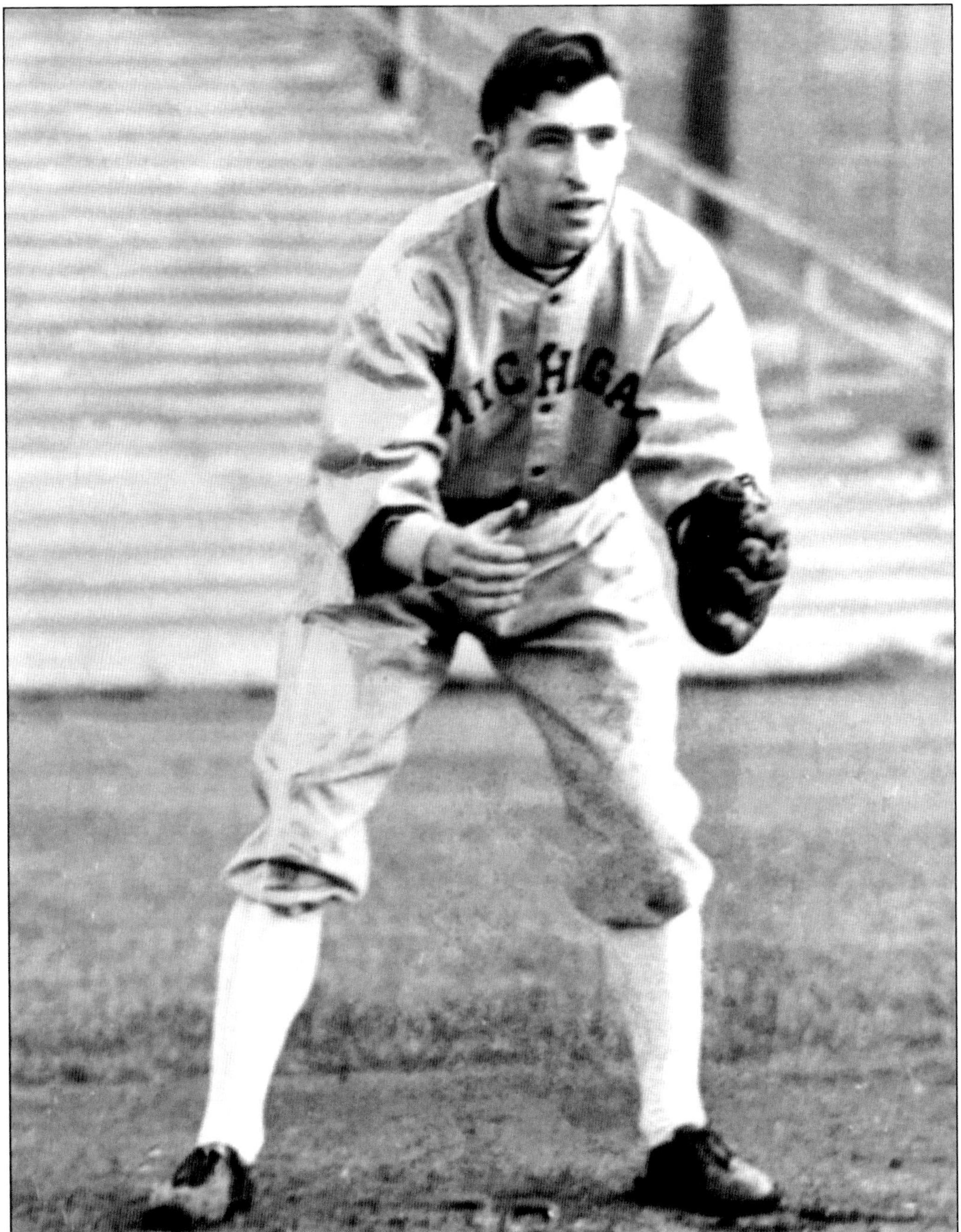

Walter Peckinpaugh held down third base three seasons for Michigan (1937–1939). Son of former major leaguer Roger Peckinpaugh, Walt was known primarily for his defensive ability at the "bag." He did hit .327 in 1938, and .290 in 1939, as well as serving as team captain that year. (Courtesy of the Bentley Historical Library.)

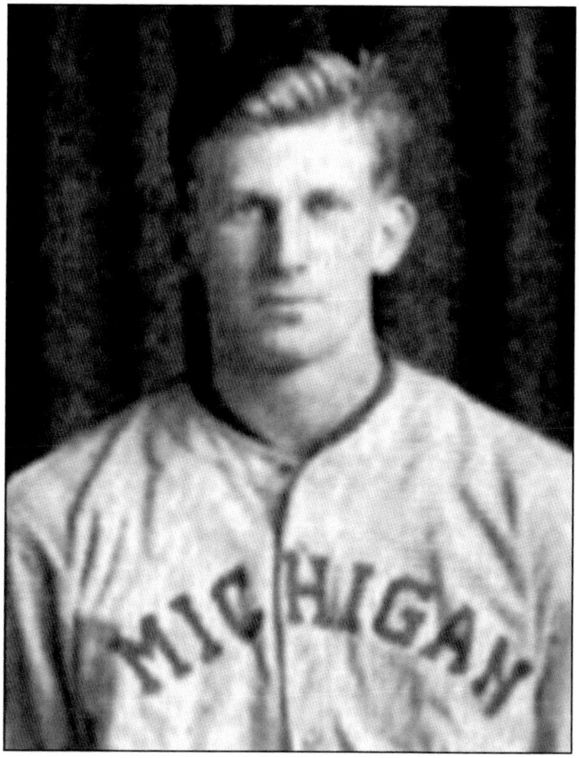

Elmer Gedeon is one of the more tragic figures to have graced Michigan diamonds. The 6'4" first baseman earned three football letters as an end, plus an additional two in both baseball and track. In both 1938 and 1939, Gedeon was the Big Ten champion in the indoor 70-yard hurdles for which he was also co-holder of the U.S. record, and outdoor 120-yard high hurdles. On several occasions he ran hurdles in the morning, and played baseball in the afternoon. In 1939, his final season with Ray Fisher, Gedeon batted .320. Following the season, Gedeon signed with the Washington Senators. After a short stretch with Orlando in the Florida State League, Gedeon was promoted to the parent Senators. His major league statistics consisted of 3 hits in 15 at bats, while playing in five games. Gedeon spent 1940 playing with Charlotte in the Piedmont League, batting .271. (Courtesy of the Michiganensian.)

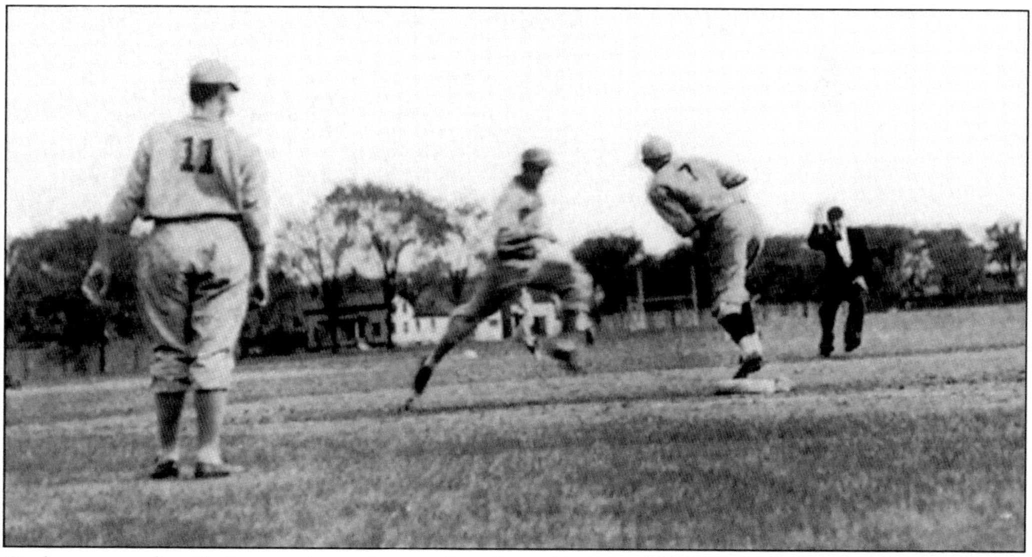

Gedeon, number 7, is seen in action at first base. In March 1941, Gedeon was inducted into the army, and volunteered for pilot training in the Army Air Force. In 1943, he was decorated for heroism for the rescue of a pilot from a plane, which had crashed and burned. Badly burned himself, Gedeon spent three months in the hospital. Gedeon returned as a bomber pilot, participating in action over Europe. In April 1944, Gedeon was killed when his plane was shot down over St. Pol, France. (Courtesy of the Michiganensian.)

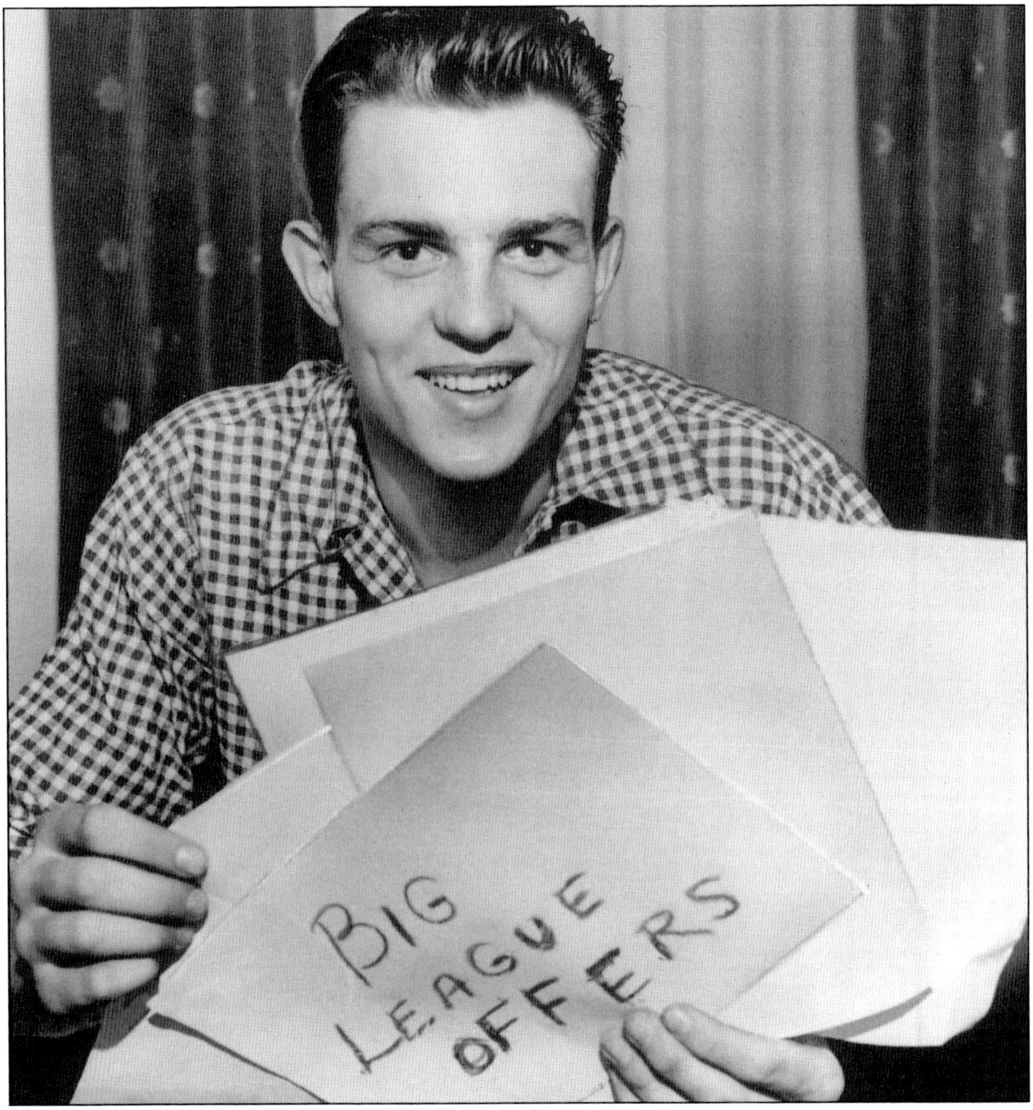

Ray Fisher considered Dick Wakefield to be one of the strongest hitters ever to play on one of Michigan's teams. The 6'4", 200-pound sophomore outfielder hit .372 in 1941, a major factor in Michigan's conference title that season. Wakefield's nine home runs included several over 400 feet. Numerous major league teams expressed interest in signing him, and the Detroit Tigers were the winners in the bidding war, signing Wakefield to a contract of $52,000 plus an automobile. To place the bonus in perspective, most established stars in the majors were making less than $10,000. After a brief time with Detroit that season, Wakefield enlisted in the Navy, volunteering for flight school. But the program was temporarily canceled and Wakefield returned to the Tigers. In 1943, he batted .316, leading the league with 200 hits. The following year, Wakefield returned to the Navy in time to lead the Iowa Pre-Flight School in hitting. Wakefield returned to the Tigers in 1946, but his years in the Service had diminished his abilities as well as his desire to provide a maximum effort towards the game. He briefly played with both the New York Yankees and Giants before retiring in 1952. Altogether, Wakefield played parts of nine years in the majors, producing a lifetime average of .293. Heart disease cut his life short in 1985. (Courtesy of the National Baseball Hall of Fame and Museum.)

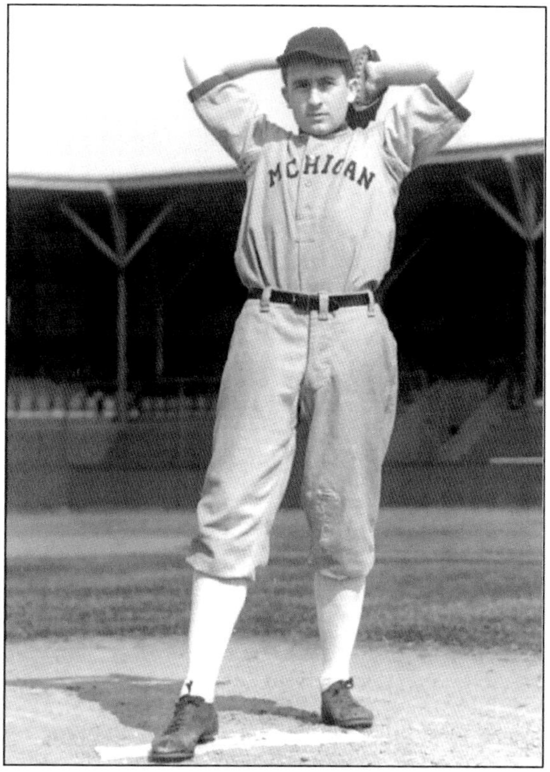

Dick Savage was typical of the many veterans who returned to school after the war to complete their education. A pitcher for three seasons (1942, 1943, 1946), his two victories in his final season contributed to the team's overall record of 18-3, and 2nd place finish in the Big Ten. (Courtesy of the Bentley Historical Library.)

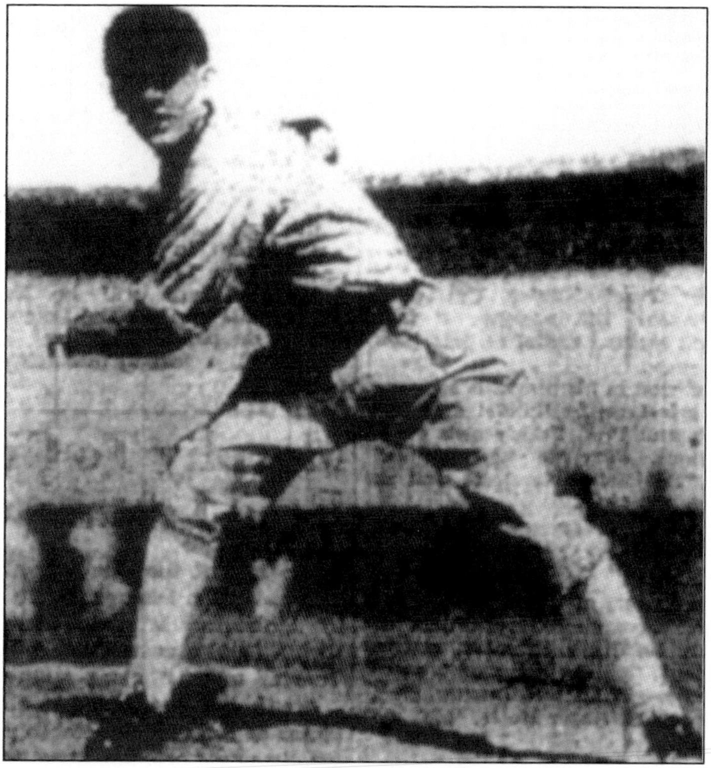

Bliss "Bo" Bowman was the left-handed "ace" of the staff from 1944 to 1946, compiling a record of 16-4 for the three seasons. His 4-2 victory against Purdue on June 10, 1944, helped clinch the conference championship for Michigan. In 1945, his 6-1 record included an ERA of 1.89. (Courtesy of the *Michigan Daily*.)

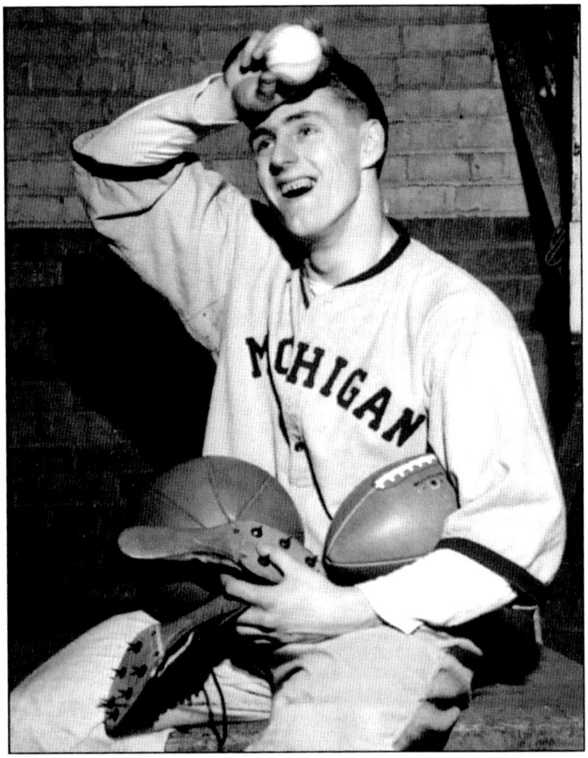

Better known for his football exploits at the University of Wisconsin (and the origin of his nickname), as well as with the professional Rams, Elroy "Crazy Legs" Hirsch attended the University of Michigan in 1943 and 1944 as a Marine Corps trainee. The primary starting right-handed pitcher on the 1944 baseball squad, Hirsch had a record of 6-1 for the conference champions. He also batted .355 (11 for 31) in the nine games in which he appeared. Hirsch went 2 for 3 in the championship clinching conference final against Purdue. Released from the Service in 1946, Hirsch briefly played with the Chicago Rockets of the All-America Football Conference, but spent most of his professional career with the Los Angeles Rams. He was athletic director at the University of Wisconsin from 1969–1987. Hirsch died in 2003. (Courtesy of the Bentley Historical Library.)

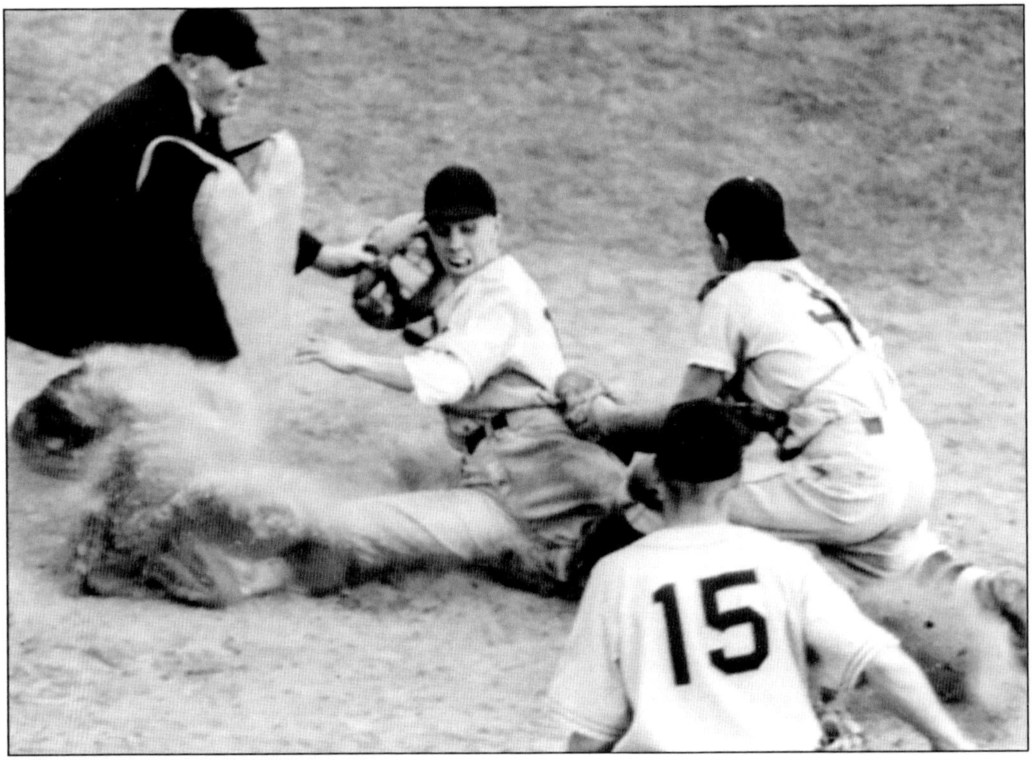

Walter Kell is tagged out in action at home plate.

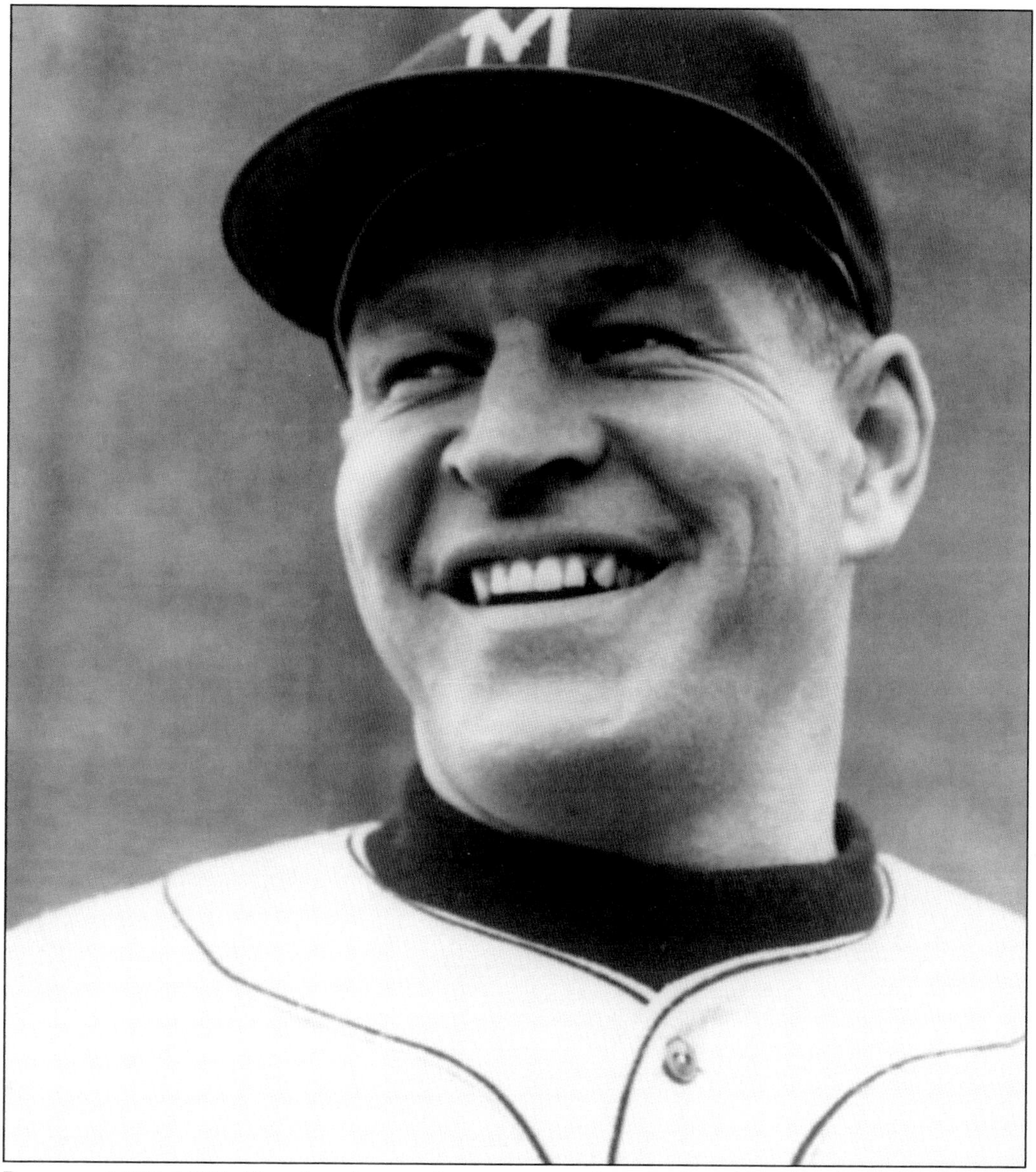

Between 1943–1945, Don Lund earned nine varsity letters: 3 each in baseball, football and basketball. In 1945, he was elected captain of the baseball team. As a centerfielder, Lund had two perfect seasons in the field (1944–1945), as well as hitting .348 for the 1944 conference champion team. It was on June 10th that year, that a double-header victory over Purdue clinched the title. Lund's barehanded catch in the second game was a key to the victory, a catch which Coach Ray Fisher stated was one of the best he ever saw. Elroy Hirsch, the pitcher in that victory, reportedly bowed down to Lund afterwards.

Following graduation, Lund was signed by Branch Rickey for the Brooklyn Dodger organization. He played three seasons in Brooklyn, moving to the St. Louis Browns on waivers in 1948. Lund finished his Major League career with the Detroit Tigers in 1954, compiling a lifetime average of .240. His best season was in 1953, when he batted .257 with 9 home runs in 131 games for the Tigers. Lund continued with the Tigers as a coach. (Courtesy of the Bentley Historical Library.)

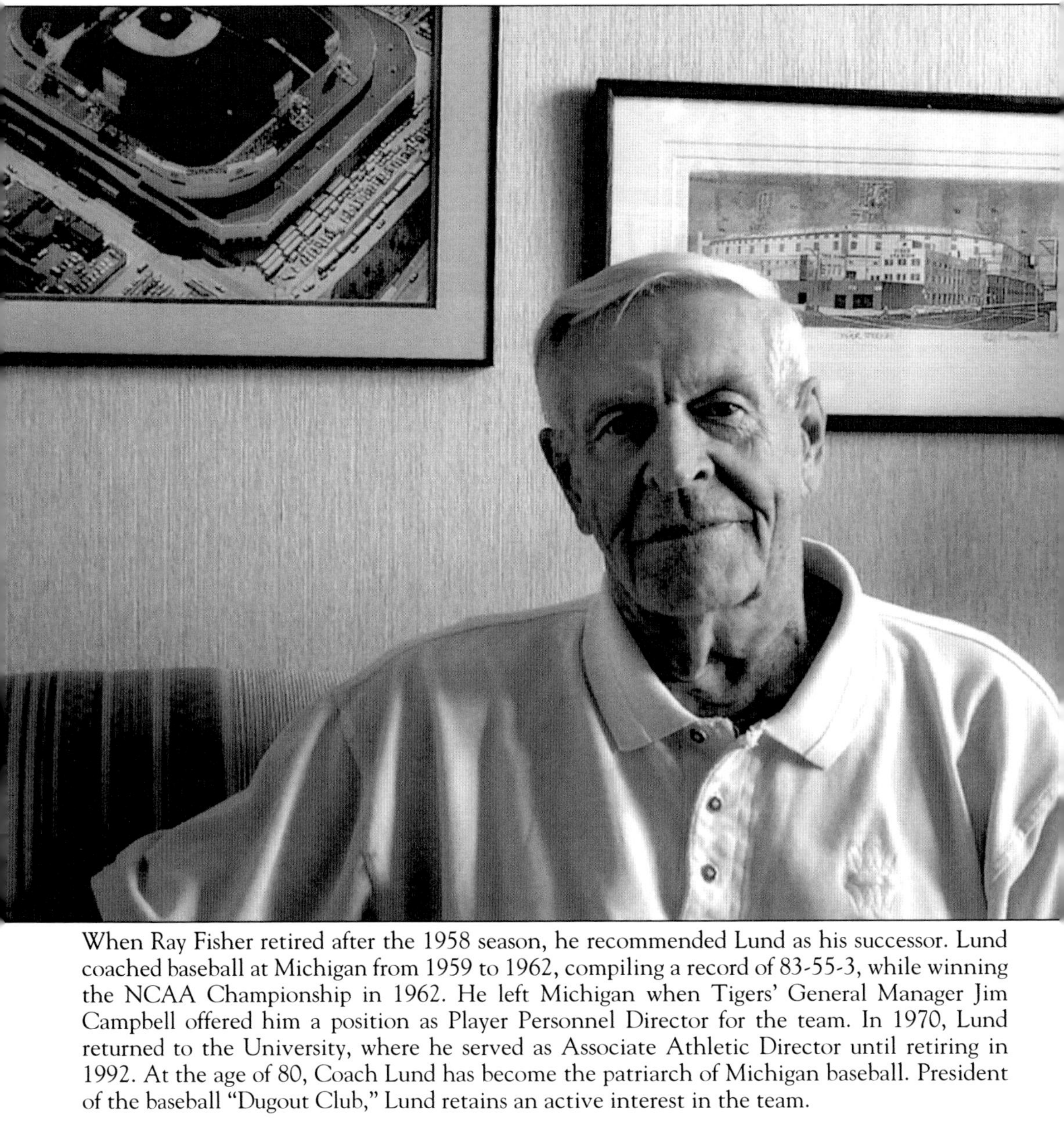

When Ray Fisher retired after the 1958 season, he recommended Lund as his successor. Lund coached baseball at Michigan from 1959 to 1962, compiling a record of 83-55-3, while winning the NCAA Championship in 1962. He left Michigan when Tigers' General Manager Jim Campbell offered him a position as Player Personnel Director for the team. In 1970, Lund returned to the University, where he served as Associate Athletic Director until retiring in 1992. At the age of 80, Coach Lund has become the patriarch of Michigan baseball. President of the baseball "Dugout Club," Lund retains an active interest in the team.

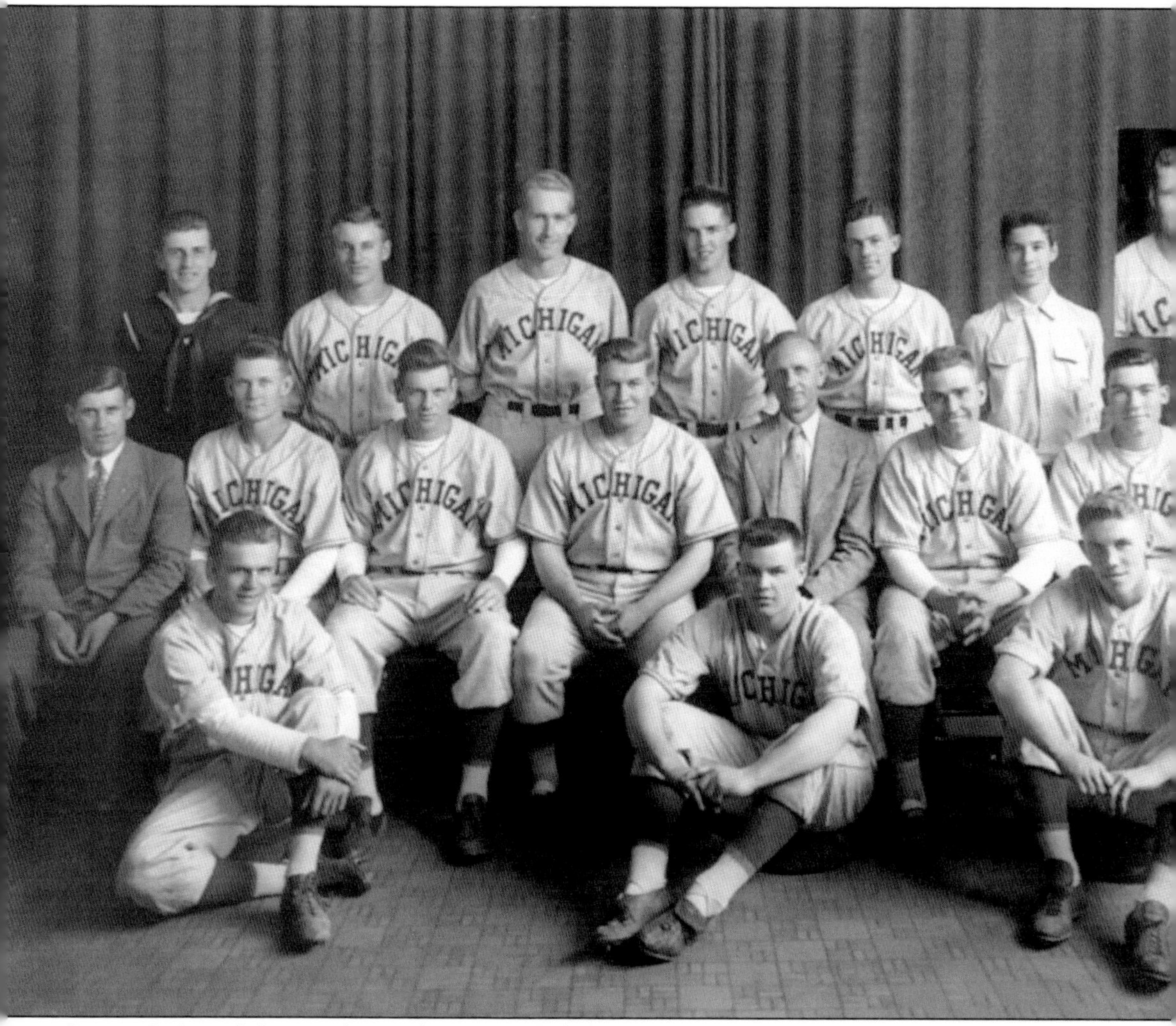

Pictured, from left to right, is the 1945 Michigan team: (front row) Bowman, Tomasi, and Kell; (middle row) Heyliger (Hockey coach), Nelson, Hackstadt, Lund, Fisher, Stevenson, and Gregor; (back row) unknown, Soboleski, Rosema, Wisenbergen, Peddy, unknown, and Louthen (Inset). A 5-4 loss to Western Michigan in the opening game was the only blemish on a 20-1 season, which included a record of 8-0 in conference action. The championship season represented the beginning of what would stretch into the following year as a 27 game winning streak. Team captain Don Lund batted .291, and for the second consecutive season had no errors in the outfield. Pitcher "Bo" Bowman produced a 6-1 record and an ERA of 1.89. Bowman was also the leading hitter on the team with an average of .444 (12 for 27). Ray "Red" Louthen, a multi-sport athlete from Western Michigan University assigned to Ann Arbor by the Navy, led the staff with an 8-0 record, and an ERA of 1.13. Louthen also struck out 96 batters in fewer than 80 innings. John Hackstadt contributed 4 victories. Third baseman Walter Kell led the position players with a .348 average. (Courtesy of the Bentley Historical Library.)

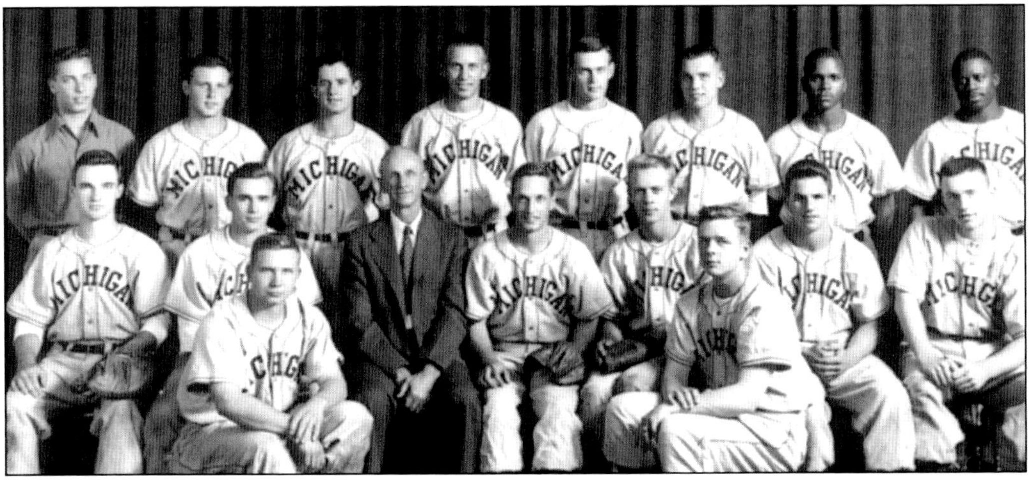

Pictured, from left to right, is the 1952 Michigan team: (front row) Billings and Lepley; (middle row) Peck, Goulish, Fisher (coach), Haynam (cap.), Mogk, Yirkoski, and Corbett; (back row) Mazer (mgr.), Sabuco, Harrington, Wisniewski, Fancher, Leach, Eaddy, and Howell. Despite losing three games with weaker Big Ten teams to rainouts, Michigan finished in a first place tie with Illinois. The hitting attack was led by first baseman Bill Mogk (.300 average), and freshmen Paul Lepley (.343) and Don Eaddy (.337). Frank Howell hit 3 home runs in conference play. Jack Corbett hurled three shutouts in Big Ten play, compiling a conference record of 4-2. He also pitched a two-hitter against Minnesota, but lost when Paul Giel pitched a 2-0 shutout for the opponents. Marv Wisniewski pitched three shutouts in Big Ten play. (Courtesy of the Bentley Historical Library.)

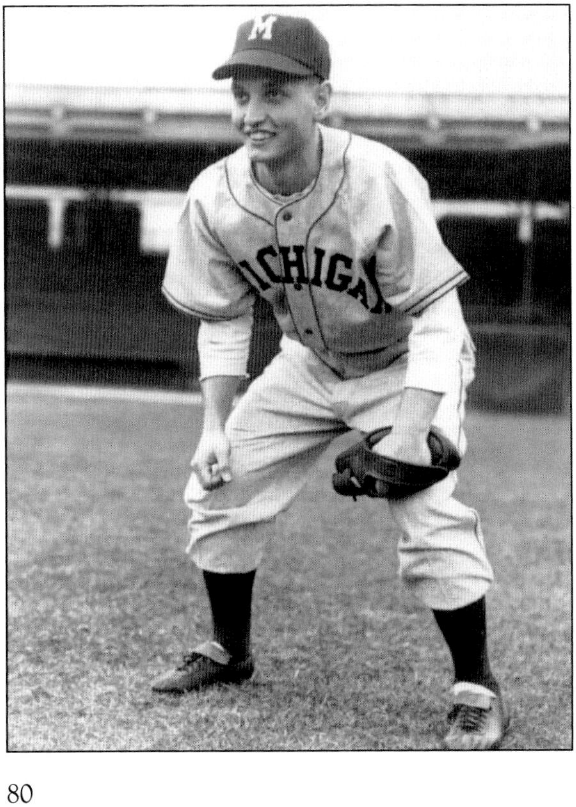

Bruce Haynam played three seasons at Michigan (1951–1953), and is considered by some to be the greatest shortstop in team history. Though only 5'9", 160 pounds, Haynam hit .360 for the 1953 national champions, and was named an All-American at his position. As a junior (1952), he was elected team captain. (Courtesy of the Bentley Historical Library.)

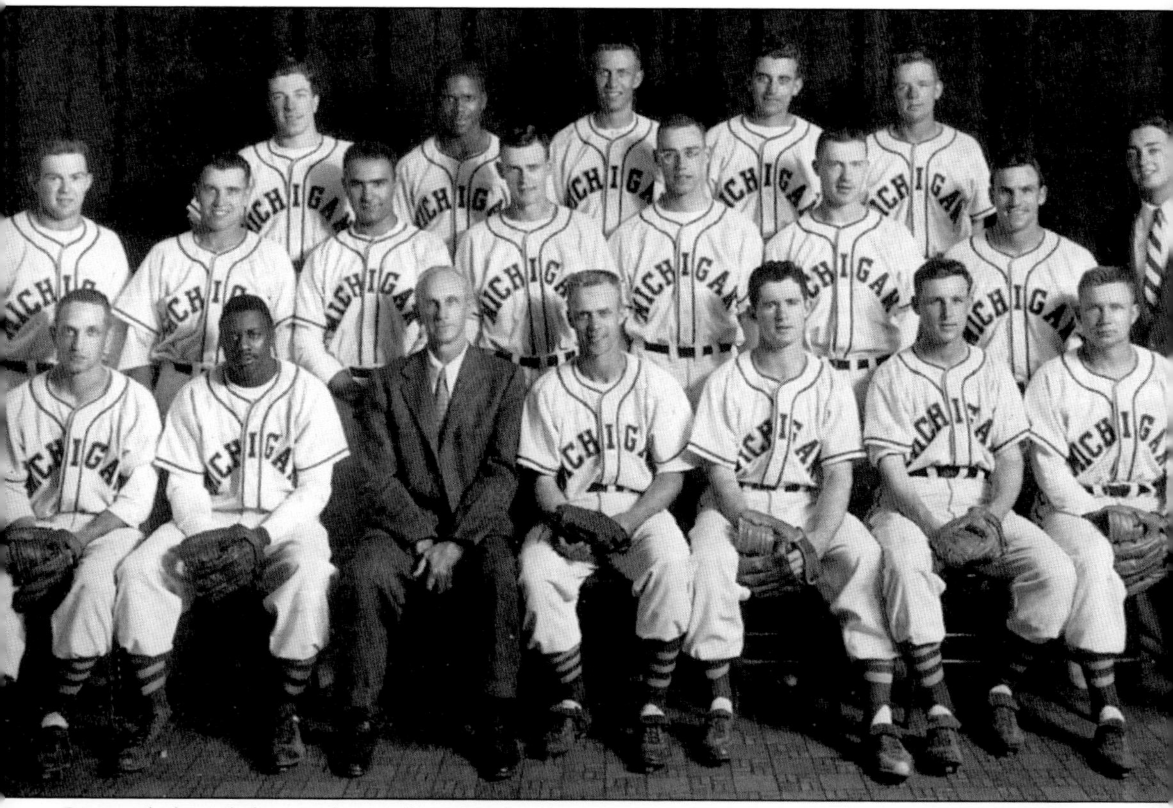

Pictured, from left to right, is the 1953 Michigan team: (front row) Haynam, Howell, Fisher (coach), Mogk (cap.), Harrington, Sabuco, and Billings; (middle row) Ritter, Leach, Tadian, Fancher, Woschitz, Corbett, Yirkosky, and Margolin (mgr.); (back row) Cline, Eaddy, Wisniewski, Pavichevich, and Lepley. The nucleus of the 1952 team, which had tied for the Big Ten championship, returned in 1953. The title was not decided until the last weekend of conference play, as both Michigan and defending champion Illinois remained in contention. Michigan was assured of at least a tie for the title by twice defeating Northwestern in a double-header. In the first game, Jack Ritter went nine innings in a close 3-2 victory. The game was decided in the 6th, as a Haynam single, Mogk double, a sacrifice fly by Eaddy and another single by Lepley brought in the winning runs. Michigan won the second game 5-3, as Dick Yirkosky relieved Marv Wisniewski in the 2nd inning and held off Northwestern the rest of the way. Illinois also won, however, and the title ended in a tie. Michigan advanced to the College World Series by defeating Midwest Conference champion Ohio University in the NCAA Playoff. Dick Yirkosky again relieved (Corbett) in the 5th, as Michigan went on to win 6-5. Michigan advanced to the World Series with a second victory over Ohio, as Wisniewski threw a 2-hit, 11-strikeout shutout, 7-0. In the College World Series, Wisniewski, Jack Corbett and Ritter all hurled complete games. In the final game against Texas, Wisniewski again came through, as Danny Cline knocked in the winning runs for a 7-5 victory. Cline hit .500 during the championship series (7 for 14). Between 1953 and 1955, he would earn three letters in both football and baseball. During his senior year, he led the Big Ten in kick-off return yardage, while serving as captain of the baseball team. (Courtesy of the Bentley Historical Library.)

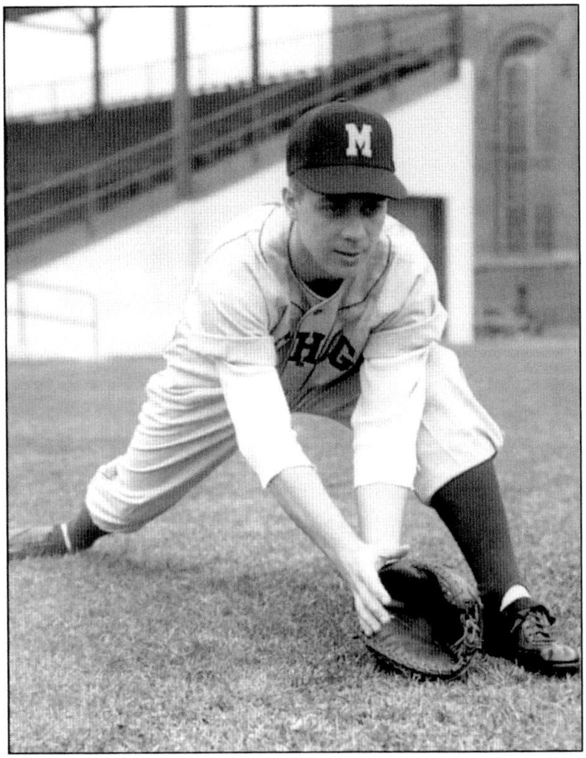

First baseman Bill Mogk was captain of the 1953 team, the first to win an NCAA championship. (Courtesy of the Bentley Historical Library.)

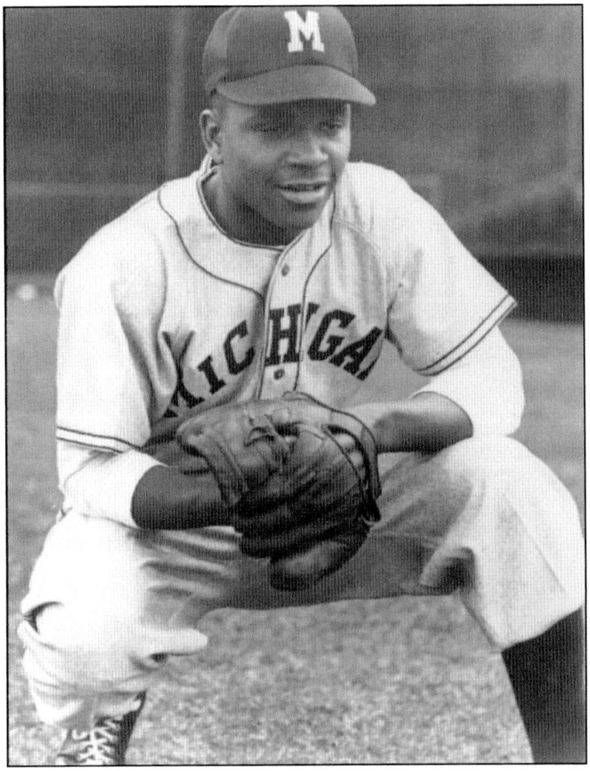

Third baseman Don Eaddy was named to the Big Ten first team at his position four consecutive years (1952–1955), as well as being selected for All-American honors his senior year. That season Eaddy hit .324, with 3 home runs and 25 RBI. Eaddy appeared briefly with the Chicago Cubs in 1959, striking out in his only appearance at the plate. (Courtesy of the Bentley Historical Library.)

Fisher's 1953 team not only tied for the Big Ten championship for the second consecutive season, they went on to become Michigan's first NCAA champion. (Courtesy of the Bentley Historical Library.)

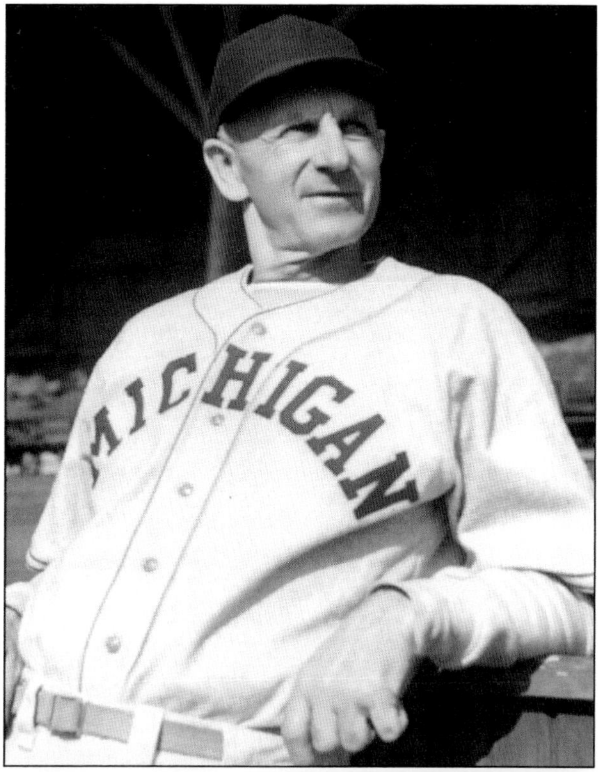

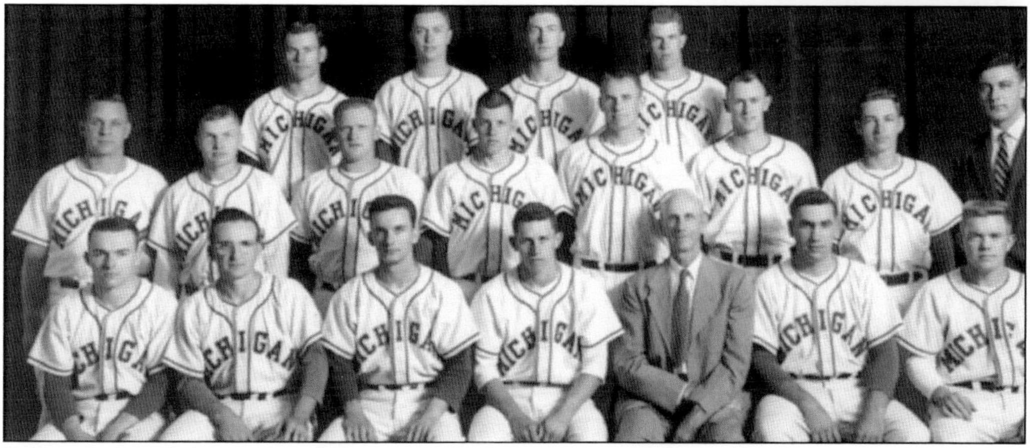

Pictured, from left to right, is the 1956 Michigan team: (front row) Girardin, Ferrelli, Ronan, Benedict, Fisher (coach), Peterjohn, and Tommelein; (middle row) Snider, Tippery, Sigman, Poloskey, Clark, Thurston, Fox, and Koplin (mgr.); Boros, Finkbeiner, Sealby, and Rembiesa. The 1956 squad finished fourth in Big Ten action with a record of 6-5. Two of those losses were one run affairs with conference champion Minnesota. The hitting attack was led by second baseman Ken Tippery, who batted .380 in conference play, and .345 for the year. Pitcher and center fielder Bill Thurston hit .459 against Big ten opponents, and .407 overall. His 370 foot home run against Purdue was a deciding factor in a 3-1 win. Thurston also won three of four decisions against Big Ten opponents. Future coach Moby Benedict hit .283, and future Detroit Tiger Steve Boros hit .274 against Big Ten opponents. Utility infielder Frank Ronan capably filled in for an injured Tippery, hitting .400. (Courtesy of the Bentley Historical Library.)

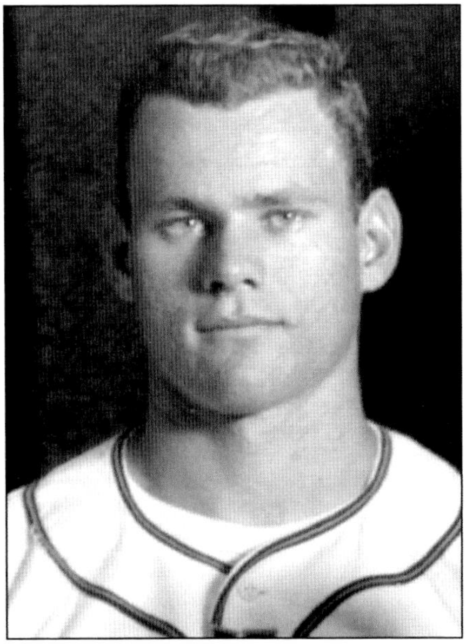

Shortstop Steve Boros was one of the more colorful characters to play for Ray Fisher. During his two years with the team (1956–1957), Fisher was never quite sure when Boros would show up for spring training. However, his outstanding play allowed for some leeway with the schedule. In 1956, Boros hit .311 (.274 against Big Ten opposition). He followed this up in 1957, with a Big Ten average of .400, and along with teammate Ken Tippery, led the Big Ten in hits with 18. In June, at the end of the season, Boros signed a bonus contract for $25,000 with the Detroit Tigers, and within three days was pinch-hitting against the Yankees. Coach Fisher was far from happy at losing Boros with a year of eligibility remaining. "They use the army threat as a pry. They sell the youngsters on giving up on college . . . to get established in baseball before they get their service call." Ironically the man Boros replaced on the Tigers, Reno Bertoia, had been a Michigan freshman in 1953, when he signed with the Tigers. Boros never lived up to the team's expectations. He spent seven seasons in the majors, primarily with the Tigers, producing a lifetime average of .245. His best season was 1961, when he hit .270 as a full-time third baseman. In recent years, Boros has held a number of administrative positions with the Tigers, including the job of Director of Player Development, and in September 2003, an appointment as special assistant to the General Manager. (Courtesy of the Bentley Historical Library.)

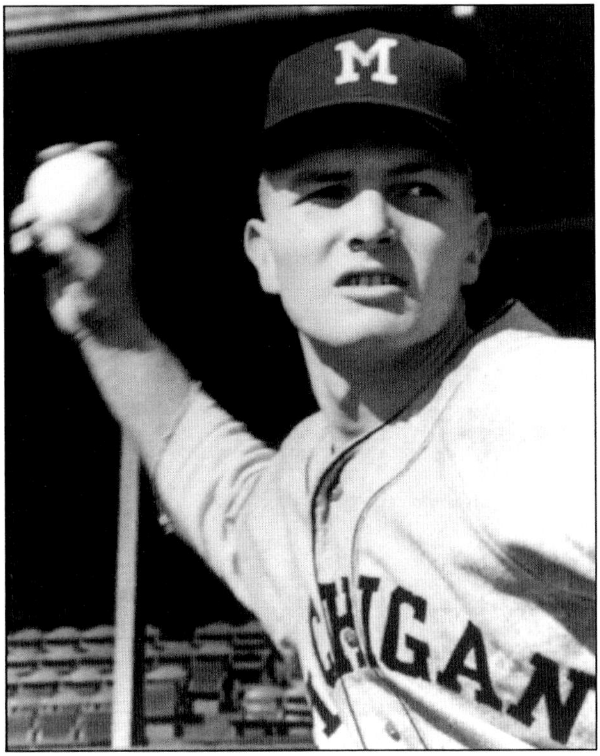

Second baseman Ken Tippery (1955–1957) had a career year in 1957, batting .400 for a Michigan team which finished 17-7. During the previous season (1956), injuries limited his playing time, but he still managed to hit .345. He also led the Big Ten in 1957 with 5 home runs and 14 RBI. His batting average in conference play was just behind the leader, Jerry Kindall of Minnesota (.440). Following the season, Tippery was signed by the Baltimore Orioles. (Courtesy of the Bentley Historical Library.)

FIVE

Champions: Not Just of the West

1950s–1979

In 1947, the NCAA established a tournament to decide a national champion in college baseball. The College World Series, the more popular name for the tournament, was held in Kalamazoo, Michigan, the first two years. Initially, eight teams were selected and divided into two divisions. The two winners met in a best-of-three final. That first year, California defeated Yale in two games; the first baseman for Yale was a future president, George Bush.

In 1950, the tournament was moved to its current location in Omaha, Nebraska, with an eight team, double-elimination format. The country was divided into eight districts, with one team chosen by committee from each district. In 1953, Michigan appeared for the first time.

Under the direction of Coach Ray Fisher, and with the strong pitching of Jack Corbett, Jack Ritter and Marvin Wisniewski, Michigan first defeated Stanford and Boston College. In the finals against Texas, Michigan split the first two games, winning 12-5, and losing 6-4. The pitching of Wisniewski and Ritter, and a clutch single by Dan Cline to drive in the winning runs in the eighth inning, resulted in a 7-5 victory in the final game, and Michigan's first NCAA Championship.

Ray Fisher retired after the 1958 season, and his logical successor was Don Lund. Lund had played for Fisher during the war years, and had played professionally in both the Tigers and St. Louis Browns organizations. His playing career over by the end of Fisher's tenure, Lund had remained with the Tigers as first base coach. "Fritz" Crisler, Athletic Director at Michigan was a strong supporter of Lund, and with approval of the university, offered the coaching position to him for 1959.

Lund began his coaching career somewhat inauspiciously. John Herrnstein, who had alternated the previous year as one of Ray Fisher's pitching "mainstays", as well as a slugging outfielder, signed with the Philadelphia Phillies. Catcher Jim Dickey, one of the leading batters in the Big Ten the previous two years had graduated. The season's low point was a 21-0 loss to Notre Dame. It would be several years before a strongly competitive team would be ready.

Lund's strongest teams were the 1961 and 1962 squads. Led by the pitching of lefty Fred "Fritz" Fisher and Mike Joyce, and the slugging of catcher Bill Freehan, Michigan won the Big Ten title. Fisher's three-hit, eleven strikeout performance against Illinois to clinch the title was considered one of Coach Lund's greatest thrills. The team did not fare as well in the District 4 Regional Tournament. The pitching staff was simply worn out. Mike Joyce pitched twice, losing to Cincinnati 3-1, then defeating Detroit 6-3. But the team was then scheduled for three games in two days. Despite one day of rest due to rain, Michigan was eliminated in the regionals by Western Michigan.

The 1962 squad fared better. A double-header loss to Wisconsin late in the season resulted in Michigan finishing one game behind Illinois in the Big Ten. Nevertheless, the NCAA selection committee included Michigan for the regional tournament in Kalamazoo following a sweep of the undefeated Western Michigan team.

After a loss to Western in the regional opener, Michigan won four straight over Detroit, Illinois and Western Michigan twice. Because of the setup for the tournament, John Kerr pitched five hours of baseball in the double-header sweep of Illinois and the first defeat of Western, a total of 17 innings. "Fritz" Crisler's response to Lund: "Slap a steak on his arm and send him out again."

In the finals at Omaha, Michigan won three straight over Texas, Holy Cross and Florida State. Following a loss to Texas (which subsequently was eliminated by Santa Clara), Michigan defeated the Santa Clara team to win the College World Series. Jim Bobel won the game in relief, while tripling in a lead run and subsequently scoring the winning run in the fifteenth inning. Michigan then moved on to win the International Collegiate World Series title in the tournament held in Hawaii, defeating Japan's Hosei University in three of five games. "Fritz" Fisher won two of the three games, and was named tournament MVP.

In 1962, Jim Campbell of the Tigers offered Lund a position as Tiger Farm Director, an offer which Lund accepted. He was replaced as coach by Moby Benedict. Benedict had been a scrappy shortstop at Michigan from 1954–1956, and following a short minor league career in the Tiger organization and a stint in the army, was hired as Lund's assistant.

During Benedict's 17 year tenure as coach at Michigan, the Wolverines won three Big Ten titles, and finished second six times. Twenty-five players from those teams eventually played in the Major Leagues. From 1975 to 1978, Michigan won the title three times and finished second once, their strongest showing since the World War II years.

Benedict's 1975 team finished 28-12 (13-3 Big Ten), the team's second best record in its history, and first Big Ten title since 1961. They were quickly eliminated in the NCAA Mideast Regional Tournament, however, as future major leaguers Bob Welch and Bob Owchinko helped Eastern Michigan University twice defeat the Wolverines in regional play.

Michigan was back again in 1976. The Big Ten title came down to the last week of action, as Minnesota, Michigan State and Michigan each had the opportunity to win the title. Minnesota split a double-header with Iowa that last week, while Michigan likewise split a double-header with Michigan State. An 11-3 victory clinched the title for Michigan, the first time they repeated as champions since 1945.

Despite the title, Michigan entered the tournament with an overall 19-18-1 record, and was clearly an underdog. The pitching staff was led by Lary Sorenson (8-2 entering the tournament), and the offense was led by Rick Leach and Rich Walterhouse, each of whom hit over .340 for the year. But again Eastern Michigan was the nemesis, as Bob Owchinko twice shut the Wolverines down by 6-0 scores, on his way to a 12-3 season.

The 1978 season began with Michigan again favored for the Big Ten title. A week of wet grounds delayed the home opener, but then Michigan ran off a streak of eleven victories in twelve games in Big Ten play. Rick Leach hit .457 in Big Ten play, his 55 hits eclipsing the record by Bill Freehan in 1961. Overall, Leach hit .404 for the season. Michigan's 13-3 record again led the Big Ten.

In the NCAA regionals, Steve Howe pitched a four-hitter as Michigan defeated Texas A&M. Their old nemesis, MAC champion Eastern Michigan, was beaten 6-4, and Tom Owens pitched a nine hit shutout to eliminate Texas A&M. Right fielder Tom Parker won two games with clutch hits, and was named tournament Most Valuable Player. The College World Series began on a high note, as Steve Howe pitched a one-hitter against Baylor, Michigan winning 4-0 as Vic Ray slugged a three-run homer. But defeats at the hands of Southern California, the eventual champion, and North Carolina ended the season for Michigan.

The 1979 Big Ten championship again came down to a series with Michigan State the last week of the season. Despite home runs by Rick Leach and Jim Paciorek, a six-run third by Michigan State against Steve Howe was too much to overcome, and Michigan was eliminated from title contention by an 8-5 loss.

Benedict retired at the end of the season, finishing with a final record of 367-251-5, a win total second only to Ray Fisher. He returned twice in subsequent years, assisting coaches Bill Freehan (1990) and Goeff Zahn (1996).

Year	Overall: Won	Lost	Conference: Won	Lost	Position	Coach
1959	10	17 (2 Tie)	5	7	7th	Lund
1960	19	12 (1 Tie)	7	7	5th	Lund
1961	20	11	10	2	1st	Lund
1962	34	15	12	3	2nd[7]	Lund
1963	21	11	7	7	6th	Benedict
1964	19	16	10	4	2nd	Benedict
1965	18	14	10	5	2nd	Benedict
1966	22	11	10	3	3rd	Benedict
1967	24	12	10	4	2nd	Benedict
1968	17	16	9	5	4th	Benedict
1969	14	21 (1 Tie)	8	8	5th (Tie)	Benedict
1970	16	18	7	7	5th	Benedict
1971	23	13 (1 Tie)	10	5 (1 Tie)	2nd	Benedict
1972	18	13 (1 Tie)	9	5	3rd	Benedict
1973	22	16	12	6	2nd	Benedict
1974	18	14 (1 Tie)	7	5	3rd	Benedict
1975	28	12	13	3	1st	Benedict
1976	22	19 (1 Tie)	9	4	1st	Benedict
1977	33	15	14	4	2nd	Benedict
1978	30	17	13	3	1st[8]	Benedict
1979	22	14	10	4	3rd	Benedict

[7] NCAA Champion
[8] Regional Champion; 5th place, College World Series

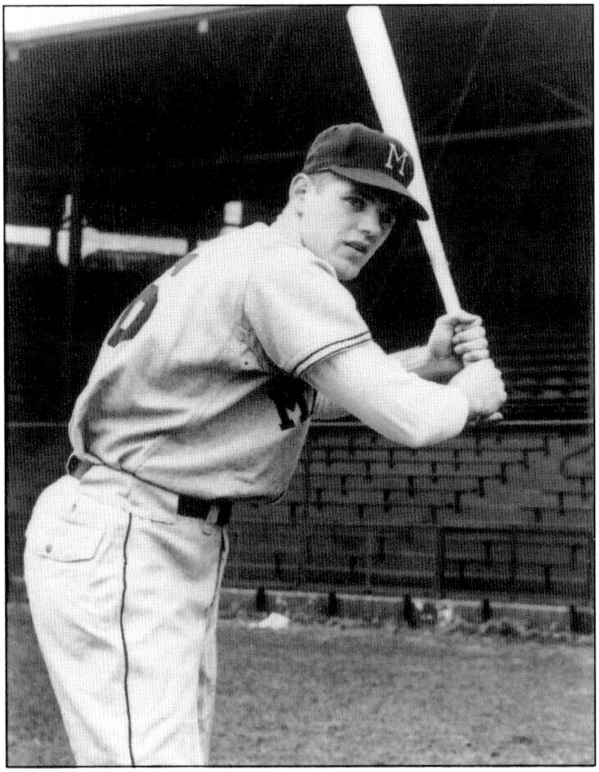

John Herrnstein played two seasons with Michigan (1957–1958). As a pitcher/outfielder in 1958, he hit .287 while compiling a pitching record of 4-4. His victory total included a 1-0 no-hitter against Bradley. Following the season, he signed with the Philadelphia Phillies. His five-year major league career lasted from 1962–1966. Herrnstein's best year was 1964, when alternating between first base and the outfield he hit .234. (Courtesy of the Bentley Historical Library.)

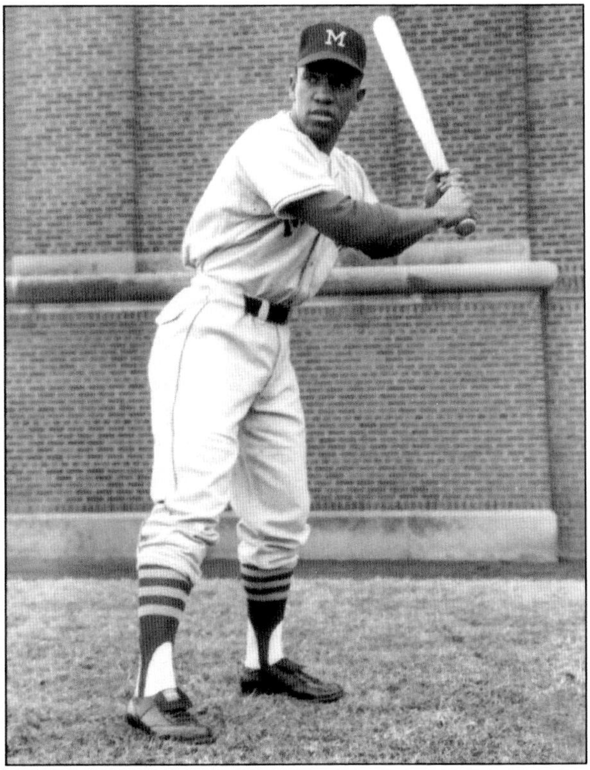

Outfielder Wilbert Franklin led Michigan in batting both seasons with the team: 1959 (.347) and 1960 (.383), for a career average of .367. (Courtesy of the Bentley Historical Library.)

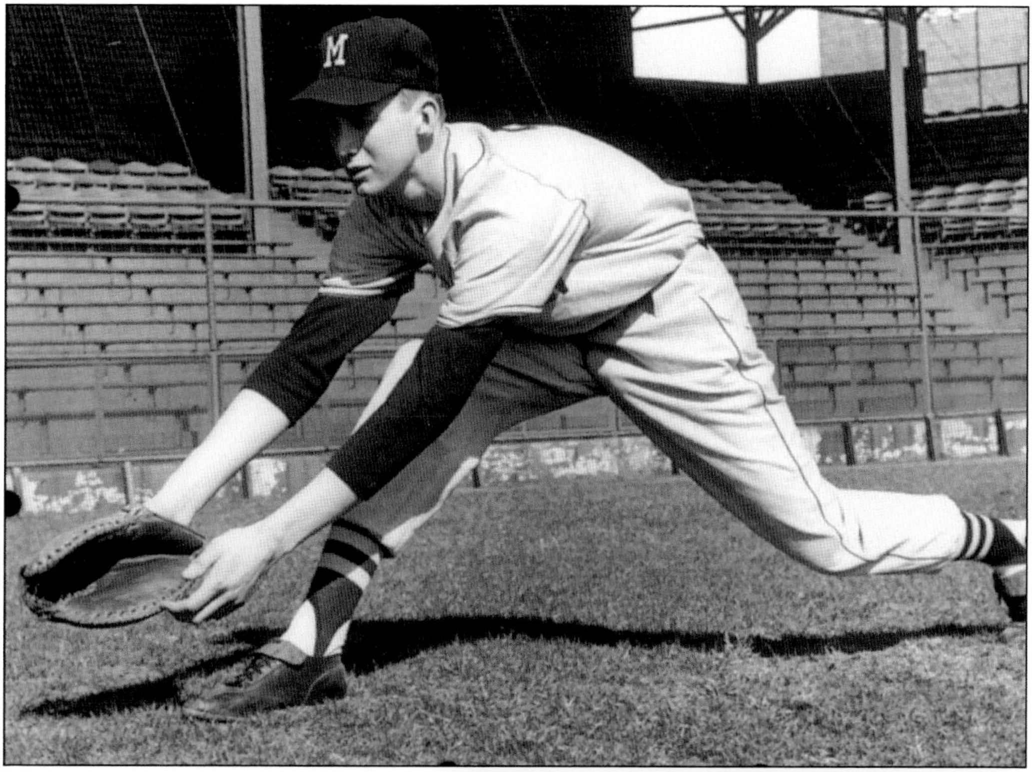

(*above*) The 6'4" Roman held down first base for Michigan for three years (1958-1960). In 1960, he was captain of the team. Though he hit only .209 in Big Ten action during 1959, he followed this up with an overall average of .333 the following season (.340 in Big Ten play). Following the season, Roman signed a contract with the Detroit Tigers for a reported $30,000. Roman only played two seasons in Detroit: 1964–1965, hitting .143 in 24 games. However, his start was auspicious: In his first at bat in the major leagues, he hit a home run against the New York Yankees. (Courtesy of the Bentley Historical Library.)

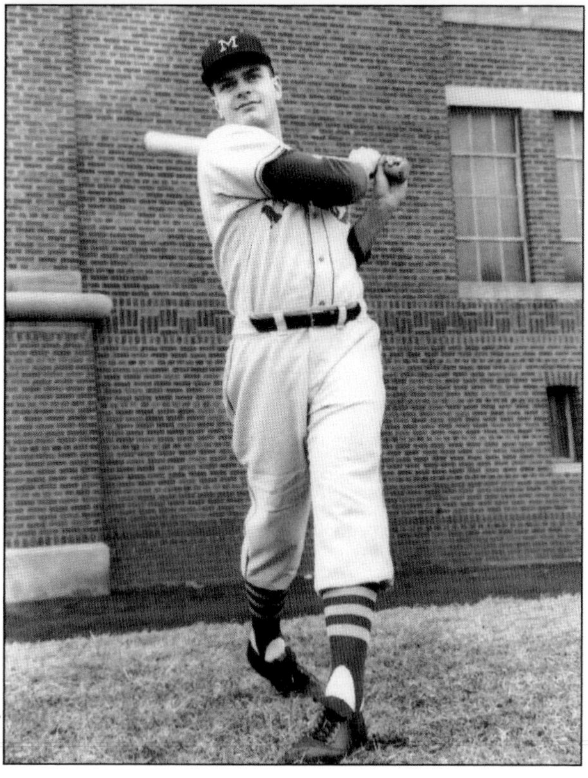

(*right*) Between 1958 and 1960, third baseman Dave Brown compiled a lifetime average of .353, including a team leading average of .397 in 1958. In 1960, he led the team with ten home runs.(Courtesy of the Bentley Historical Library.)

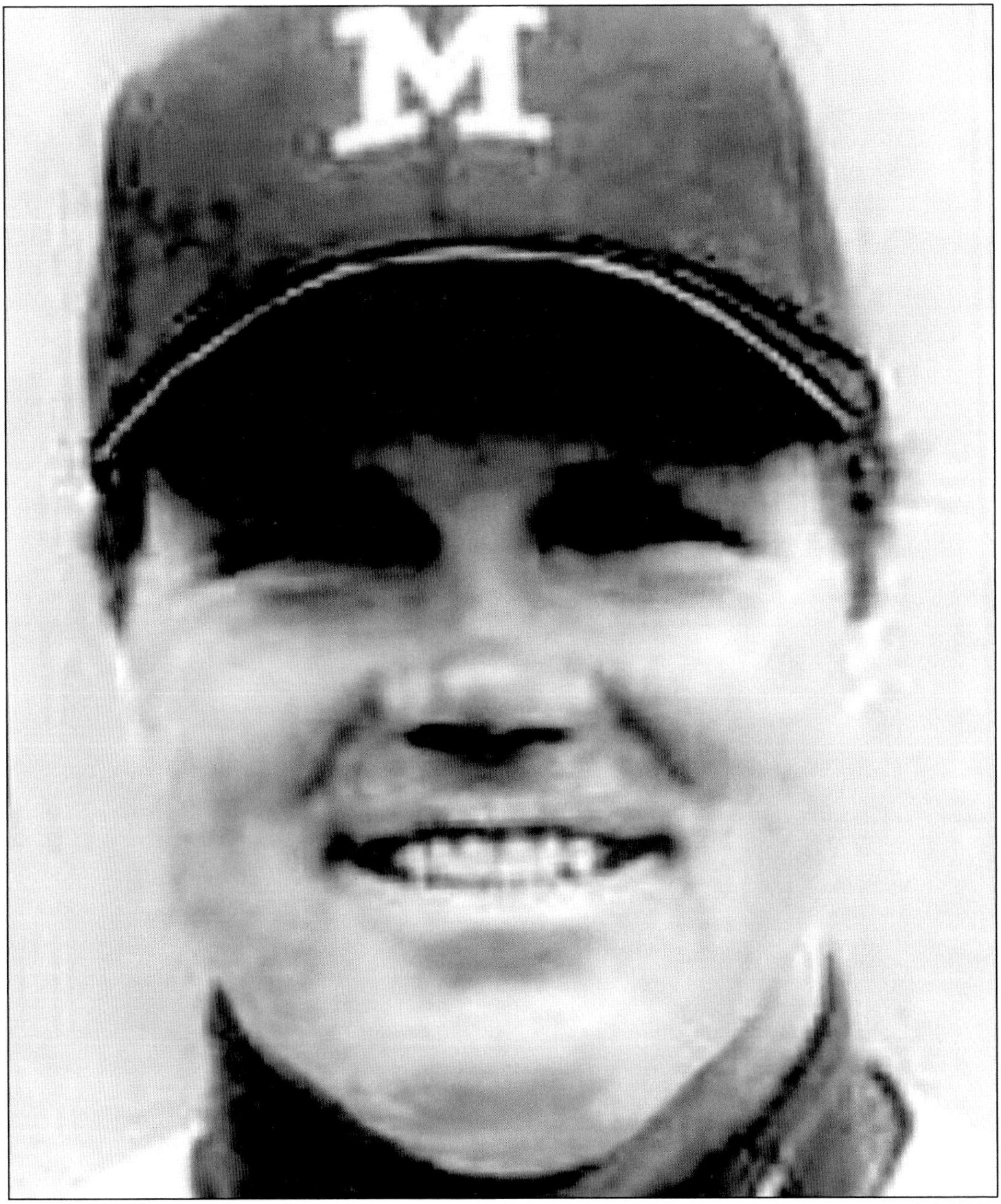

Bill Freehan played only one season at Michigan: 1961. But what a season it was! A solid 6'3" catcher, he hit Big Ten pitching for a .585 average (21 for 41). The record still stands 42 years later. Freehan was only the second man to hit over .500 in the conference, easily eclipsing the mark of Purdue's Bill Skowron, who hit .500 in 1950. Overall in 1961, Freehan hit .476, with 10 home runs and 41 RBI. Following the season, Freehan signed with the Detroit Tigers for a $100,000 bonus. His 15 years with the Tigers between 1961 and 1976 established Freehan as one of the greatest catchers in Detroit history. Three times he led the league in fielding, and was a major factor in the championship season of 1968. Though he had never coached college baseball, Freehan was recommended by Don Lund to replace Bud Middaugh as Michigan coach after the 1989 season. (Courtesy of the *Michigan Daily*.)

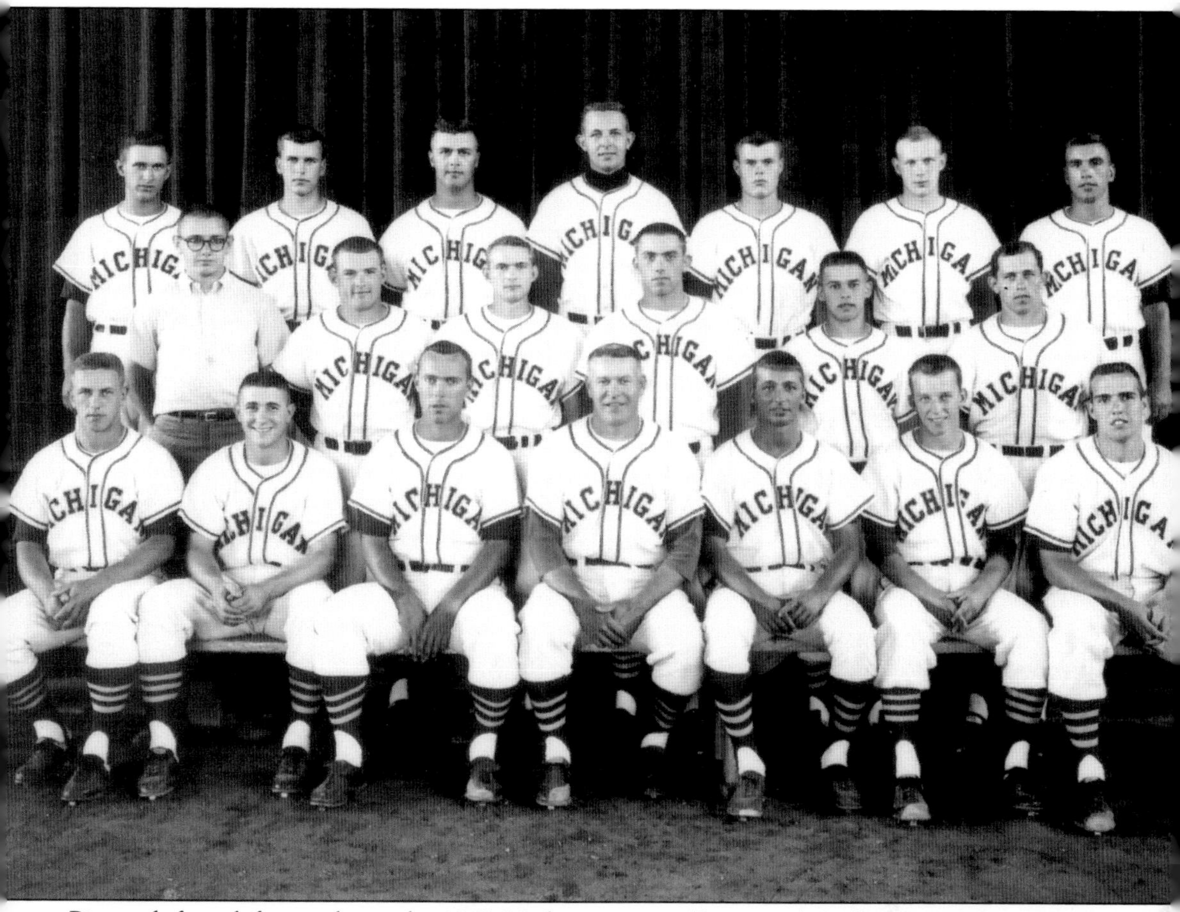

Pictured, from left to right, is the 1962 Michigan team: (front row) Stalla, Honig, Kerr, Lund (Coach), Merullo, Slusher, and Roebuck; (middle row) Kropschot (mgr.), Post, Jones, Tate, Newman, and Benedict (asst. coach); (back row) Steckley, Bobel, Lauterbach, Dunston, Campbell, Fisher, and Chapman. A double-header loss to Wisconsin cost Michigan the Big Ten title. Nevertheless, Michigan finished one game behind champion Illinois, with a record of 12-3, and received an at-large invitation to the District 4 NCAA Regional Tournament at Kalamazzoo. In the regional finals, John Kerr pitched both games of the double-header (17 innings), first defeating Illinois 5-1, and then host Western Michigan 3-2. It was Kerr's sacrifice fly that represented the winning run. In the College World Series championship game against Santa Clara, Harvey Chapman scored in the 15th inning on pitcher Jim Bobel's triple. Bobel came in on a wild pitch with what would prove to be the winning run in a close 5-4 game, and Michigan was the national champion for the first time since 1953. Following the season, Michigan traveled to Honolulu, Hawaii, for the International Collegiate World Series tournament. Michigan won the world crown while defeating Hosei University in three of five games. "Fritz" Fisher, tournament Most Valuable Player, finished the season with a record of 8-6, and an ERA of 2.67, which included a 2-1 victory in the final game against Hosei. Bobel had a 4-3 record in an injury plagued year, while Wayne Slusher had a perfect 5-0 record. While in Hawaii, Michigan played several service teams, winning six of seven. Including all post-season games, Michigan had a season record of 40-16, a victory total which would not be surpassed until 1981. Future major leaguers in what would be Don Lund's last year as coach were "Fritz" Fisher (Detroit) and future sportscaster Dave Campbell (Detroit, San Diego, St. Louis, Houston). (Courtesy of the Bentley Historical Library.)

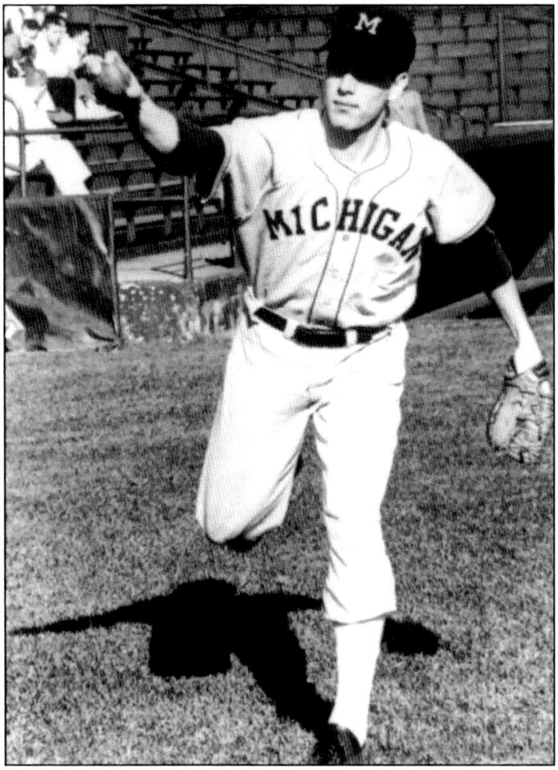

Injuries hindered Jim Bobel during the championship season of 1962, limiting him to a record of 4-2 in the regular season. However, in the College World Series, Bobel won two games in relief, including the 15-inning, 5-4 victory over Santa Clara in the final. Bobel himself scored the winning run. Bobel went on to pitch two more seasons for Michigan. (Courtesy of the Bentley Historical Library.)

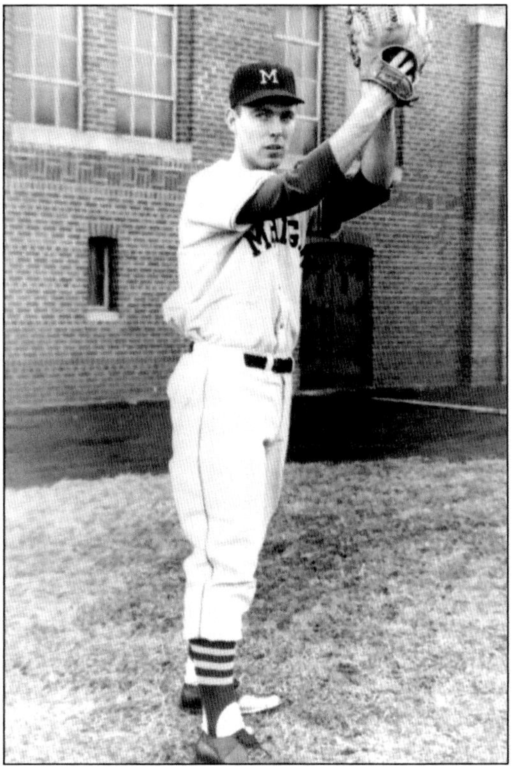

Including the post-season, John Kerr won ten games as a senior for Coach Lund's NCAA champion Michigan team in 1962. He pitched 17 innings in a regional final double-header, first defeating Big Ten champion Illinois, 5-1, and then returning to pitch Michigan to a 3-2 victory over Mid-American Conference champion Western Michigan. Kerr lettered for three seasons at Michigan (1960–1962). (Courtesy of the Bentley Historical Library.)

Dave Campbell came to Michigan as a shortstop, but was switched to first base his first season. Against Wisconsin, he hit two home runs in a 6-5 loss. Nevertheless, Campbell's strong hitting and defensive play were important factors in Michigan advancing to the NCAA Championship. His home run against (seventh ranked nationally) Western Michigan aided Michigan's victory and resultant invitation to the tournament. In 1964, Campbell returned to shortstop as the team was hit by graduation losses. He also served as captain that year. Campbell entered the majors with Detroit in 1967. He played eight seasons in the majors with four different teams. Primarily a utility infielder, Campbell's only season as a full-time second baseman came with San Diego in 1970; he hit .219 with 12 home runs. Campbell's career average was .213. In recent years, Campbell has been known best as a sports analyst with ESPN. (Courtesy of the Bentley Historical Library.)

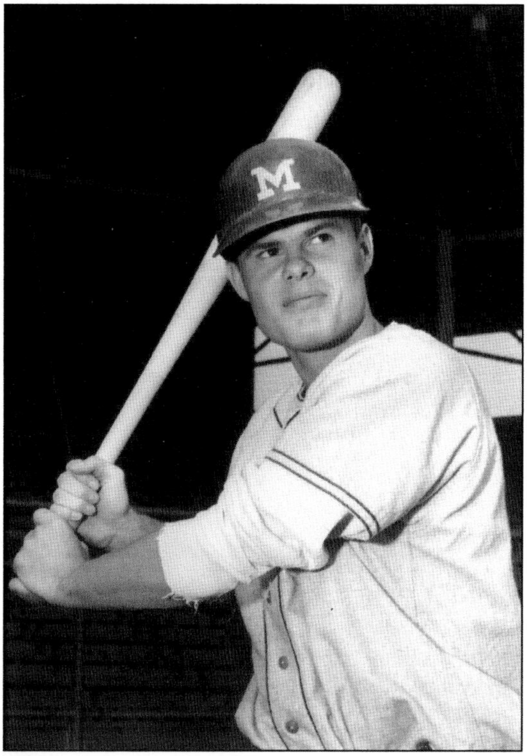

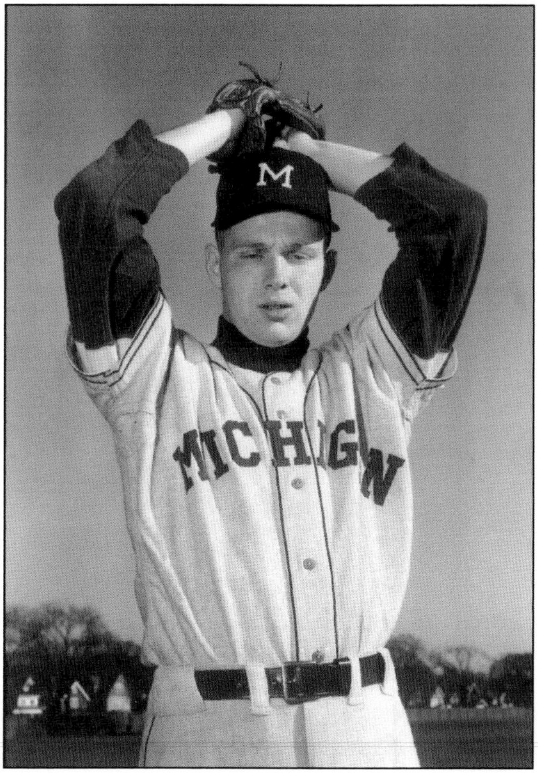

Fred "Fritz" Fisher was a key player during the 1962 championship season, during which he won eight games in fourteen decisions. The following season he compiled a record of 9-1. His 70 strikeouts in 79 innings pitched that year, including 16 against Central Michigan, caught the eyes of professional scouts. Fisher's career record of 21-9 represents the tenth highest career win total in Michigan team history. Following the season, Fisher signed a $30,000 bonus contract with the Detroit Tigers. He only appeared once in the majors (1964), striking out Harmon Killebrew while walking two and allowing two hits. (Courtesy of the Bentley Historical Library.)

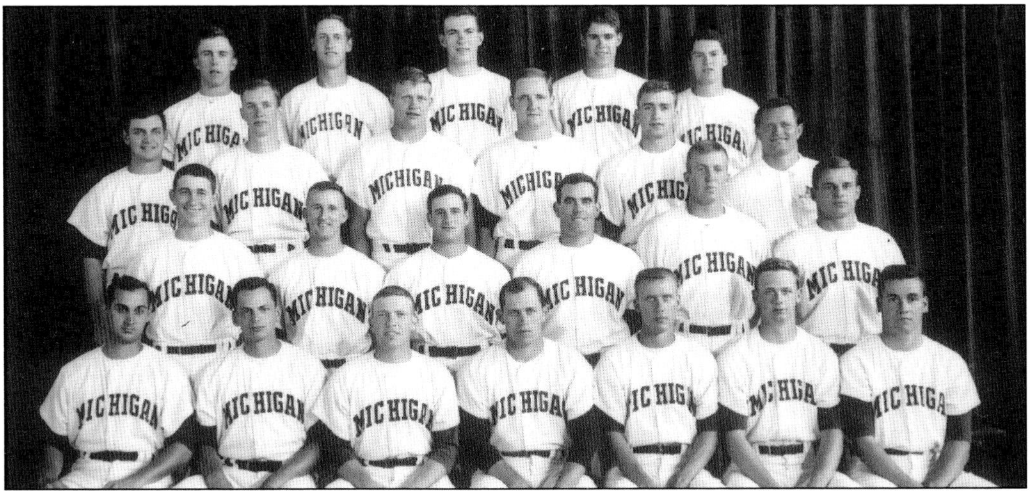

Pictured, from left to right, is the 1965 Michigan team: (first row) Dinunzio, Skaff, Sizemore (cap.), Benedict (coach), Pemberton, Wahl, and Barnhart; (second row): Honig (asst. coach), Reed, Kerr, Pascal, Meyers, and Sygar; (third row) Gilhooley, Lyijynen, Nunley, Tanona, Bara, and Shilling (trainer); (last row) Schryer, Cmejrek, Zepp, Volk, and Simonds. The 1965 squad produced an overall record of 18-14, with a record of 10-5 in the Big Ten—good enough for second place for the second consecutive year. Catcher and team captain Ted Sizemore won the second of three varsity letters in baseball (1964–1966), earning a position on the All Big Ten team for the first of two consecutive years. Sizemore later played 12 seasons in the major leagues, winning the Rookie-of-the-Year award while playing second base with the Dodgers in 1969. Sizemore's best professional years were with the Cardinals, with whom he played from 1971–1975. In 1982, Michigan established the Ted Sizemore Award to honor the team's top defensive player each year.

Other members of the team who played in the majors included Bill Zepp (Minnesota, Detroit) and Bob Reed (Detroit). (Courtesy of the Bentley Historical Library.)

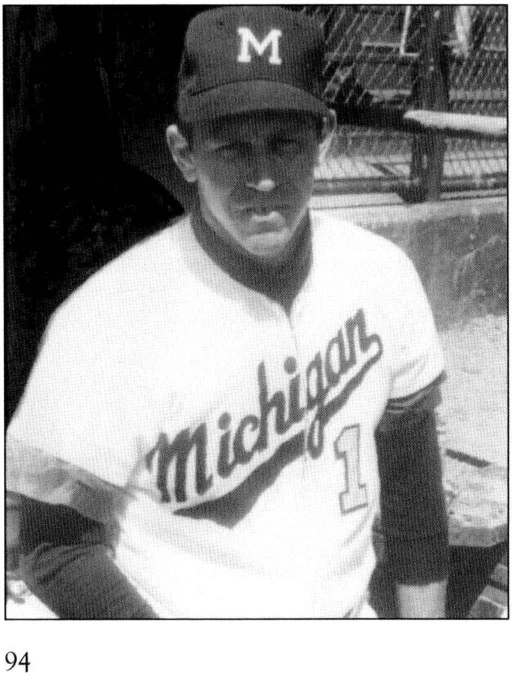

Milbry "Moby" Benedict lettered three years (1954–1956) at shortstop for Michigan under Ray Fisher. After a short professional career in the Detroit Tigers' system, Benedict returned to Michigan as an assistant coach under Don Lund. Following Lund's resignation in 1962, Benedict became the head coach. Between 1963 and 1979, Benedict produced a record of 367-251-5, which included three Big Ten championships. (Courtesy of the Bentley Historical Library.)

Elliott Maddox played one season at Michigan, 1968, during which he hit .393. That summer he was picked in the amateur draft by the Detroit Tigers. In 1970, Maddox was part of the trade in which Denny McClain was sent to the Washington Senators in exchange for Aurelio Rodriguez and others. In 1974, Maddox's contract was purchased by the Yankees, and it was in New York that he had his best seasons. In 1974, he batted .303, and in 1975, .307. Maddox played a total of 11 seasons in the majors, compiling a lifetime average of .261. (Courtesy of the Bentley Historical Library.)

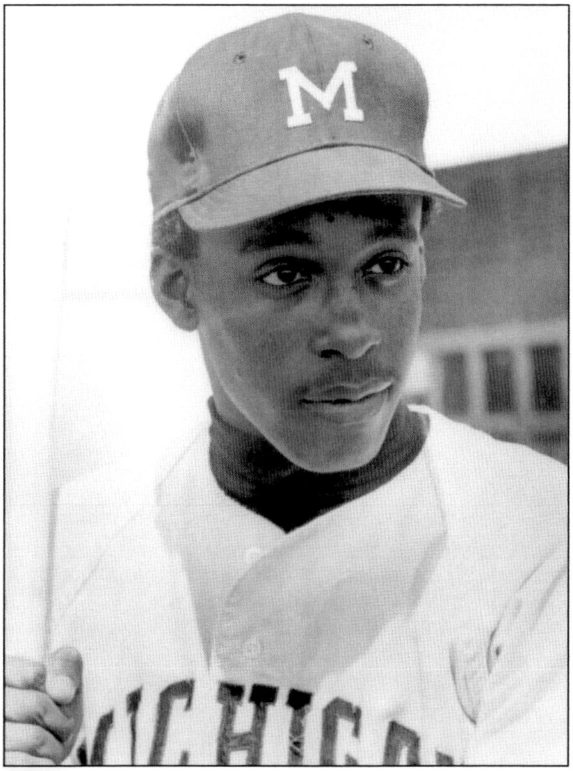

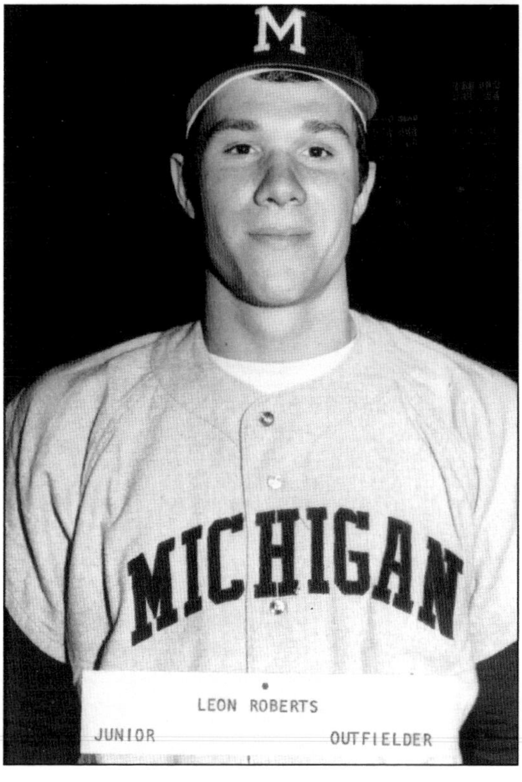

In 1972, outfielder Leon Roberts hit .422 in Big Ten competition, second highest in the conference, and was named to the All-Big Ten team. That summer he was picked by the Detroit Tigers in the tenth round of the amateur draft. Roberts played 11 seasons in the majors, between 1974–1984. His best year was with Seattle in 1978, hitting .301 with 22 home runs and 92 RBI. His lifetime average in the majors was .267. (Courtesy of the Bentley Historical Library.)

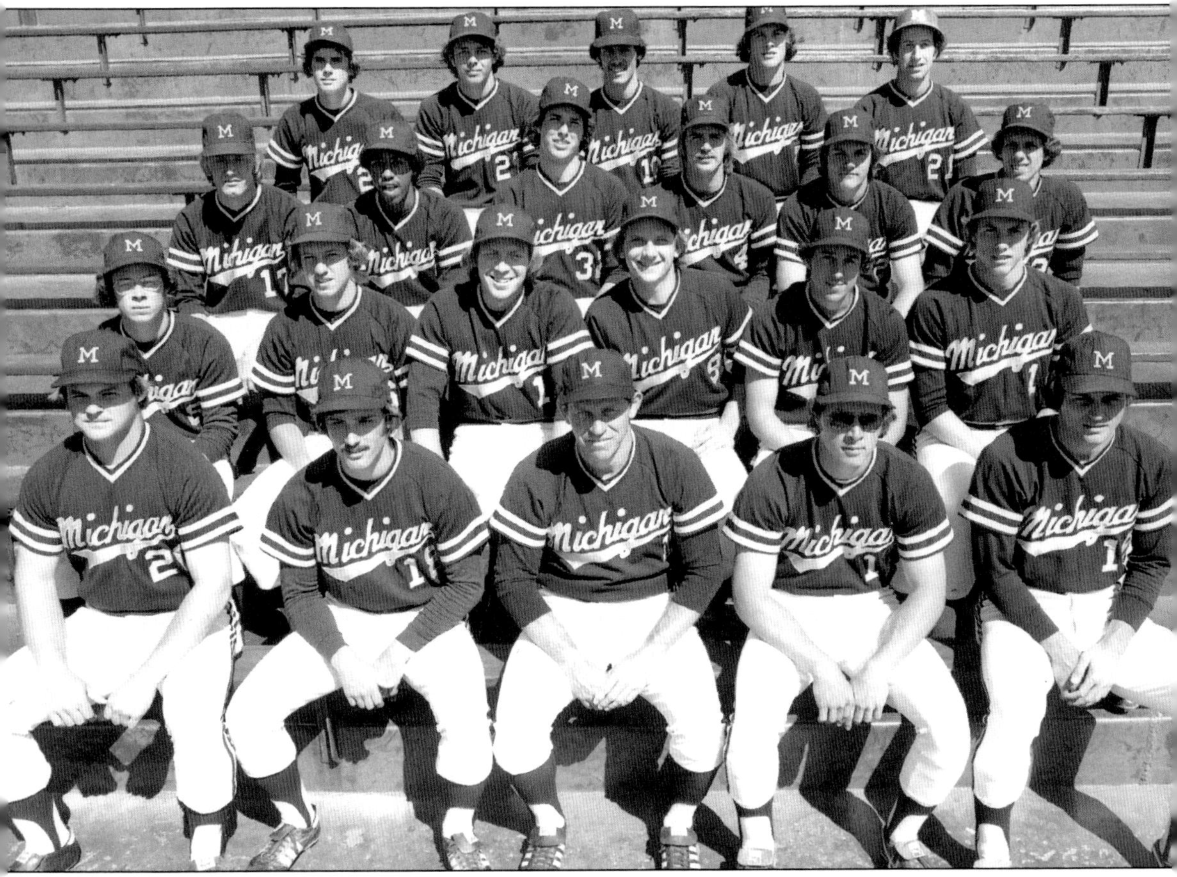

Pictured, from left to right, is the 1976 Michigan team: (first row) Pete Ross (asst. coach), Mark Weber, Moby Benedict (coach), Dick Walterhouse (cap.), and Dan Damiani; (second row) Dan Chapel, Steve Seyferth, John Jagels, Greg Lane, Mark Grenkoski, andLary Sorensen; (third row) Bill Stennett, Bill Haslerig, Craig McGinnis, Dave Chapman, Bob Wasilewski,, and Jim Berra; (last row) Tom Owens, Steve Perry, Chris Martucci, Rick Leach, and Jim Capoferi. Despite the second best record in Michigan baseball history (28-12), the 1975 Big Ten champions had been eliminated in the NCAA Mideast Regional Tournament by the Hurons of Eastern Michigan. EMU pitching in 1975 was led by future major leaguers Bob Welch and Bob Owchinko. The 1976 Michigan team consisted of many of the same players as the previous year, and with a record of 9-4, was once again the champion of the Big Ten. With an overall record of 19-18-1 to that point, Michigan entered the tournament as an underdog. The opening match was again against EMU (40-13): Lary Sorenson (8-2, 2.64 ERA) and Owchinko (10-3, 1.29 ERA as the tournament began). Owchinko pitched a two-hit, 6-0 shutout. Still, Michigan reached the tournament finals by shutting out Southern Illinois (2-0) and defeating Illinois State (5-4). But a 6-0 shutout again at the hands of Bob Owchinko and EMU eliminated Michigan with their second loss in the tournament. For the year, Michigan (22-19-1 overall) was led by Rick Leach (.345) and Dick Walterhouse (.342). Mark Weber was 3-2 in Big Ten competition, and 5-4 overall. Sorenson led the staff with a 4-2 record in the Big Ten, and 9-3 overall, with an ERA of 2.52. Both Leach and Sorenson went on to play in the "Majors." Sorenson was drafted in the eighth round by the Milwaukee Brewers. Between 1977 and 1988, he played with seven teams, compiling a record of 93-103. His best year was 1978, when he was 18-12 with the Brewers and pitched in the All-Star game. Between 1995–1998, Sorenson was a radio broadcaster with the Detroit Tigers. (Courtesy of the Bentley Historical Library.)

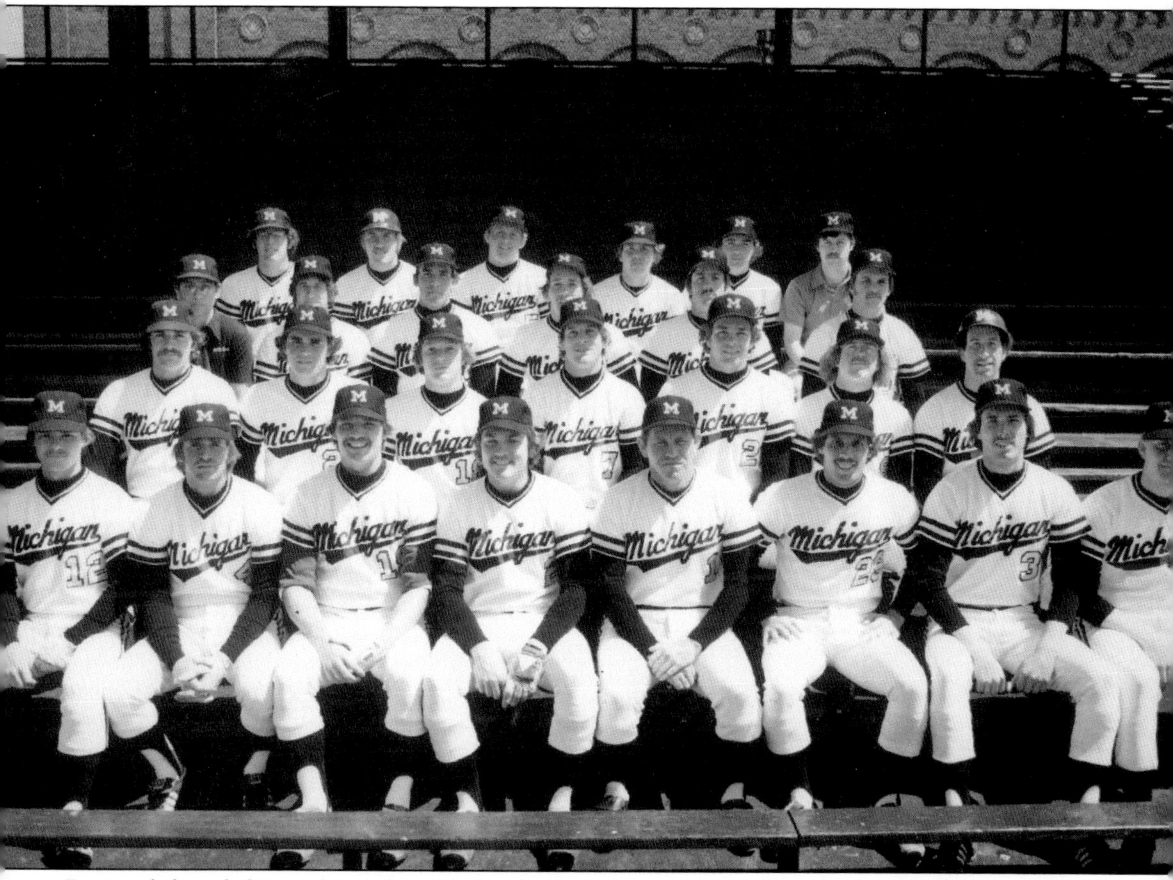

Pictured, from left to right, is the 1978 Michigan team: (front row) Anderson, Chapman, Parker, Wasilewski, Benedict (coach), Berra, McGinnis, Stennett; (second row) Forhan (asst. coach), Owens, Howe, Leach, Perry, Cooperrider, and Capoferi; (third row) Young (mgr.) McEldowney, Foussianes, Ray, Mason, and Bryant; (last row) Thomas, Hool, Wroten, Henderson, Clinton, and Campbell (trainer). The 1978 squad led the Big Ten for the third time in four years. Success was slow as the team ended its southern trip with a record of 7-8. Then wet grounds forced the postponement of the home opener for another week. But Michigan quickly began to dominate the Big Ten, winning 11 and losing once, eventually finishing with a record of 13-3 in conference play. Michigan began the NCAA Midwest Regionals with an 8-1 victory over Texas A&M, as Steve Howe pitched a four-hitter. This was followed by a 6-4 victory over the MAC champions, Eastern Michigan, and a nine hit shutout (3-0) by Tom Owens, again against Texas A&M. Tom Parker had two game winning hits, and scored five runs as he was named tournament Most Valuable Player. In the College World Series, Michigan shut out Baylor, 4-0, behind Howe's one-hitter and Vic Ray's three-run homer, but was eliminated by consecutive losses to USC and North Carolina. Rick Leach, more famous at the time for his football exploits, hit .457 in Big Ten play, collecting 55 hits and breaking the record held by Bill Freehan. Overall Leach hit .404. Leach's career batting average with Michigan was .348 during his three seasons of play (1976–1979). Drafted by the Detroit Tigers in the first round of the 1979 amateur draft, Leach played ten seasons in the majors, primarily with Detroit and Toronto, and had a lifetime batting average of .268. As a Michigan ballplayer, Leach was following family tradition, as both his father and uncle had preceded him in that endeavor. (Courtesy of the Bentley Historical Library.)

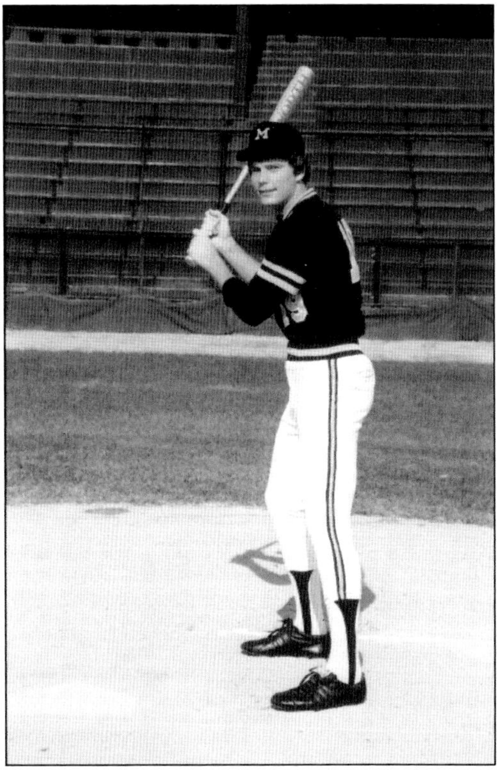

In Jim Paciorek's four seasons at Michigan (1979–1982), he produced hitting records which rank near the top in team history. His batting average of .443 in 1982 is second only to that compiled by Bill Freehan in 1961 (.446), while Paciorek's slugging average of .824 that season is third highest in team history. He hit 17 home runs that season, and drove in 65 runs. Paciorek's career batting average of .375 is second to that of Ken Hayward among modern players, while his career total of 32 home runs ranks fourth. In 1982, Paciorek was chosen in the eighth round of the amateur draft by the Milwaukee Brewers. He played one season in the majors, 1987, hitting .228 in 48 games. Paciorek was much more successful in Japan, where he played for six seasons (1988–1993). He led the Central League there in hitting in 1990 (.326), compiling a lifetime average of .315, with 86 home runs and 431 RBI. (Courtesy of the Bentley Historical Library.)

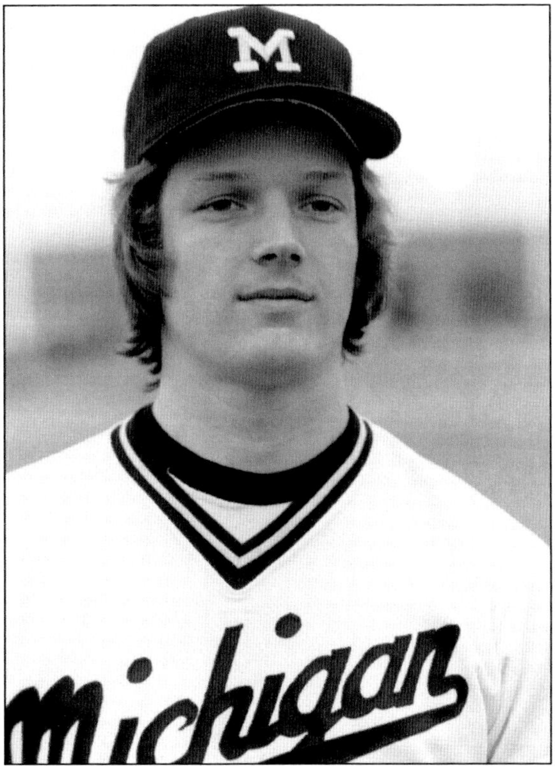

In three years at Michigan (1977–1979), Steve Howe compiled a career record of 27-8, including 196 strikeouts in 265.6 innings pitched. His best season was 1978, when he was 11-3, with 92 strikeouts in 98 innings, the third highest number of wins in a season for a Michigan pitcher. Following the 1979 season, one in which he had a record of 7-2, Howe was chosen in the first round of the amateur draft by the Los Angeles Dodgers. Howe played 12 seasons in the major leagues between 1980–1996. His primary success was with the Dodgers (1980–1985) and Yankees (1991–1996), with whom he signed as a free agent. Used entirely in relief, Howe had 91 career saves, and a record of 47-41. (Courtesy of the Bentley Historical Library.)

SIX

Scandals and Rebirth

1980–2003

As a result of the retirement of Moby Benedict, Don Canham, Michigan Athletic Director had to find a replacement before the upcoming season. Upon the recommendation of football coach Bo Schembechler, Canham offered the job to Bud Middaugh. Middaugh was a graduate of Miami University of Ohio, where he had been a four-year letterman at shortstop. After briefly playing in the Baltimore Oriole minor league system, and coaching high school baseball, Middaugh returned to Miami in 1967, becoming baseball coach the following year. He spent twelve years in that position, producing a record of 359-173. His Miami teams won three MAC championships and appeared in NCAA tournaments four times. It was during this period that he met Schembechler.

During the 1980s, Michigan won seven Big Ten titles in ten years, and participated in the College World Series four times. Middaugh was a no-nonsense type of coach. But as noted by Casey Close, whose Michigan hitting records were accomplished under Middaugh, "when you're winning, you don't mind the work." Once when Middaugh was not satisfied with the pitching mechanics exhibited during a spring trip to Florida, he had the bus stop at a rest stop, where the pitchers practiced their windups with the curb as the pitching rubber.

Middaugh's tenure began on a high note as Michigan ended the 1980 season as Big Ten champion once again. They followed this up with a sweep of the Mid-east regional. Steve Ontiveros pitched six innings of strong relief as Michigan first defeated MAC Champion Central Michigan 9-4, then swept two from Nebraska: a 7-0 shutout behind Mark Clinton and Ontiveros, followed by a 12-3 pounding led by Jim Paciorek's 5 RBI. Catcher Gerry Hool's three-run double in the 11th and Clinton's pitching produced a 9-8 victory over California in the first game of the College World Series. But with Clinton pitching again on only twenty hours rest, Miami defeated Michigan, 3-2. Michigan was then eliminated as Arizona, featuring a three-run home run by Terry Francona, shut out the Wolverines 8-0. Despite the losses, Paciorek was outstanding as he reached base nine times in succession, and produced a game saving catch against California.

In 1981, the Big Ten instituted a divisional format for determining the conference champion. A similar system to name the champion would be followed until 1992. The two top teams in the East Division would play their equivalents from the West Division in a single elimination at seasons end. Once again, Michigan led the Big Ten. In tournament play, Michigan swept Illinois, Purdue and Minnesota to head for the Mid-east Regional Tournament.

The regionals began with a loss to New Orleans. Michigan followed this with victories over Nevada-Las Vegas and New Orleans. They clinched the tournament with a double-header shutout of Eastern Michigan: a 10-0 shutout by Bill Shuta, and 4-0 behind Scott Elam, Elam's 11th victory of the year. Jim Paciorek was named tournament MVP. However, Michigan was quickly eliminated from the College World Series, as they fell to Miami once again, and Arizona.

In 1982, Michigan continued its domination of the Big Ten during regular season play. A sweep of Michigan State resulted in a tie with Ohio State for the title. They opened the Big Ten playoffs by defeating Ilinois 4-2, as Rich Stoll established a Michigan record with his 12th victory. But losses to Ohio State and Minnesota ended Michigan's season.

Michigan continued as either Big Ten champion or East Division champion for most of the decade. In 1988, the Big Ten eliminated the East-West format, and tournament play was based upon the four top teams. Michigan again had the best record in the conference, but lost the title in the tournament to Minnesota. Nevertheless, the team still received an at-large bid for the regional tournament. Losses to California and Texas ended their season at the regional level.

Despite disquieting rumors concerning some of Coach Middaugh's practices, the 1989 Big Ten season again ended with Michigan on top. Michigan was defeated for the Big Ten championship by Illinois, but still moved on to the NCAA West II regionals where they were eliminated by consecutive losses to Wichita State.

Scandal ultimately disrupted the team. Middaugh was accused of diverting revenues from program sales at football games to replace baseball scholarships held by players. Players allegedly received payoffs ranging as high as $4,500.00 for doing little or no work, or as substitutions for scholarships. Middaugh was accused of providing over $80,000.00 to players. He initially denied the charges. But the evidence was overwhelming, and in July, Middaugh was asked to resign by Bo Schembechler, Canham's successor as Athletic Director.

Michigan baseball was placed on probation by the NCAA for two years. The University imposed its own, harsher, penalties: all scholarships were cut for two years, postseason play was banned for three years, and off-campus recruiting was ended for a year. The result was the program was badly crippled. It would take a decade to fully recover.

In September 1989, Michigan graduate and former Tiger catcher Bill Freehan was named as Middaugh's replacement. Freehan had never previously coached. But Schembechler felt Freehan's strong character and clear abilities would be necessary to restore the proper image to Michigan baseball. Though the initial one-year "contract" was merely a handshake, Freehan would remain as coach through the 1995 season.

While Freehan's tenure re-established a sense of integrity and credibility to the program, the difficulty in recruiting outstanding athletes limited the ability of the team to compete with strong opposition. His 1995 team had been picked to finish as high as second in conference play. Instead, it finished last, and Freehan by then had had enough. In July, Freehan resigned, leaving as the first Michigan baseball coach with a losing record.

Freehan was replaced by Geoff Zahn. Zahn had been a Michigan graduate (Class of 1968), and followed this with thirteen years as a Major League pitcher. In 1996, he finished the Big Ten season with a 17-11 record, sufficient for 4th place, and followed this with a 1st place finish the following year. In 1999, Michigan won the Big Ten tournament, its first such triumph in twelve years.

Following the 2001 season, Zahn suddenly resigned, and was replaced on an interim basis by Chris Harrison for the 2002 season. Rich Maloney was hired as permanent coach prior to the 2003 season. Led by senior third-baseman Brock Koman and junior Jake Fox, another in a line of slugging catchers who have played at Michigan, the team finished third in the conference and once again qualified for the playoffs.

Year	Overall: Won	Lost	Conference: Won	Lost	Position	Coach
1980	36	18 (1 Tie)	14	2	1st [9]	Middaugh
1981	41	20	10	4	1st [10]	Middaugh
1982	44	10	13	3	East Div. Champion – tie	Middaugh
1983	50	9	13	2	Big Ten Champ. [11]	Middaugh
1984	43	20	11	5	Big Ten Champ. [12]	Middaugh
1985	55	10	14	2	East Division Champion	Middaugh
1986	47	12	13	3	Big Ten Champion	Middaugh
1987	52	12	13	3	Big Ten Champion	Middaugh
1988	48	19	20	8	1st [13]	Middaugh
1989	49	16	21	6	1st [13]	Middaugh
1990	33	24	14	14	5th (Tie)	Freehan
1991	34	23 (1 Tie)	15	13	5th	Freehan
1992	21	32	11	17	8th (Tie)	Freehan
1993	25	30	13	14	7th	Freehan
1994	29	29	13	15	3rd (Tie) [14]	Freehan
1995	24	29	10	16	10th	Freehan
1996	24	30	17	11	4th [15]	Zahn
1997	33	22	17	9	1st [16]	Zahn
1998	21	27 (1 Tie)	9	15	6th (Tie)	Zahn
1999	34	30	15	13	4th [17]	Zahn
2000	20	32 (1 Tie)	10	18	8th	Zahn
2001	28	28	10	14	6th	Zahn
2002	21	32	14	17	8th	Harrison
2003	30	27	16	14	3rd [18]	Maloney

[9] Regional Champion; 5th Place, College World Series
[10] Regional Champion; 7th Place, College World Series
[11] Regional Champion; 3rd Place, College World Series
[12] Regional Champion; 7th Place (tie), College World Series
[13] Regular Season Champion
[14] Big Ten Playoff, 2nd
[15] Big Ten Playoff, 4th
[16] Big Ten Playoff, 2nd
[17] Big Ten Playoff, 1st; NCAA Regional, 2nd
[18] Big Ten Playoff, 4th

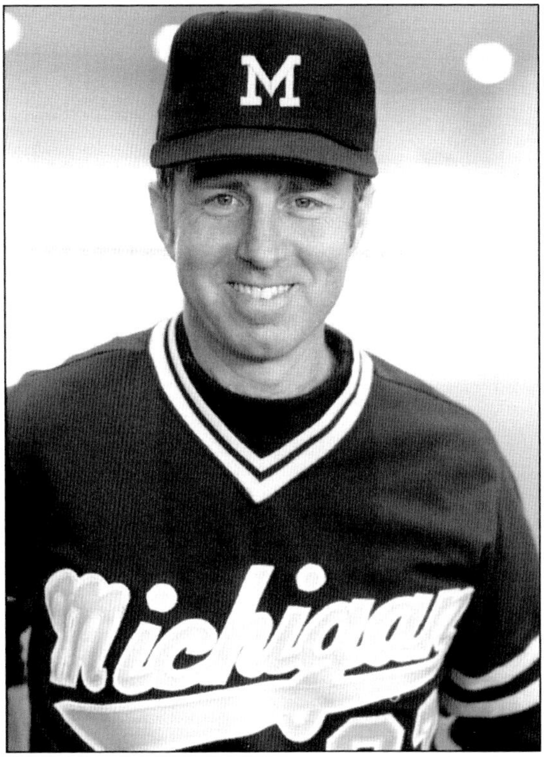

Forest "Bud" Middaugh's successful reign as baseball coach at Michigan was ultimately tempered by controversy. Hired to replace Moby Benedict, Middaugh produced a recordof 465-146-1 between 1980–1989. The total included eight conference championships and four regional titles. Middaugh was a tough perfectionist, and thought nothing of pulling his team off a bus while traveling to practice in a parking lot. As former Wolverine Mike Ignasiak described him, "Think Bobby Knight in a baseball uniform." But you couldn't argue with Middaugh's success in the coaching ranks. Middaugh's coaching career at Michigan came to a sad end in 1989. He was accused of diverting proceeds from the sale of sports programs into payoffs for players, and was forced to resign. (Courtesy of the Bentley Historical Library.)

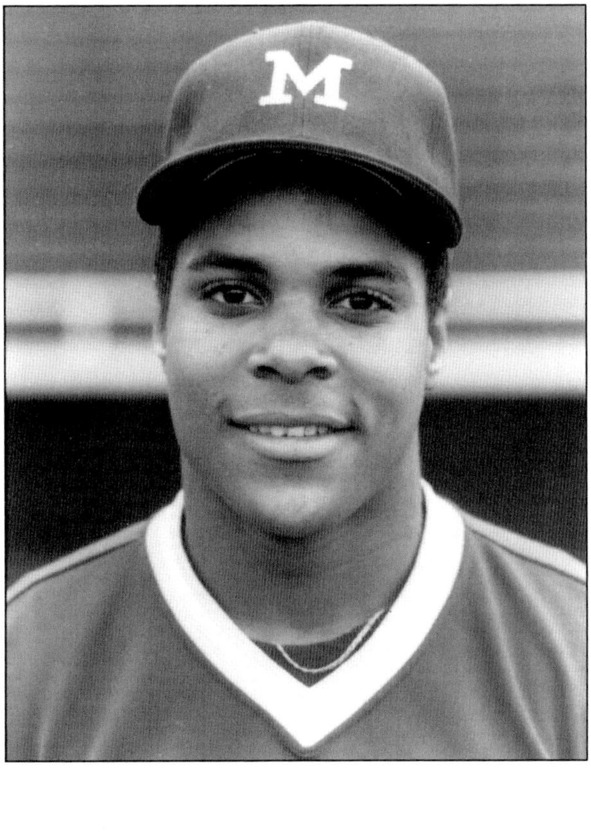

Barry Larkin played three seasons at shortstop for Michigan (1983–1985), producing a career batting average of .361 (8th highest); his first year with the varsity resulted in an average of .352, including 5 home runs and 37 RBI. Larkin's career totals ranked among the team's top ten in several additional areas, including fifth in runs scored (172), eighth in home runs (26), tenth in RBI (136) and ninth in hits (203). Larkin was chosen by Cincinnati in the first round of the 1985 draft. This previous season (2003), he completed his 18th year in the major leagues, all with the Reds. Larkin's contributions to the team have been steady throughout his career, as indicated by his lifetime average of .295, with over 2,200 hits. (Courtesy of the Bentley Historical Library.)

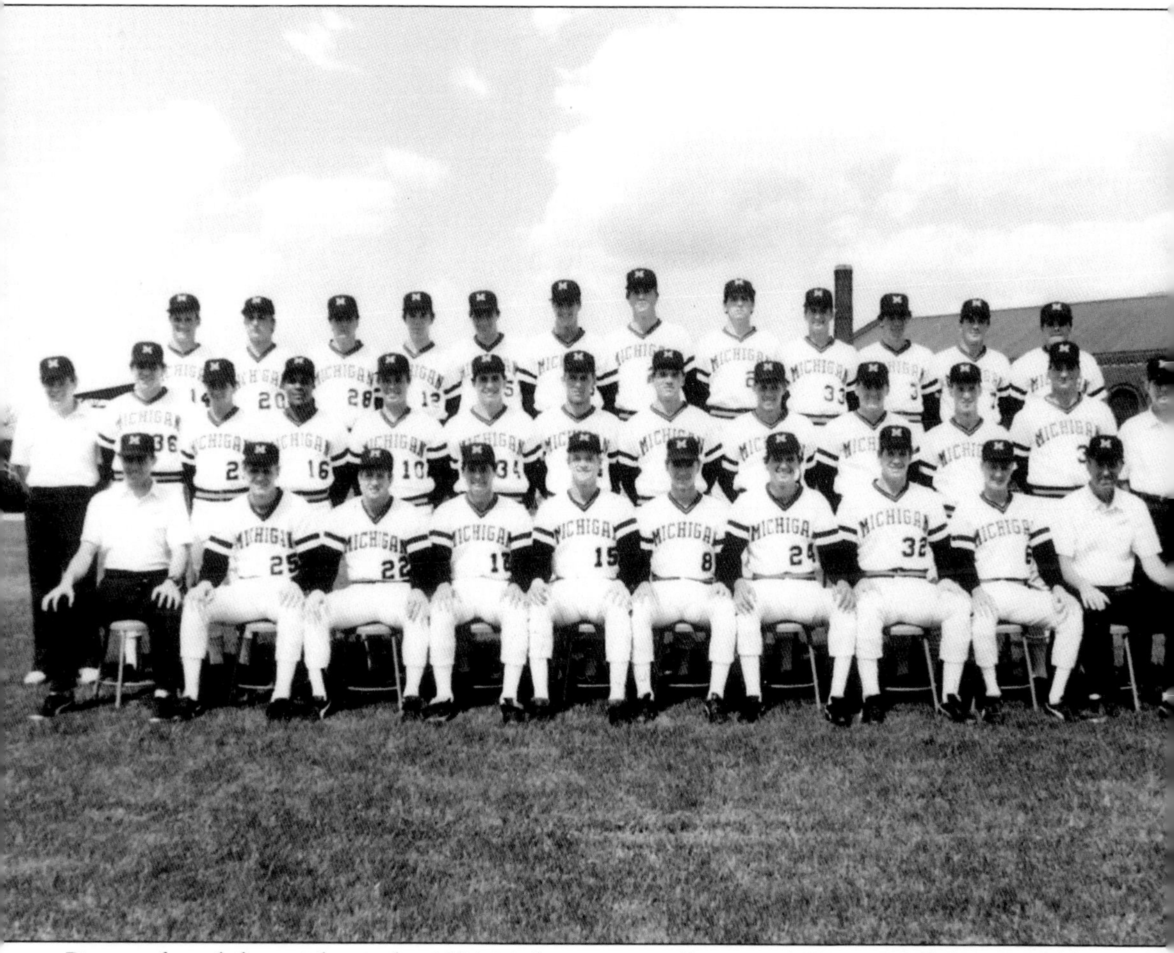

Picture, from left to right, is the 1984 Michigan team: (front row) Danny Hall (asst. coach), Randy Wolfe, Jeff Minick, Bill Shuta, Rick Bair, Chuck Froning, Gary Wayne, Ken Hayward, C.J. Beshke, and Bud Middaugh (coach); (middle row) Jim Neidert (equipt. mgr.), Gary Murphy (asst. coach), Chris Gust, Barry Larkin, Eric Sanders, Casey Close, Mike Watters, Dan Disher, Kurt Zimmerman, Scott Kamieniecki, Derek Kerr, John Young (general asst.), and Rex Thompson (trainer); (back row) Dave Karasinski, Paul Wenson, Mike Betz, Jon Wood, Jerry Wolf, Paul Kaspar, Kevin Gilles, Hal Morris, John Grettenberger, Buddy Dodge, Rob Huffman, and Matt Siuda. After compiling a season record of 43-20, including a record of 11-5 in Big Ten competition, Michigan won the Big Ten tournament and advanced to the Regionals. Michigan defeated Central Michigan, 4-3, behind future major leaguer Scott Kamieniecki and moved on to the College World Series. Despite the hitting of Mike Watters and the strong pitching of Gary Wayne, Michigan was quickly eliminated. Future major leaguers on the team included Barry Larkin, Hal Morris, Kamieniecki and Wayne. Ken Hayward (Front row, third from right) set many of the modern Michigan hitting records during his four years on the team (1982–1985), including highest lifetime batting average (.376) and career RBI (207). His total of 33 home runs is second only to the total hit by Casey Close (46). In 1985, Hayward had a batting average of .432, fourth highest in team history.(Courtesy of the Bentley Historical Library.)

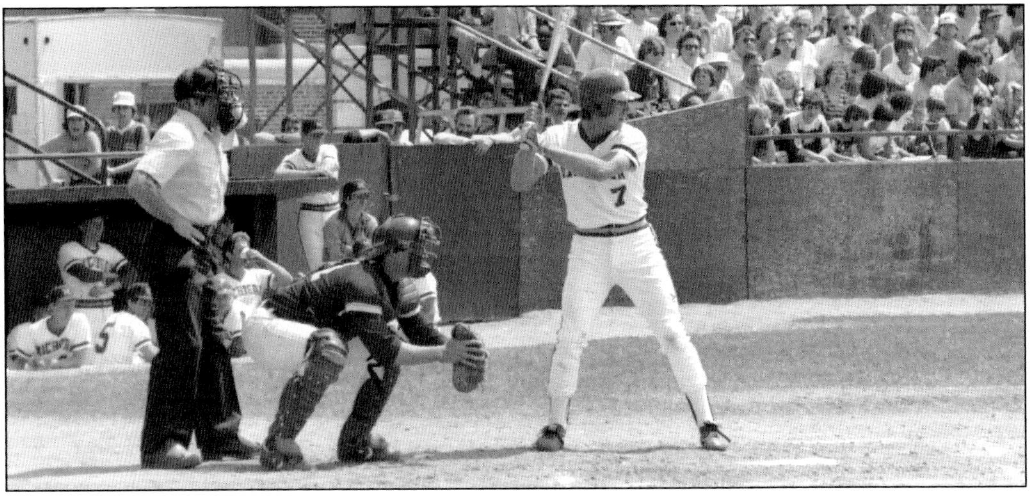

For three years (1981–1983), Chris Sabo was Michigan's third baseman. His 1982 average of .257 (4 home runs, 30 RBI) was not indicative of his hitting potential. In 1983, Sabo hit .368, with 16 home runs and 56 RBI. His play in the College World Series that year, though not enough to prevent Michigan's elimination, still resulted in his being named to the All-Tournament team. Sabo's 400+ foot home run to the Track and Field Building at Fisher Stadium in a regional match with Morehead State was one of the longest of the year. Sabo's career total of 30 home runs places him among the top ten in Michigan history. He was drafted by the Cincinnati Reds in the second round of the 1983 draft. Sabo played nine seasons in the majors, primarily with Cincinnati. His best year was 1991, when he hit .301 and was named to the All-Star team. Sabo's overall career average was .268. (Courtesy of the Bentley Historical Library.)

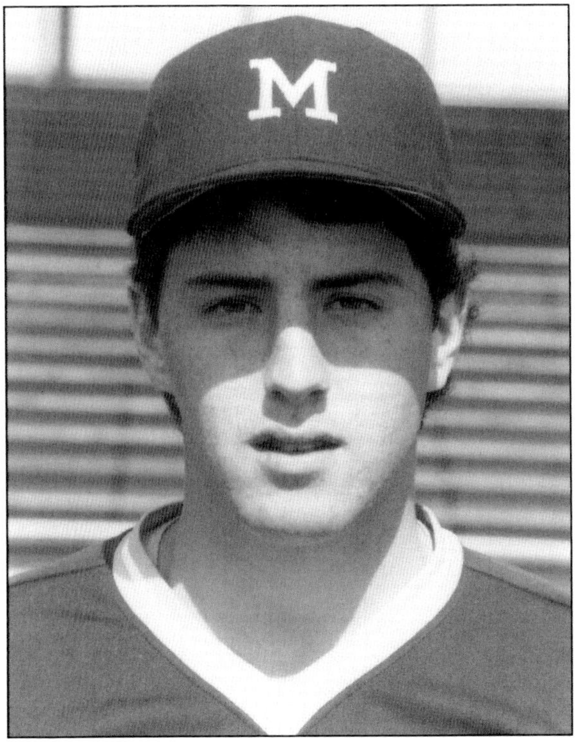

Hal Morris was one of several future major league stars to play under Coach Bud Middaugh. Between 1984–1986, Morris produced a career average of .373, including 20 home runs. His best season was 1985, when he hit .421 (fifth highest in modern team history) with ten home runs. Morris was chosen by the New York Yankees in the eighth round of the 1986 amateur draft. After two seasons in a part-time role, he was traded to Cincinnati in 1989, and it was here that Morris established himself as one of the outstanding players on the team. Five times he hit over .300, with a high of .340 in 1990. Primarily an infielder, Morris was in the "Big Leagues" for 13 seasons between 1988–2000, with a lifetime average of .304. He finished his career in 2000 with the Detroit Tigers. (Courtesy of the Bentley Historical Library.)

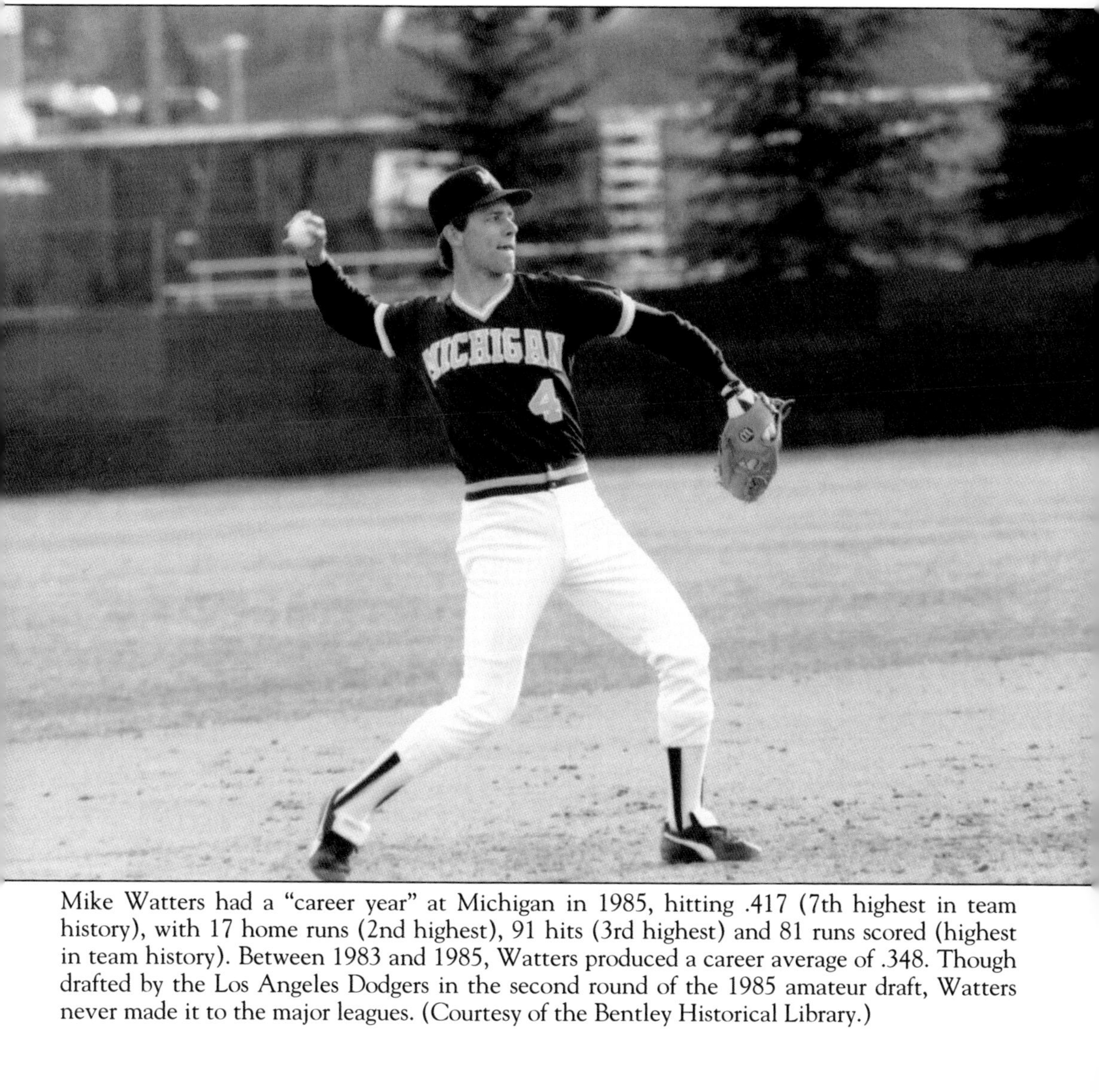

Mike Watters had a "career year" at Michigan in 1985, hitting .417 (7th highest in team history), with 17 home runs (2nd highest), 91 hits (3rd highest) and 81 runs scored (highest in team history). Between 1983 and 1985, Watters produced a career average of .348. Though drafted by the Los Angeles Dodgers in the second round of the 1985 amateur draft, Watters never made it to the major leagues. (Courtesy of the Bentley Historical Library.)

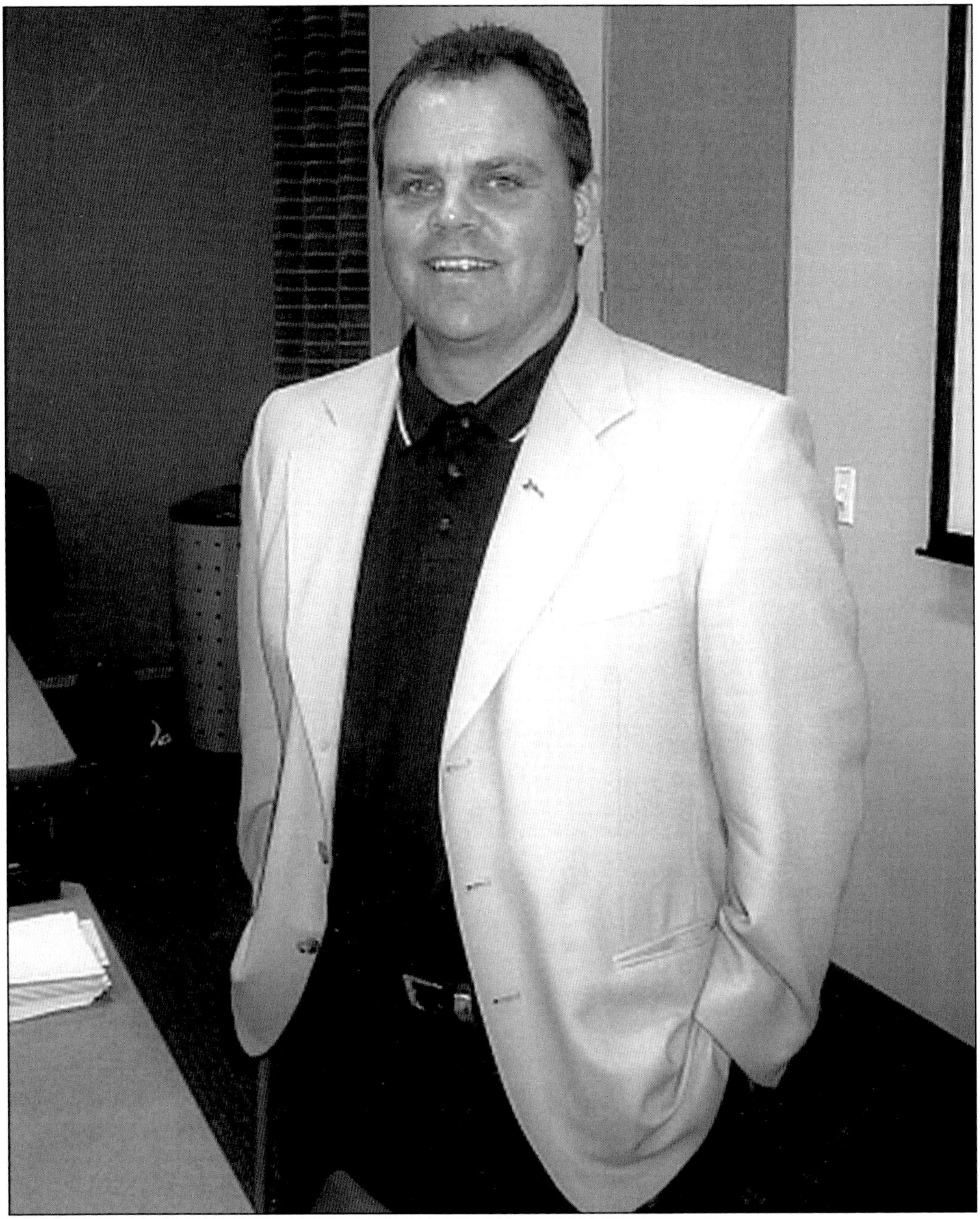

Mike Ignasiak holds many of the modern pitching records for Michigan. From 1985 to 1988, he compiled a record of 33-17, team records in both areas. In 1988, his record was 10-7, while in 1985 as a freshman, he was 9-2. His career strikeout level of 286 is two behind that of record holder Jim Burton. Ignasiak was drafted by St. Louis in 1987, but turned the offer down. In the 1988 amateur draft, he was picked in the eighth round by the Milwaukee Brewers. Ignasiak played four seasons with Milwaukee (1991–1995), compiling a lifetime record of 10-4, before injuries forced him to retire. Ignasiak is one of twelve children. His father was a member of the "Flying Tigers" during World War II. Brother Gary pitched briefly with the Detroit Tigers in 1973. (Courtesy of Jim Lannen.)

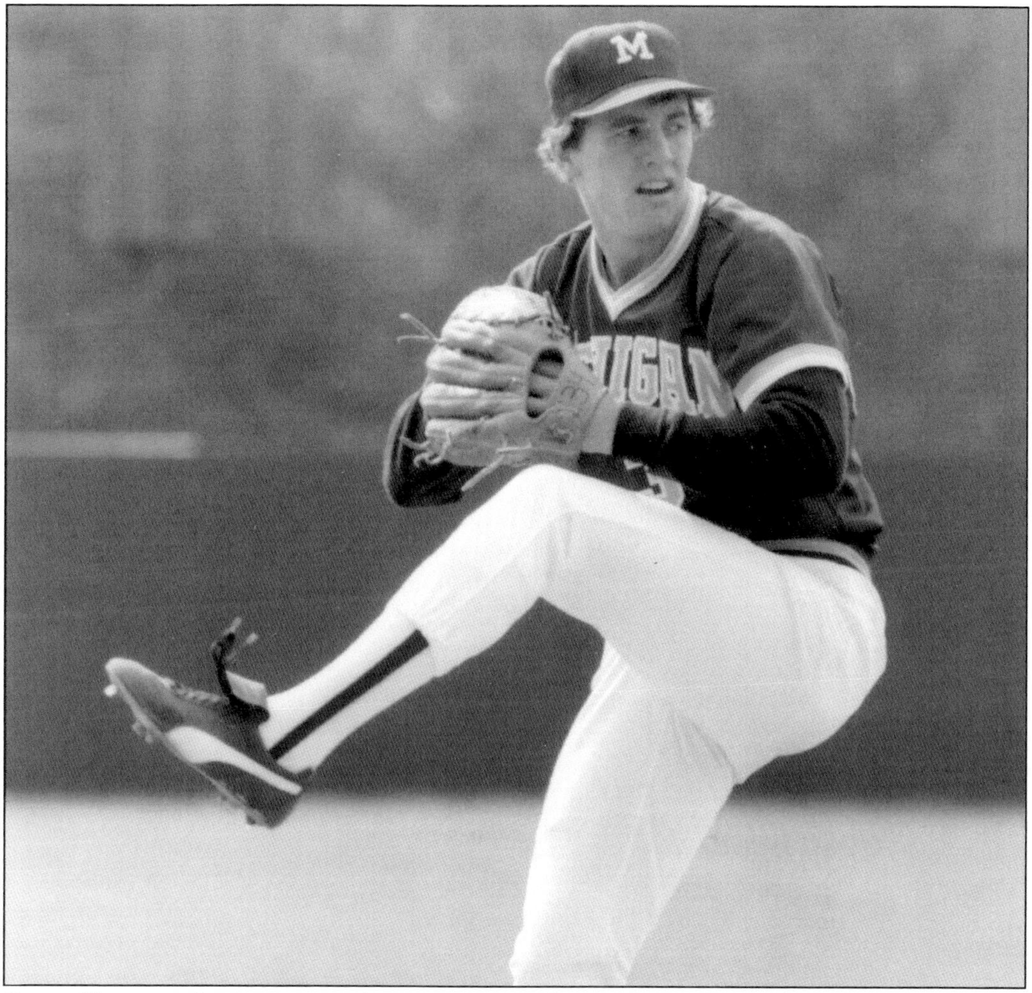

Casey Close was the dominating figure among Michigan players during the 1980s. A four-letter man in the sport (1983–1986), Close continues to hold both many season records, as well as career totals for the team. These include home runs for a season (19 in 1986) as well as career (46), RBI in a season (72 in 1986), and Slugging Percentage in a season (.869) and career (.697). During his first three seasons, Close both pitched and played the outfield. In 1985, he had a record on the mound of 6-1, with a 3.93 ERA, while hitting .388, including 16 home runs and 58 RBI. However, Close was not chosen in that year's major league draft, and he decided to concentrate during his senior year as a position player. Close began that season with an average of .543, and five home runs, during the nine game spring trip to Florida. By the end of the season, he compiled an average of .440, and team records in home runs and RBI. *Baseball America* chose Close as its player of the year. Close was always a player the team could count on in a pinch. Three of his home runs in 1986 came in the last innings of close games. During the College World Series in 1983, he hit a grand slam in leading Michigan over Stanford, 11-4. In 1984, Close pitched Michigan to a 6-3 victory over Minnesota to win the Big Ten title. Perhaps even more importantly, Close earned Academic Big-Ten honors his senior year. Close was drafted by the New York Yankees in the seventh round that year. He made it as high as Triple-A before giving up his professional aspirations. In recent years, Close has become one of the most successful sports agents, and includes Derek Jeter and Drew Henson among his clients. (Courtesy of the Bentley Historical Library.)

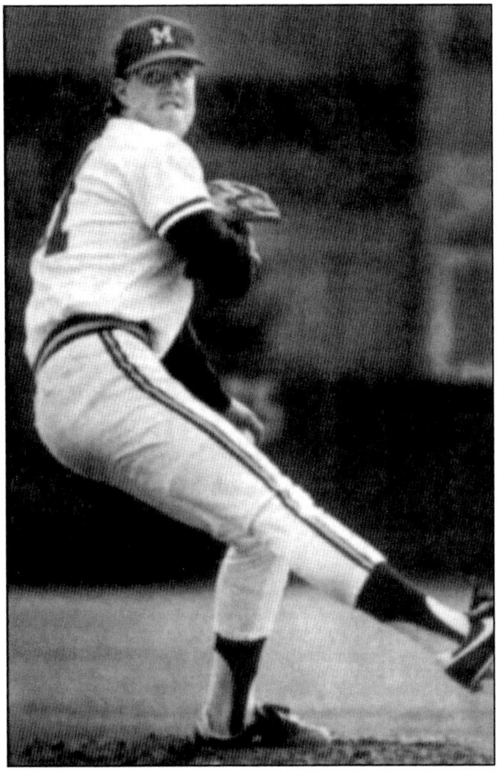

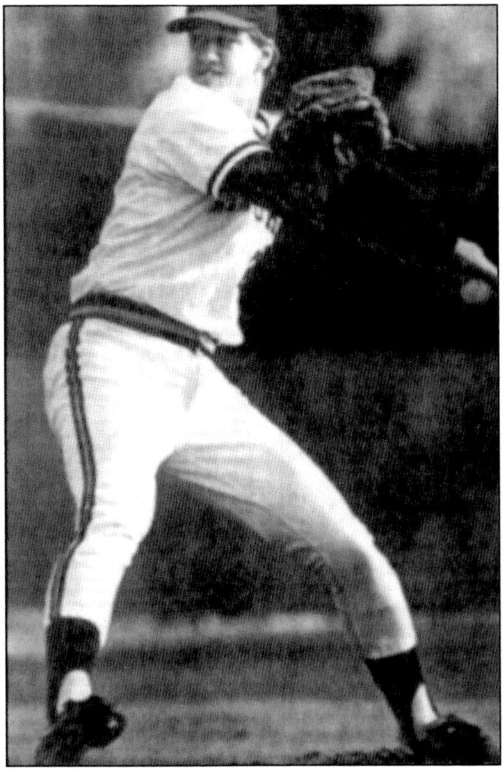

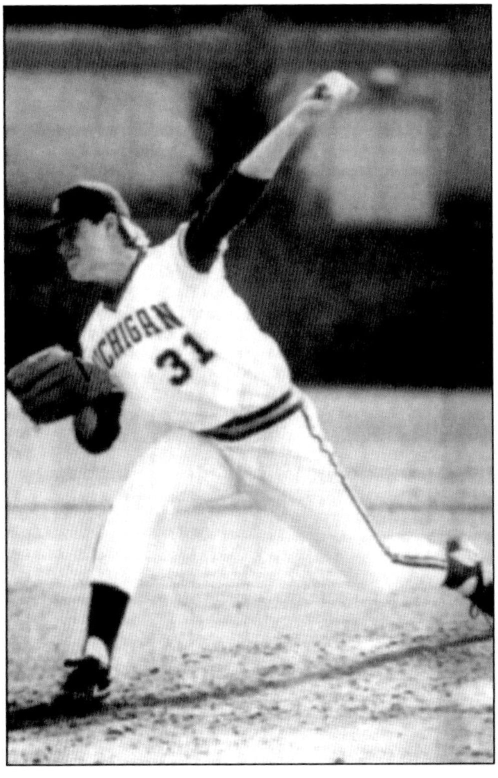

Despite being born without a right hand (one hesitates to call it a handicap), lefty Jim Abbott established himself as one of the outstanding pitchers of the 1980s. Between 1986–1988, Abbott produced a record of 26-8. In 1987, he received the Golden Spikes Award as the top amateur baseball player in the nation. He was also the winner of the James E. Sullivan Award that year as the outstanding amateur athlete in the nation. Drafted by the California Angels, Abbott finished a ten-year major league career with a record of 87-108. In 1991, Abbott won 18 games for the Angels. Traded to the Yankees in December 1992, he tossed a no-hitter against the Cleveland Indians in September of the 1993 season. (Courtesy of the *Michigan Daily*.)

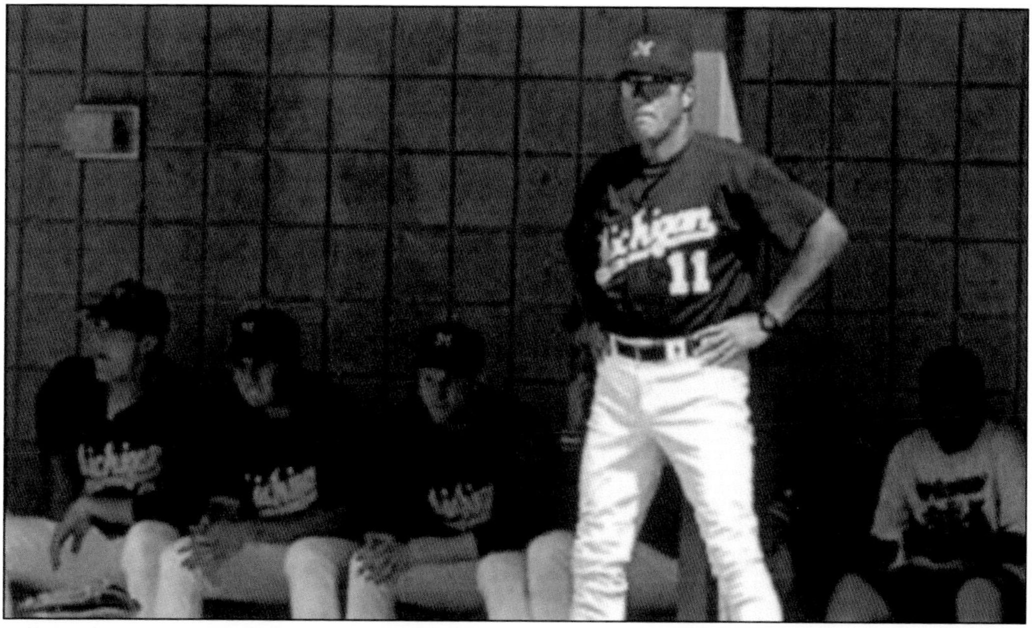

Bill Freehan coached Michigan baseball from 1990 to 1995, restoring the integrity that had been had been lost in the scandals of the 1980s. Hurt by the loss of scholarships and other penalties, the team produced a record of 166-167-1 during these seasons. (Courtesy of the *Michigan Daily*.)

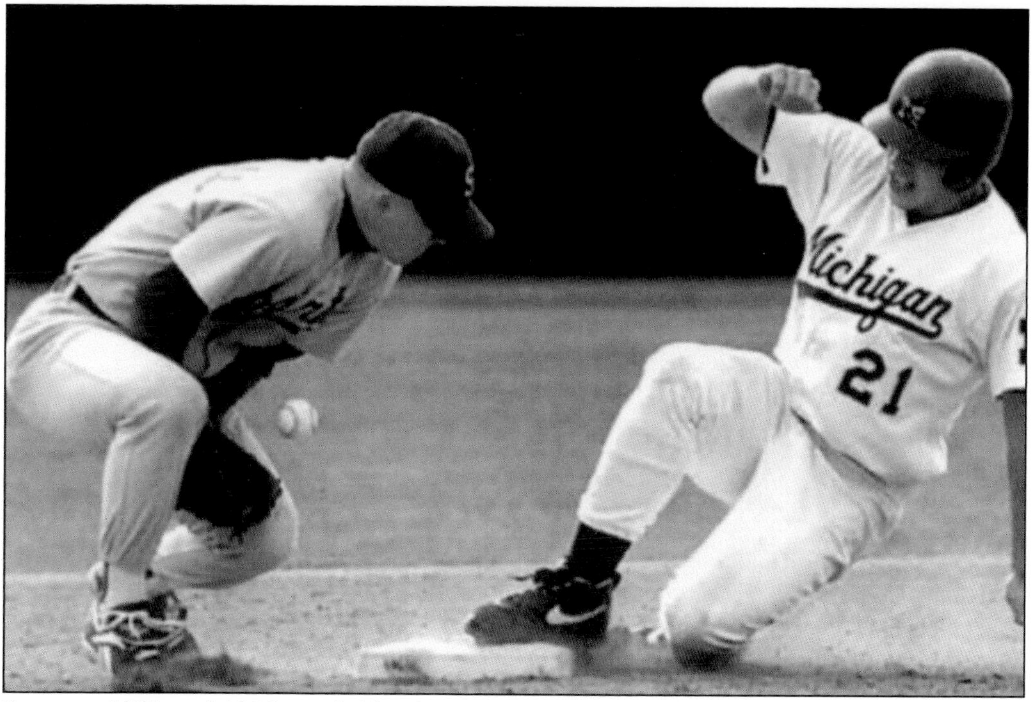

Between 1993 and 1995, outfielder Scott Weaver compiled a career average of .370, with a slugging percentage of .592. In 1995, he averaged .418 for the season, while hitting .500 against Big Ten pitching. Weaver was later drafted into the Detroit Tigers organization. (Courtesy of the *Michigan Daily*.)

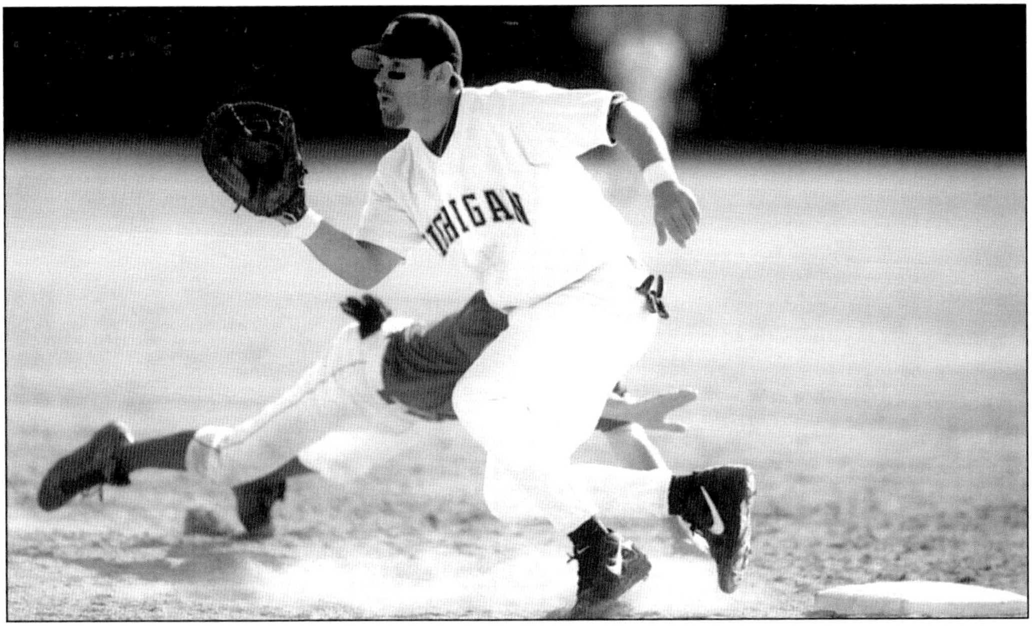

First baseman Bryan Besco (1995–1999) was at his best in tournament play. In post-season action, he hit .458 (22 for 48), including 5 home runs and 19 RBI, with a slugging percentage of .958. He finished his senior year with an average of .311. His total of 26 doubles in 1997 and 24 in 1999 represent the two highest seasonal totals for Michigan in that category. Besco's brother Derek also played for the Wolverines, from 1995–1998. (Courtesy of the *Michigan Daily*.)

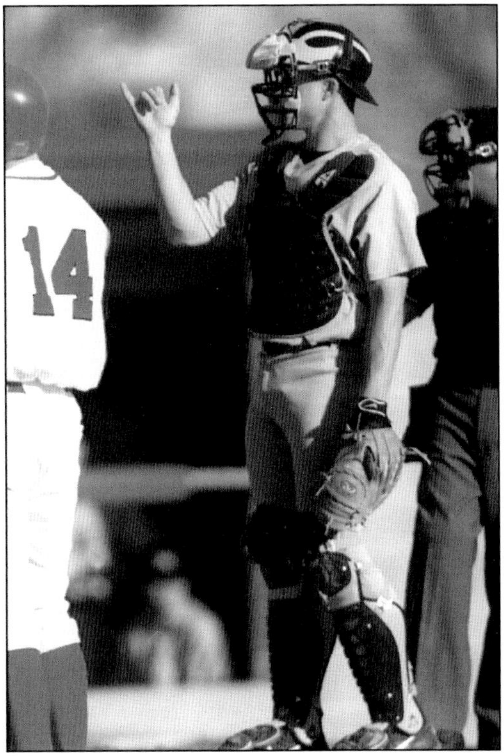

Son of former Detroit Tigers catcher Lance Parrish, David Parrish put together three strong seasons at that position with the Wolverines (1998–2000). A lifetime .325 hitter, including 25 home runs, Parrish hit .356 his senior year, with 11 home runs and 41 RBI. At 6'3", he clearly had the size and power to catch the eyes of major league scouts. Not surprisingly, he was selected in the first round of the 2000 amateur draft by the New York Yankees. Through 2003, Parrish had risen as high as Trenton of the Eastern League (Double A) in the Yankee organization. (Courtesy of the *Michigan Daily*.)

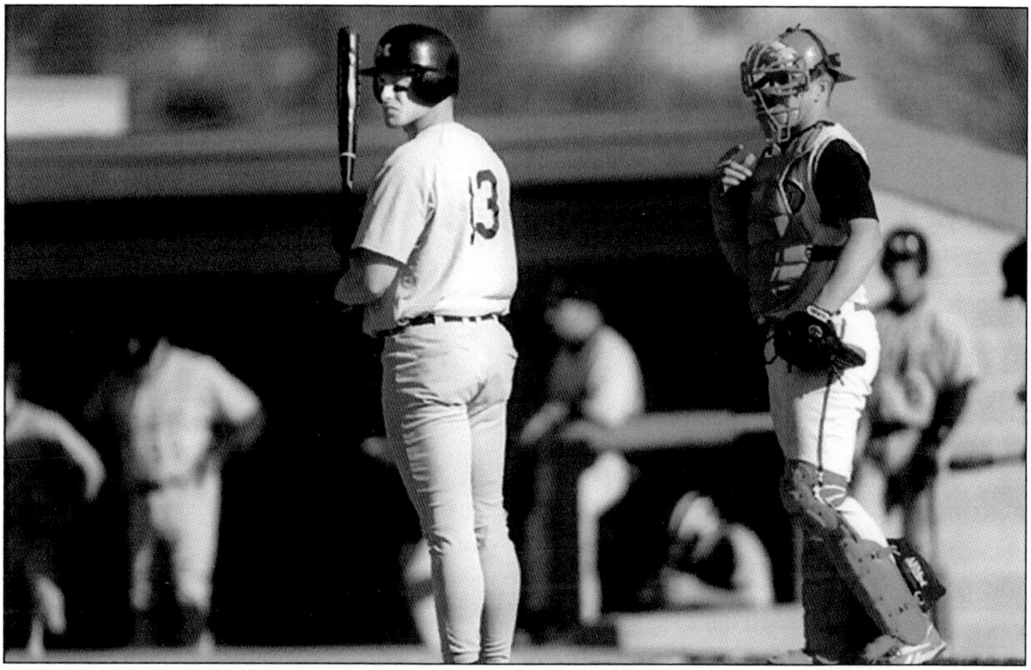

Michigan's Most Valuable Player in 2000, David Parrish became the seventh player from Michigan to be a first round choice during the major league amateur draft. (Courtesy of the *Michigan Daily*.)

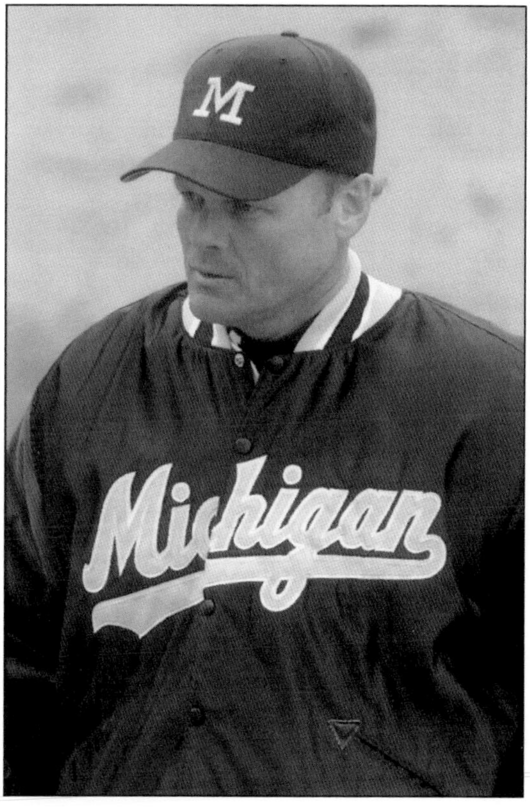

After six years as assistant coach at Michigan, Chris Harrison was hired as interim coach to replace Geoff Zahn for the 2002 season. Harrison had previously handled the hitting instruction while working under Zahn. As a first baseman/designated hitter at Oral Roberts University (1978–1982), Harrison had earned four letters in baseball. In his single season at Michigan's helm, the team produced a record of 21-32. (Courtesy of the *Michigan Daily*.)

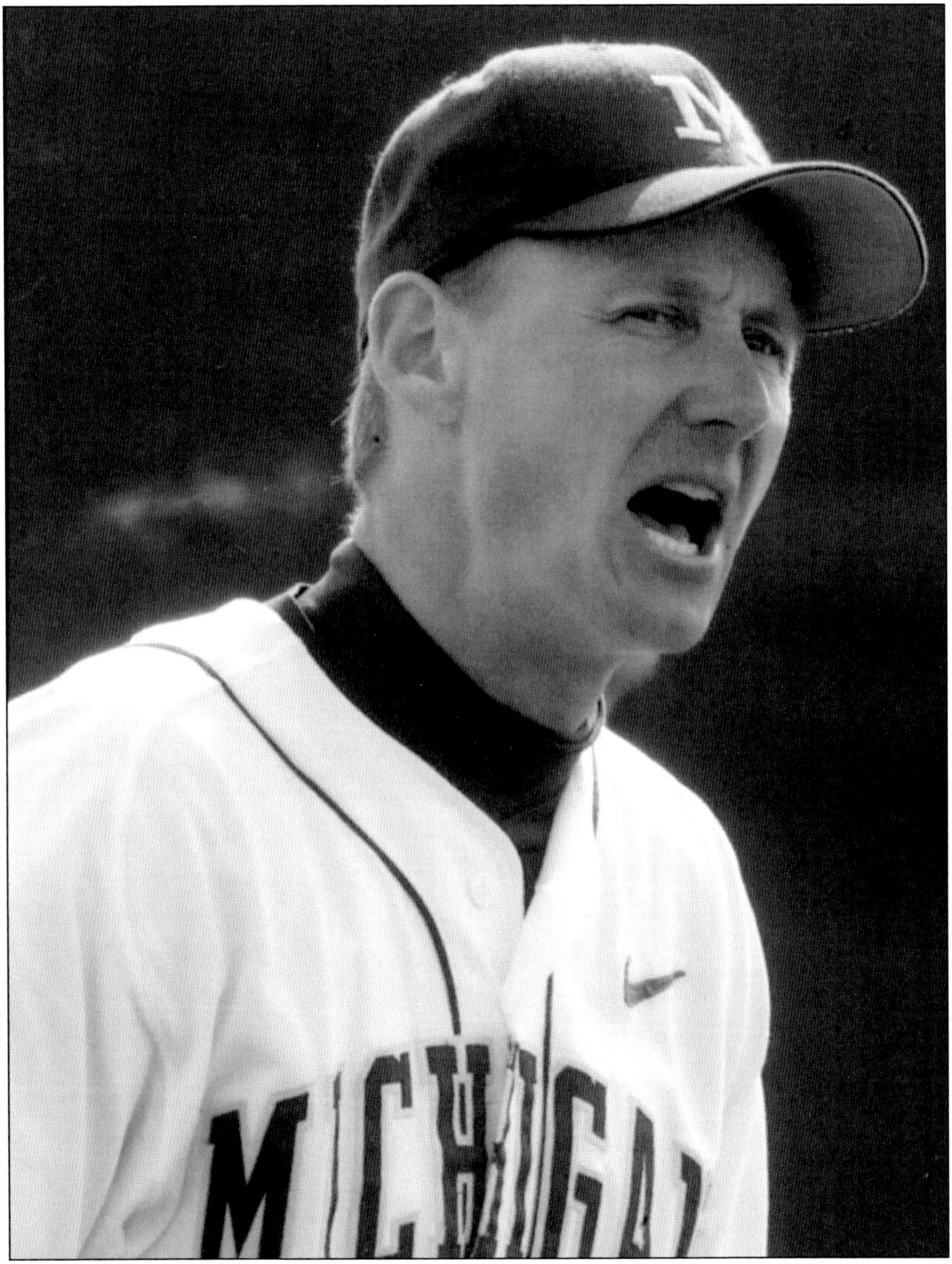

As a shortstop at Western Michigan University, Rich Maloney earned three varsity letters in baseball (1984–1986), as well as twice being elected captain. Originally drafted by the Atlanta Braves, he started his coaching career at Western Michigan (1992–1995), then accepted the position as head coach at Ball State for the 1996 season. When the same position opened up at Michigan for the 2003 season, Maloney was offered the job. In his first year as head coach, Michigan improved to 30-27, qualifying for the Big Ten playoffs. (Courtesy of the *Michigan Daily*.)

Third baseman Mike Cervenak finished his career at Michigan (1996–1999) as record holder in career hits (293) and doubles (67). His .353 career batting average is tenthhighest among modern Michigan athletes, while his 30 career home runs places him tied for fifth. He hit .385 in 1998 and .340 his senior year. Following graduation, Cervenak joined the New York Yankee organization. (Courtesy of the *Michigan Daily*.)

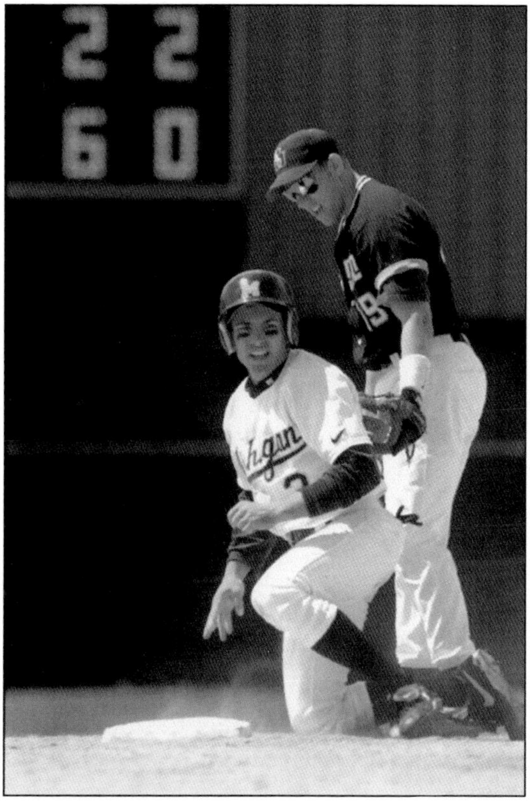

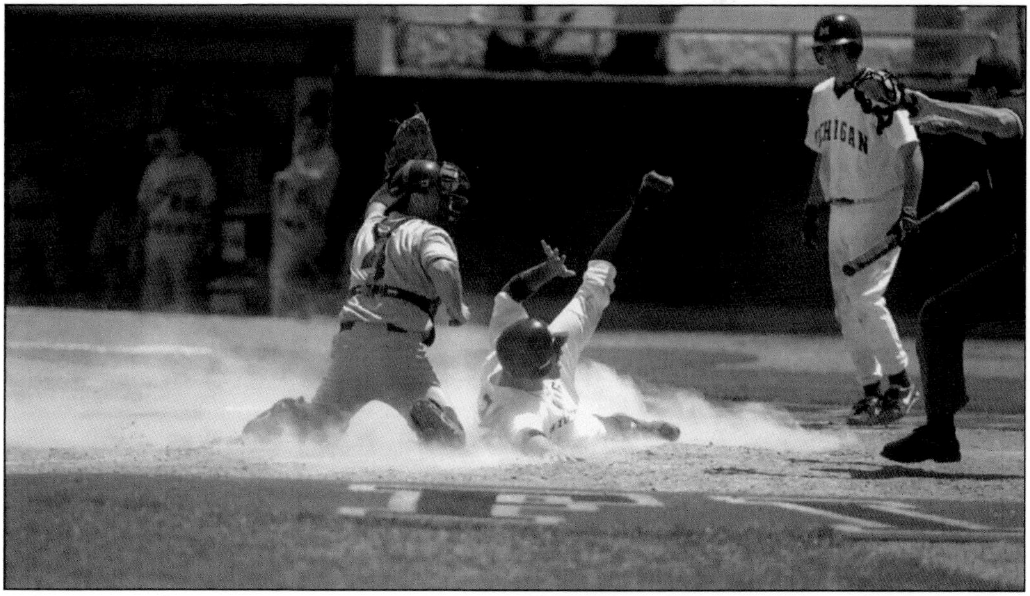

Mike Cervenak, scoring against Creighton in the 1999 South Bend Regional Tournament, finished his career with 172 runs scored, fourth highest in team history. Though Michigan *was* eliminated from the tournament, Cervenak was named to the All-Tournament team. (Courtesy of the *Michigan Daily*.)

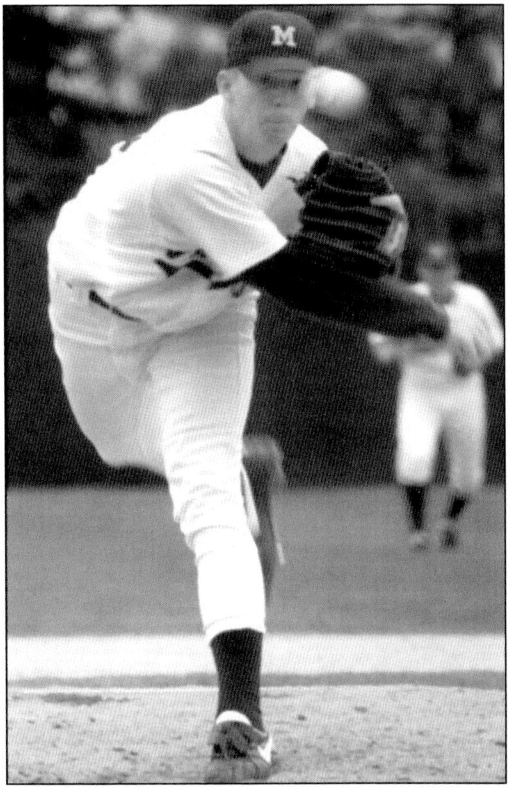

Joseph Jason "J.J." Putz won 18 of 29 decisions in his four years as a pitcher with Michigan (1996–1999). He topped off his totals with a record of 7-4 his senior year. Putz recorded two victories in the Big Ten tournament that year, only the third pitcher to do so. In his final start as a Wolverine, Putz pitched the team to a 13-5 victory over Creighton in the regional tournament in South Bend, Indiana. In 227 innings during his career at Michigan, Putz recorded 185 strikeouts. Putz was drafted by the Seattle Mariners after the season, and briefly appeared in the major leagues during the 2003 season, the 68th, and most recent, player from the Michigan varsity to reach that level. (Courtesy of the *Michigan Daily*.)

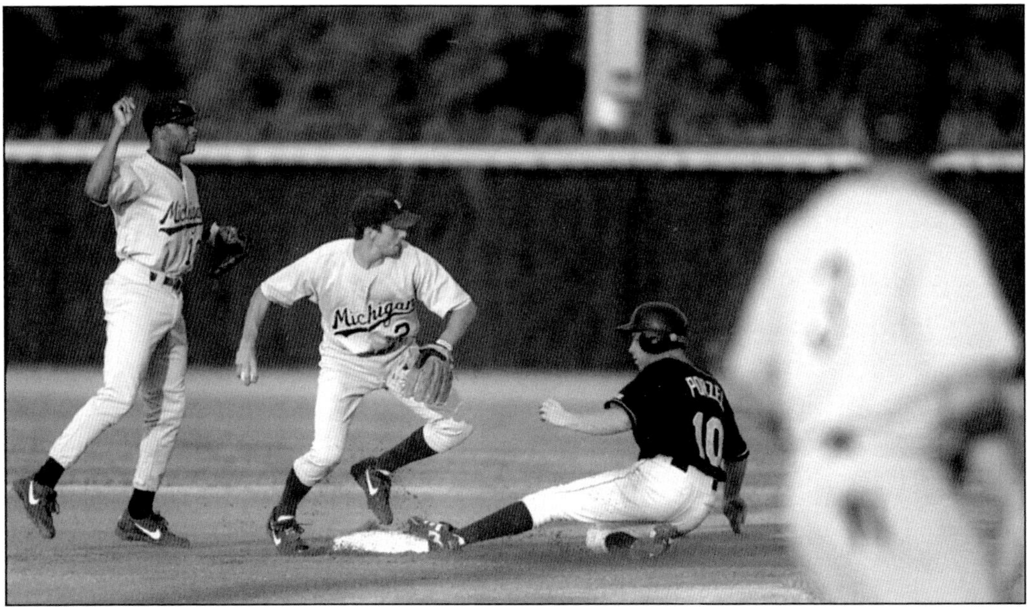

Scott Tousa (1998–2001) was the first to be named as the Ted Sizemore Award winner for outstanding defense at two different positions: shortstop (2000) and second base (2001). On offense, his career average of .311 included 217 hits (7th all-time) as well as being hit by pitches a record 27 times. In 2001, he hit .325, while leading the team with 14 stolen bases. (Courtesy of the *Michigan Daily*.)

Second baseman and senior co-captain Bobby Scales finished his four-year career (1996–1999) at Michigan with 226 hits, currently ranking seventh in career totals. As a senior, he won the Bill Freehan Award as the top hitter, with an average of .371. He also led the team in runs scored for the season (75—six behind the team record) and home runs (9). His season included a team record 18 consecutive games in which he hit safely. Scales received the Ray Fisher Award as team MVP. Following the season, Scales was drafted by the San Diego Padres. (Courtesy of the *Michigan Daily*.)

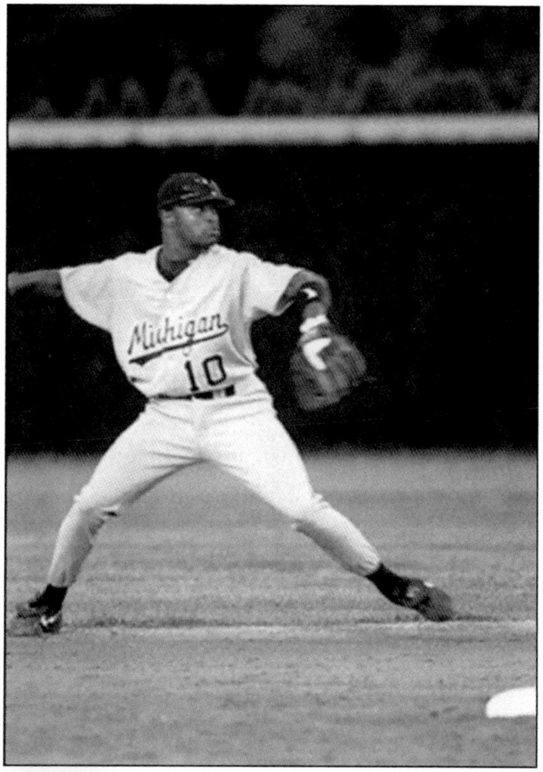

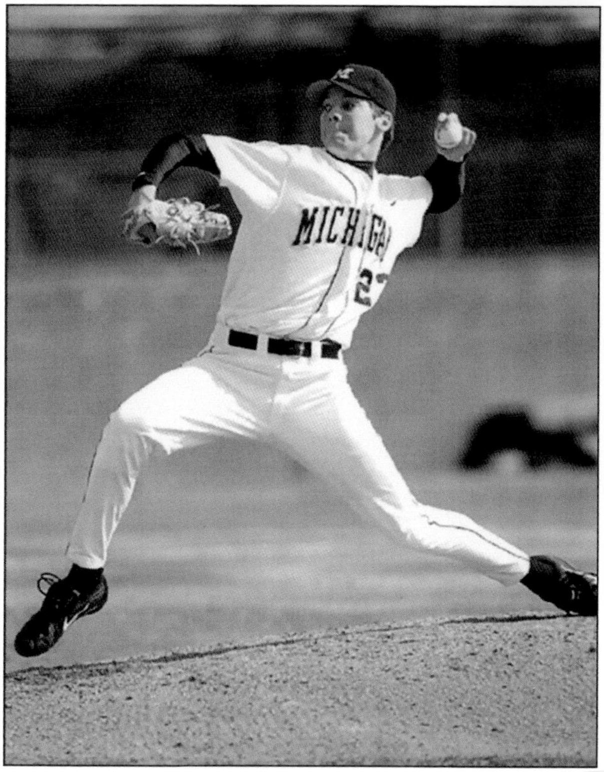

Rich Hill led the Michigan pitching staff three consecutive seasons in strikeouts (2000–2002), finishing with a career total of 229 in 177 innings. His total is fourth highest among career totals. Hill won 7 of 23 decisions during his career. Following his junior year, Hill was drafted by the Chicago Cubs. (Courtesy of the *Michigan Daily*.)

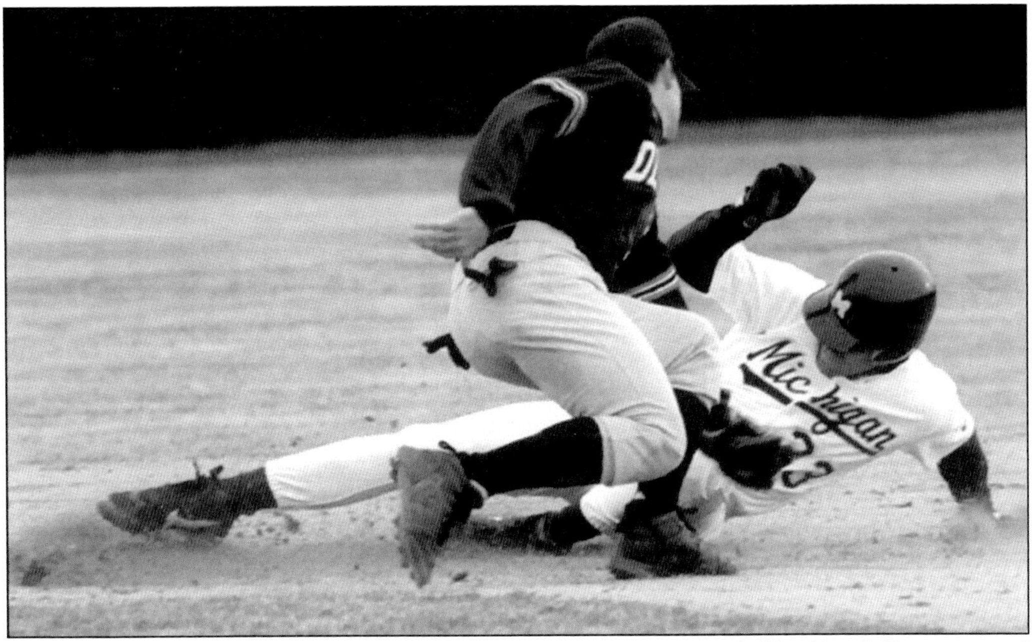

Twin brother of former Wolverine first baseman Bryan Besco, outfielder Derek Besco earned four letters from 1995 to 1998. His career batting average of .350 ranked him 13th among modern players, while his 22 career home runs is currently the 11th highest career total for the team. Besco was drafted by the Detroit Tigers in 1998. (Courtesy of the *Michigan Daily*.)

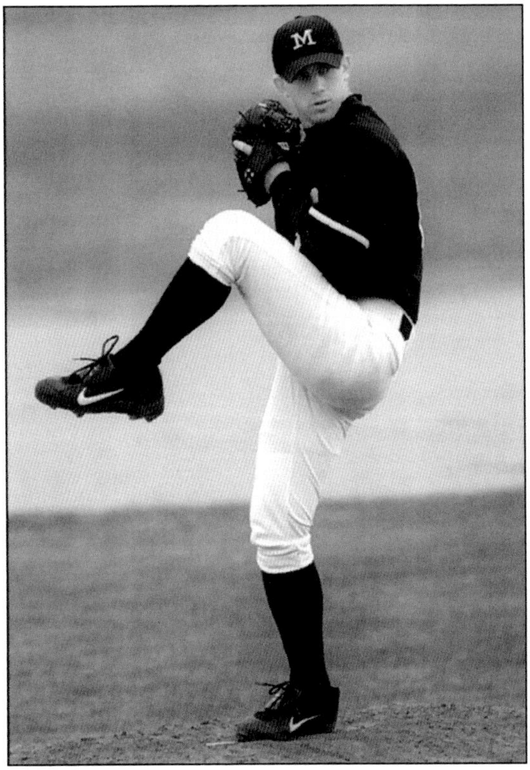

Bobby Korecky compiled a record of 17-18 during his four years with Michigan (1999–2002). His totals included 20 complete games. Korecky was named to the All-Big Ten team three consecutive seasons (2000–2002), and was elected co-captain his senior year. Korecky was picked by the Philadelphia Phillies in the 2002 draft. Through August 2003, he has compiled a minor league record of 9-8, while moving through the Phillies' farm system. (Courtesy of the *Michigan Daily*.)

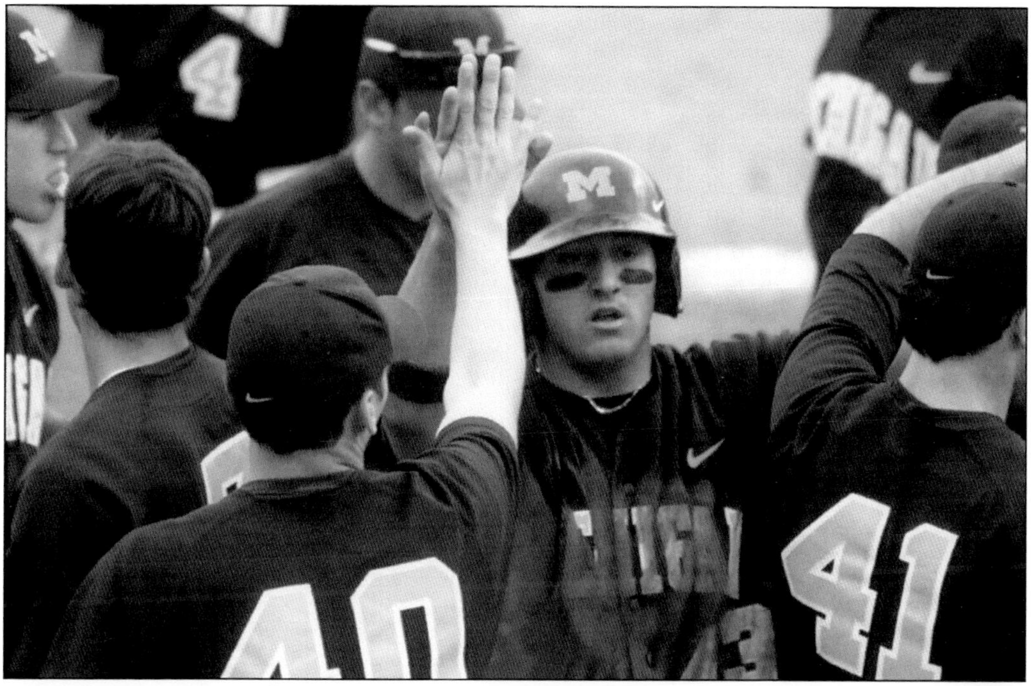

"High fives" as Gino Lollio scores against Central Michigan. The dirty uniform, acquired from an earlier steal, was a typical result of the hustle exhibited by Lollio throughout his career. (Courtesy of the *Michigan Daily*.)

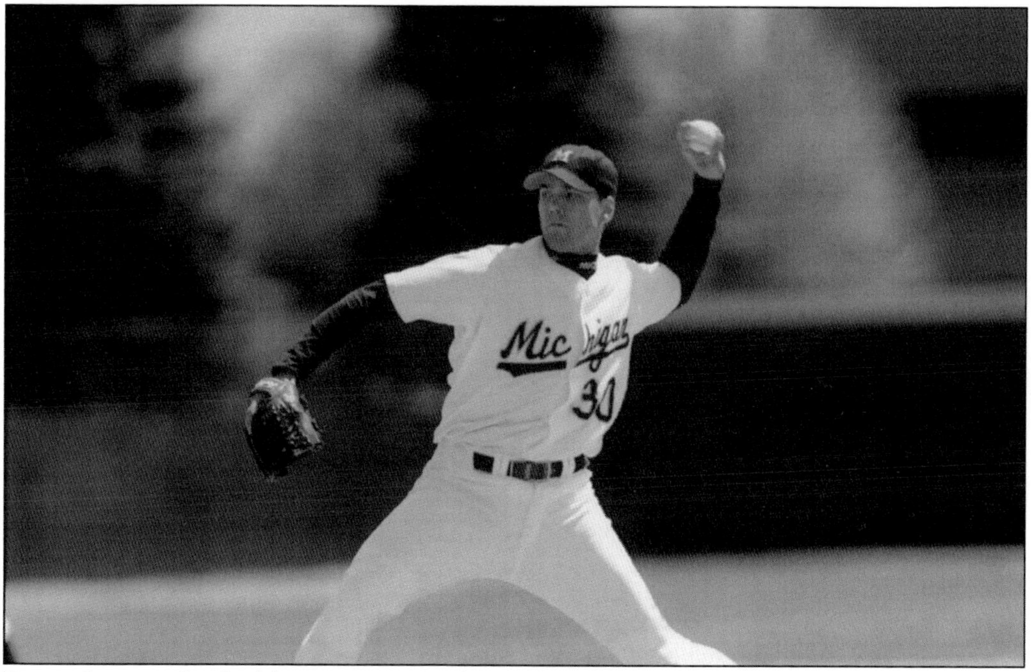

Bryan Cranson finished his career at Michigan (1997–2000) with a record of 15-17. The 15 victories was highest on the team among active players at the end of the season. Cranson's 11 starts in 1998 led the team. (Courtesy of the *Michigan Daily*.)

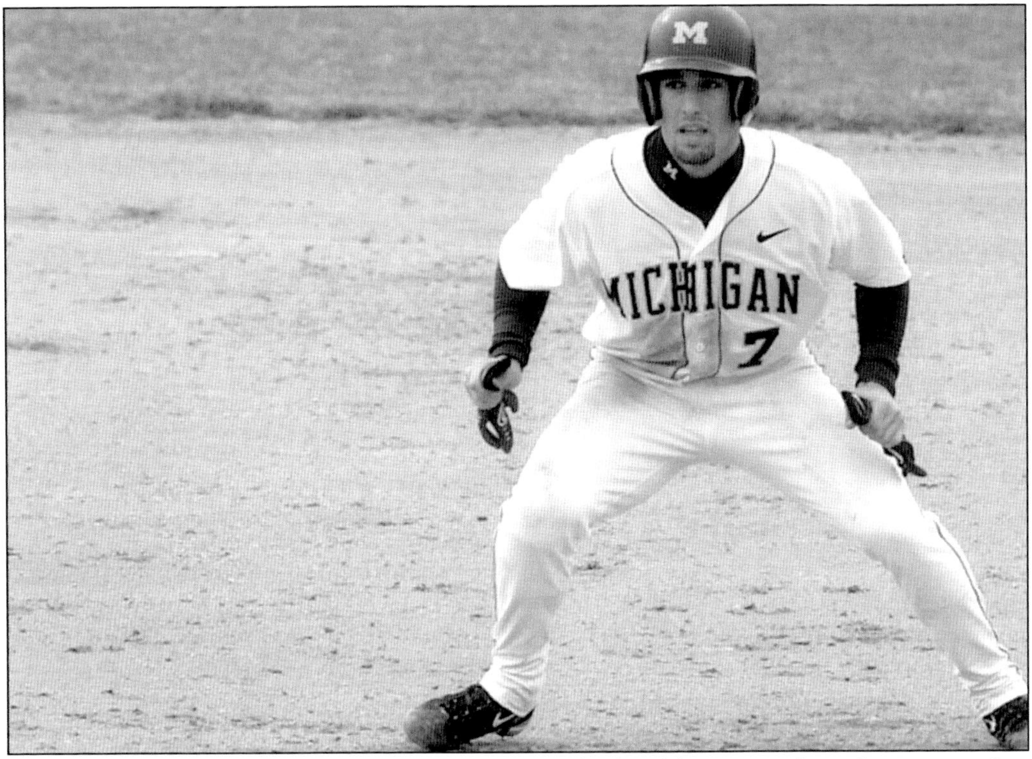

Gino Lollio's nine stolen bases his senior year (2003) placed him second on the team in that category. (Courtesy of the *Michigan Daily*.)

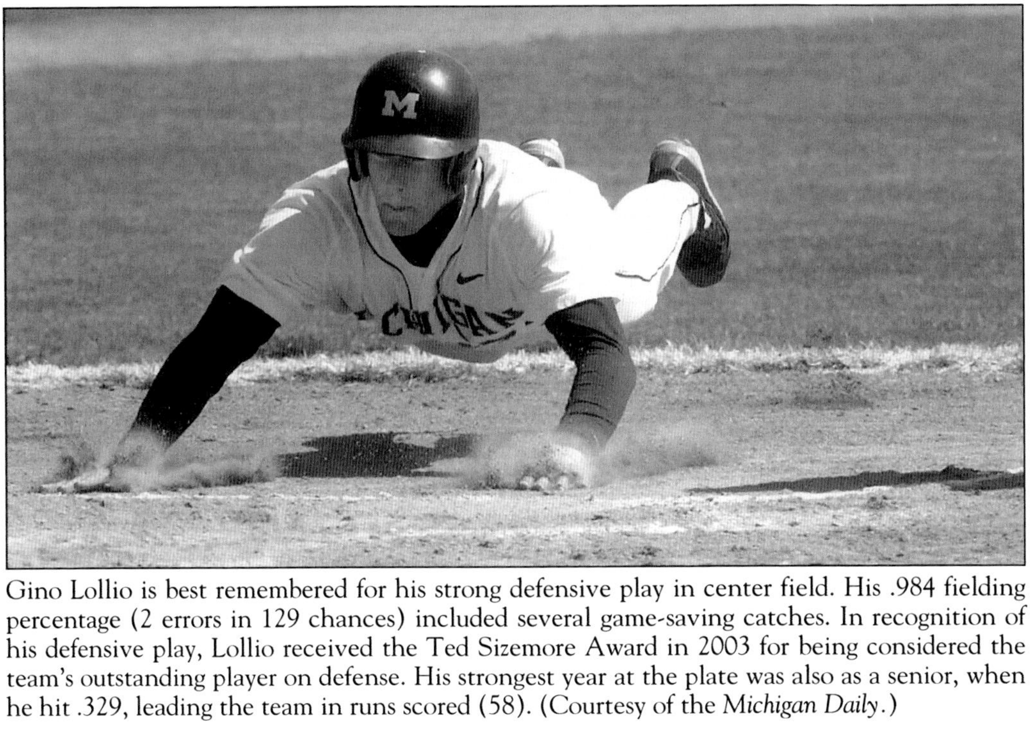

Gino Lollio is best remembered for his strong defensive play in center field. His .984 fielding percentage (2 errors in 129 chances) included several game-saving catches. In recognition of his defensive play, Lollio received the Ted Sizemore Award in 2003 for being considered the team's outstanding player on defense. His strongest year at the plate was also as a senior, when he hit .329, leading the team in runs scored (58). (Courtesy of the *Michigan Daily*.)

Powerful third baseman Brock Koman led the Wolverines three consecutive seasons (2001–2003) in hitting, becoming the first to win the Bill Freehan Award as top hitter in three consecutive seasons. In the four years in which he started at third base (2000–2003), Koman compiled a lifetime batting average of .351 (276 for 787), including an average of .383 in the 2001 season. He finished as Michigan's career leader in doubles (72), and ranked second in hits to Mike Cervenak. Koman was selected by the Houston Astros in the 2003 amateur draft. (Courtesy of the *Michigan Daily*.)

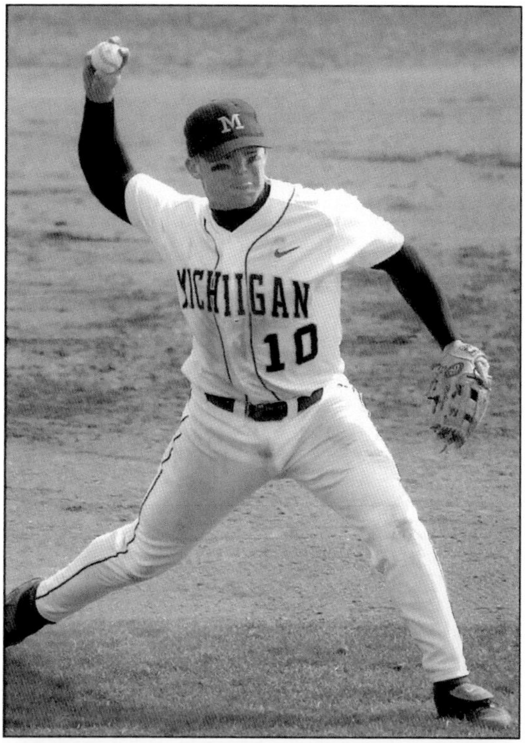

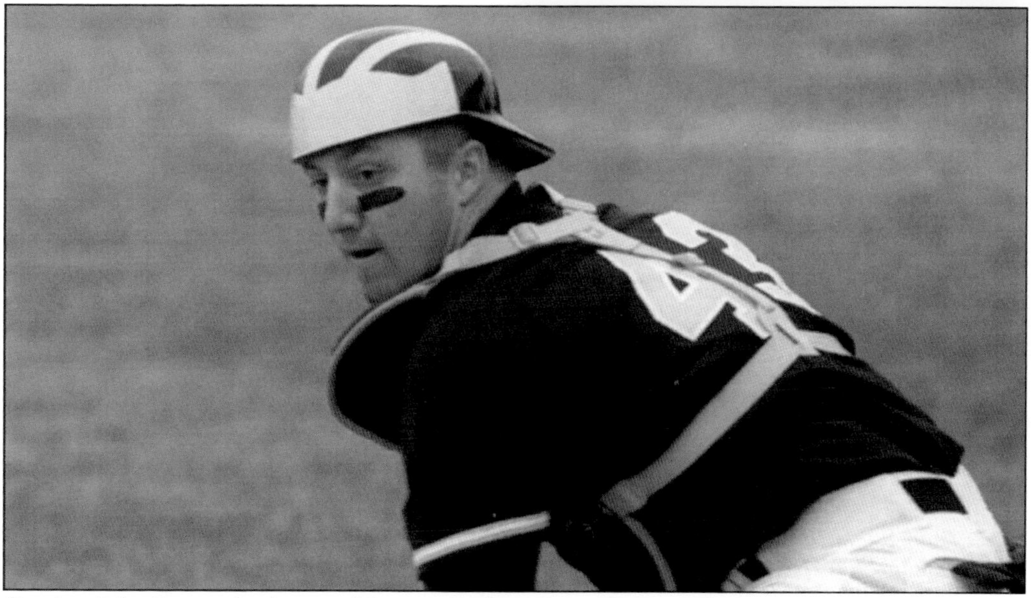

Catcher Jake Fox is the latest addition to a long line of outstanding athletes who played that position for Michigan. As a junior in 2003, Fox finished second in hitting with a .357 average, while leading the team in home runs (15) and RBI (67). He was honored with the Ray Fisher Award as MVP for the season. His career average of .333 (169 for 507) ranks him behind only Bill Freehan at that position. Following the 2003 season, Fox signed with the Chicago Cubs, the team which had chosen him in the amateur draft, deciding to pass on his final year of eligibility. (Courtesy of the *Michigan Daily*.)

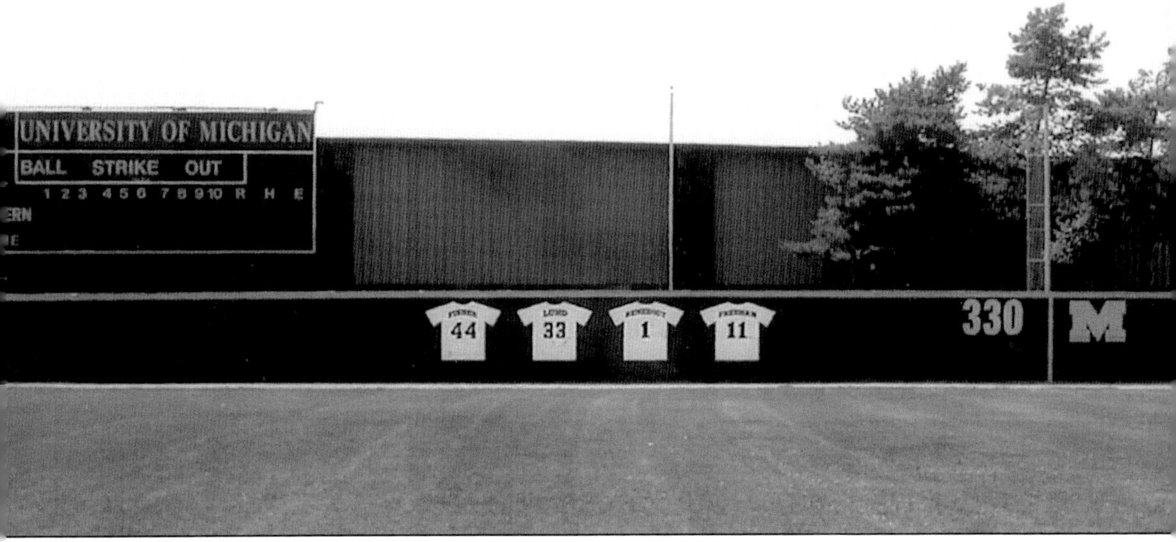

Four uniform numbers have been retired by the Michigan baseball program: Moby Benedict, number 1, was a shortstop from 1954 to 1956, later serving as head coach from 1963 to 1979, following Don Lund; Though Bill Freehan wore number 14 during the single season he played at Michigan, setting a batting mark of .446, he wore number 11 as an All-Star catcher during fifteen seasons with the Detroit Tigers. When he returned to coach Michigan in 1990, he continued to wear number11; Don Lund, number 33, is arguably Michigan's most notable all-around athlete since the days of Bennie Oosterbaan or George Sisler. Lund earned three letters in each of three sports from 1943 to 1945: baseball, basketball and football. Lund followed Ray Fisher as coach, directing Michigan to the NCAA National Championship in the 1962 College World Series; Ray Fisher, number 44, WAS Michigan baseball from 1921 to 1958. In 1967, the baseball facility was renamed in his honor. Images of the jerseys are painted on the right field wall near the foul line.

SEVEN

"Maize and Blue" Diamonds

The first "formal" baseball field on the Michigan campus was laid out in 1863 just north of the medical building, approximately the current site of the Chemistry Building and Dow Laboratory. Both intramural and varsity sports would be played there for nearly three decades—baseball in the spring and football in the fall. If an enclosed field was required, usually to handle larger crowds or to charge admission, games were played at the Ann Arbor Fairgrounds, the current site of Burns Park. On special occasions, games were also held at Recreation Park in Detroit.

With the increasing popularity of varsity sports by the 1890s, particularly baseball and football, it was clear that the existing athletic fields were inadequate. This era also represented the first period of significant endowments to the university. Among these endowments was $20,000 from Joshua Waterman to help fund a gymnasium to be built near the site of the existing diamond. The gymnasium would include both locker spaces for athletes, as well as training facilities, and the Board of Regents felt it was appropriate to establish more elaborate playing facilities.

Regent Frank Fletcher was instrumental in the purchase by the university, of ten acres of land near the bottom of the State Street hill, approximately where Schembechler Hall now stands. The field was leveled and enclosed, with bleachers added, and would serve for playing both football and baseball. A running track surrounded the fields. The facility was initially called simply the Athletic Field. Upon Fletcher's recommendation the name became Regents' Field.

Large crowds began to attend Michigan sporting events, particularly football, and Regents' Field quickly became obsolete. University sports in the beginning of the 20th Century, not unlike today, were expected to be self-supporting, a task made difficult given the small crowds which Regents' Field could accommodate. With the idea of obtaining funds to purchase land for a larger sports facility, Professor Albert Pattengill approached a possible donor, Dexter Ferry. Pattengill taught Greek at the University, but was also an avid follower of Michigan sports. Ferry was the wealthy owner of a Detroit business, the Ferry Seed Company. In the past, Ferry had sponsored his own company baseball team, the "Seeds," as well as having endowed a fellowship in botany at the University. His son was also an alumnus. In 1902, he purchased and donated to the University, twenty-one acres just north of Regents' Field. Additional purchases of land by the Athletic Association, extending as far as the railroad tracks, increased the final size to thirty-eight acres. An ornamental gate built of Bedford stone and red paving brick was designed by Albert Kahn Architects of Detroit, and completed in 1906.

The facility was named Ferry Field. It consisted of a football field surrounded by a track, with bleachers sitting at the current site of the IM building. The baseball diamond was laid out just south of the track, at the current site of Yost Arena. The first baseball game on the new diamond was played against Case for the home opener on April 25, 1908.

As the University grew, athletic demands on Waterman Gymnasium increased until it was felt a new gymnasium would be needed. Upon the recommendation of a committee headed by Fielding Yost, long-time football coach and by 1922 the Director of Athletics, a new facility would be built on the site of the Ferry Field diamond. The "Field House," a term coined by Yost, was erected and dedicated in November, 1923, as the Yost Field House, and later as Yost Ice Arena. The building necessitated the moving of the diamond some 150 feet west to its present location.

Michigan baseball has been played on the current site since 1923. Wooden grandstands were constructed in 1948, and replaced by steel in 1973. A snow fence constituted most of the outfield boundary until 1967, when the park was enclosed. That same year, the field was dedicated to Ray Fisher, acquiring its current name of Ray Fisher Stadium. The 1967 fence was replaced by the current structure in 1997. While there has been talk of replacing the entire stadium with a more modern structure, cost alone will probably ensure that baseball will continue at the present location for the foreseeable future.

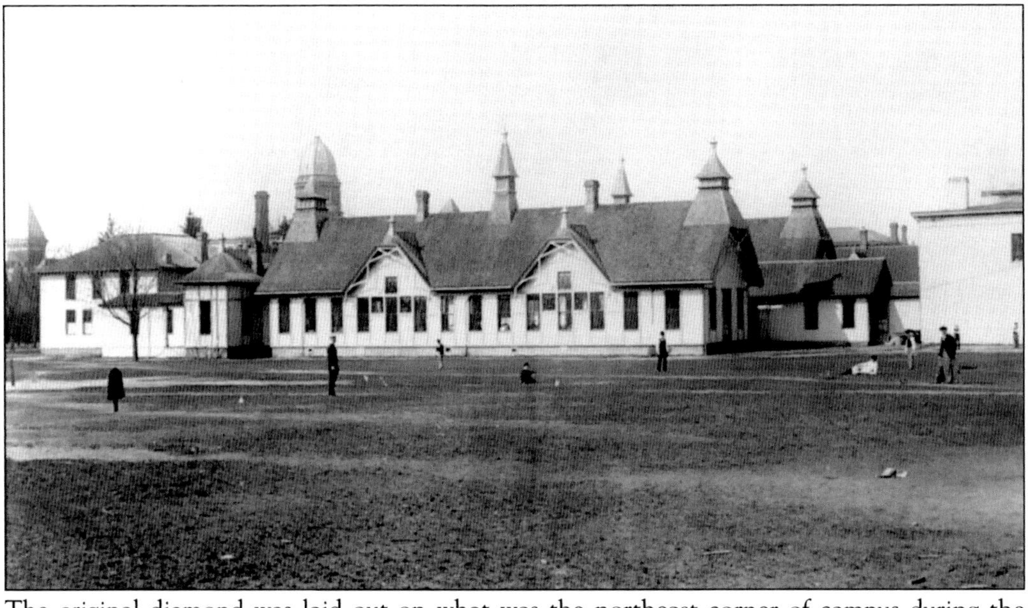

The original diamond was laid out on what was the northeast corner of campus during the 1860s, and now the current site of the Chemistry Building. Students played both baseball and football on this site until 1892, by which time the Regents' Field grounds were purchased and converted to athletic facilities. Waterman Gymnasium, the first indoor athletic facility built on campus, was completed on this site in 1894. It fell to the wrecking ball in 1977. The photograph includes an image of the medical building. (Courtesy of the Bentley Historical Library.)

The May 5, 1891 issue of *University of Michigan Daily* ran this announcement and description of the site for the new athletic fields to be built at Regents' Field. Football was played at the site until the completion of what is now Michigan Stadium, though the seating area underwent subsequent expansion from the original plans. The cinder track is still at the same site, adjacent to the Intramural Sports Building. (Courtesy of the *The University of Michigan Daily*)

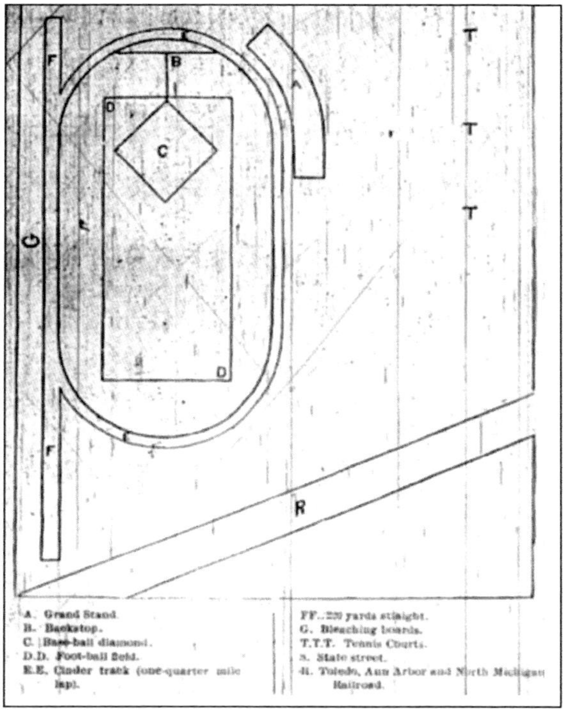

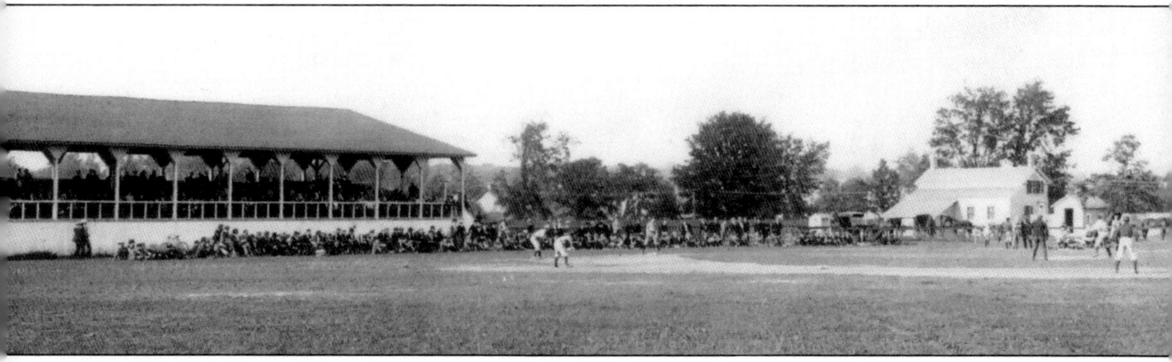

Originally named simply as the "Athletic Field," the sports facility opened in 1893 for both baseball and football. In 1894, the name was changed to Regents' Field. The grandstand originally was built to hold 400 spectators. The original grandstand burned in 1895, and was rebuilt with its capacity doubled to 800, as seen in the photo. Baseball was played here until 1907, at which time the diamond was moved several hundred feet to the new South Ferry Field. A portion of Regents' Field is now the site of Schembechler Hall. (Courtesy of the Bentley Historical Library.)

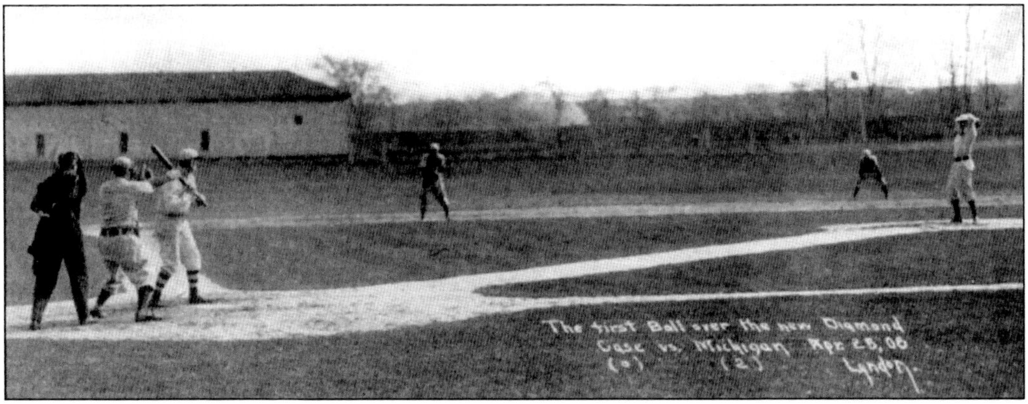

Case vs. The University of Michigan, April 25, 1908. Pitcher David Barr prepares to throw the first pitch on the new South Ferry Field diamond (currently the site of Yost Arena). Hawley, Case shortstop, is the batter. Barr threw a one-hitter on this historic day, striking out 11, as George "Pat" Kelley scored the first run on the new field. (Courtesy of the *Michiganensian*.)

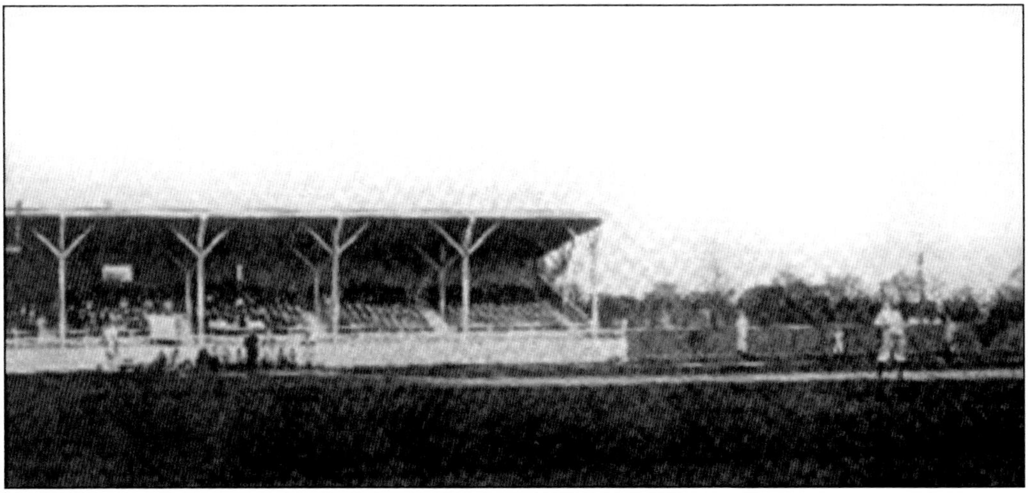

This photo captures the action on the new Ferry Field diamond, 1923. Baseball was played on the older South Ferry Field site from 1908 to 1922. Following the decision to honor Fielding H. Yost with naming rights for the new fieldhouse, the baseball diamond was moved to its current location in 1923. Yost Arena will be built just behind the grandstand and fence. (Courtesy of the *Michiganensian*.)

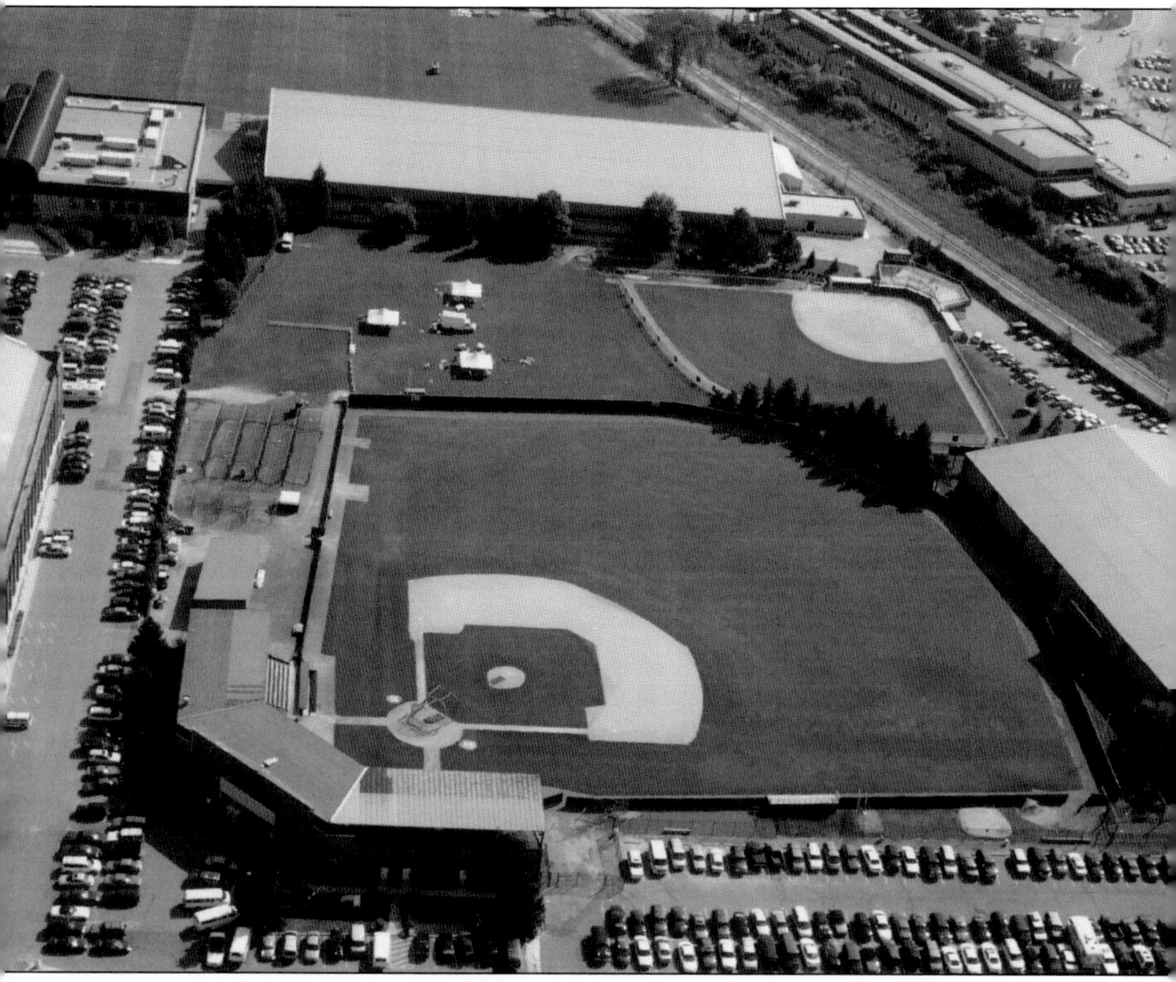

Ray Fisher Stadium is the home of Michigan baseball. Originally Ferry Field, baseball has been played here since 1923, after the field had been moved slightly north from its earlier site. (Approximately the position of the hospitality tents outside the left field wall.) A spur was attached to the railroad running through the upper left corner in the photo, allowing dirt to be brought to fill in what had been a depression in the land. Also visible is the women's softball field. The grandstand was built in 1948, and the field enclosed in 1967. Current dimensions are 330 feet down both lines, and 400 feet to dead center. (Photo courtesy of Bauer, Dunham and Barr)

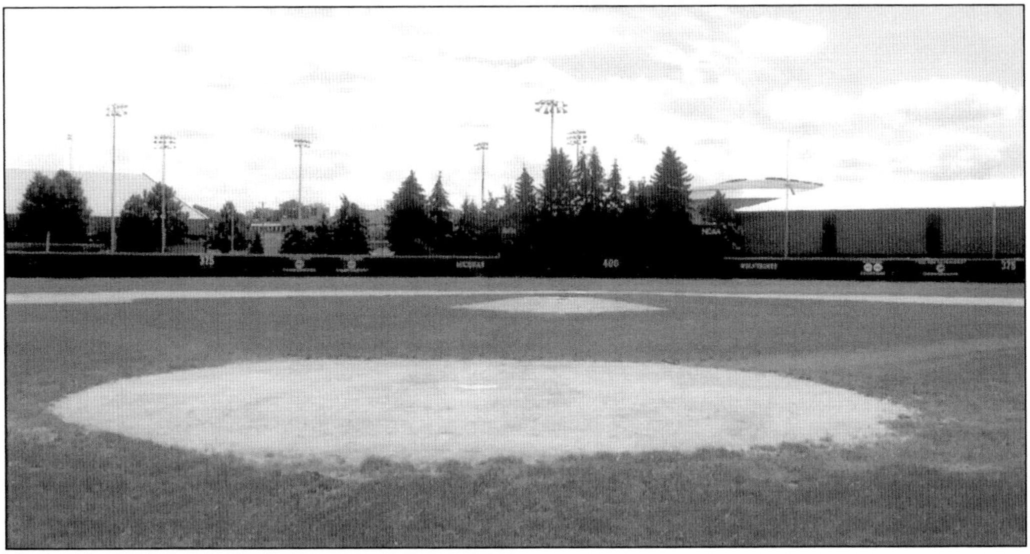

A batter's image of the mound and centerfield fence at Fisher Stadium. The building behind the fence on the right is the indoor track facility. Prior to enclosure of the field in the 1960s, a tennis court marked the site of the right field fence, with a snow fence encompassing the remainder of the outfield boundary. The women's softball facility is just beyond the 375 sign. Crisler Arena is the domed building in the background, with Michigan Stadium, home of Wolverine football, behind the Arena, but not in the photograph. (Author's collection)

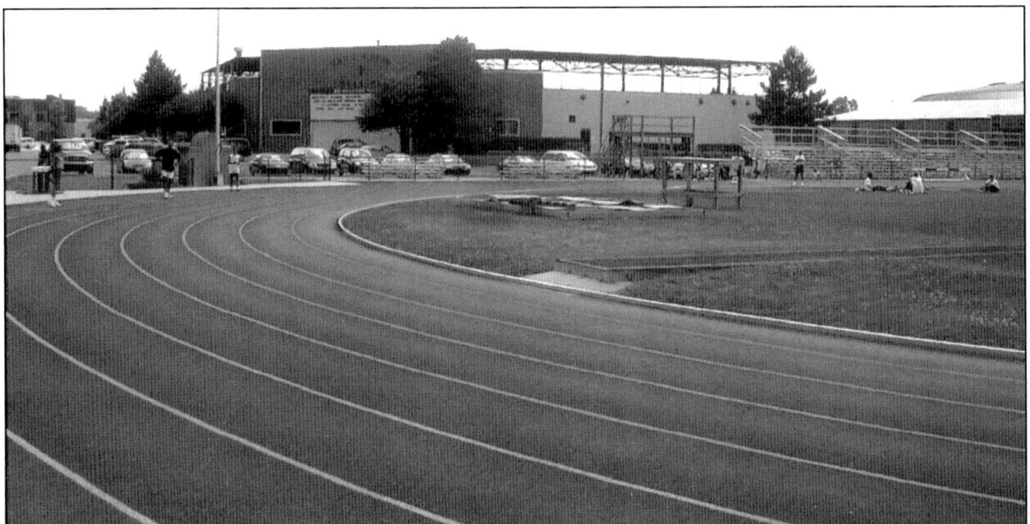

A view of Fisher Stadium from the front. The Ferry Field track in the foreground was the site of four world's records in track set by future Olympian Jesse Owens in 1935. Owens was representing Ohio State in a Big Ten track meet.

Appendix A

Michigan Coaches' Records[19]

Coach	Years	Overall	Big Ten
Peter Conway	1891–1892	22-9-1	
H. G. Cleaveland	1893	14-4	
George J. Cadwell	1894	11-8	
E. C. Weeks	1895	19-3-1	
Frank Sexton	1896; 1901–1902	38-22	15-12
Henry T. Clarke	1899	14-5	5-2
Charles F. Watkins	1897–1898; 1900	31-23-1	15-14-1
Skel Roach	1903	12-5	7-3
Jerome Utley	1904	10-5	9-3
Lew McAllister	1905–1906; 1908–1909	53-15-1	14-6
Robert Lowe	1907	11-4-1	5-3
Branch Rickey	1910–1913	68-32-4	
Carl Lundgren	1914–1920	94-33-6	27-2
Ray Fisher	1921–1958	637-294-8	269-123
Don Lund	1959–1962	83-55-3	34-19
Moby Benedict	1963–1979	367-251-5	168-82-1
Bud Middaugh	1980–1989	465-146-1	142-37
Bill Freehan	1990–1995	166-167-1	76-89
Goeff Zahn	1996–2001	163-149-2	78-80
Chris Harrison	2002	21-32	14-17
Rich Maloney	2003	30-27	16-14

[19] In Pack's *100 Years of Athletics*, as well as in Michigan baseball media guides, Watkins is listed as coach during both 1899 and 1901. However, contemporary newspapers as well as the student yearbook *Michiganensian* list the coaches as named by this author.

Appendix B

Michigan Directors of Athletics

During the earliest days of organized sports at the University, administration of athletics was primarily handled by various associations with no official standing among the administration. The first of these groups was the "Football Association," established in 1873. A "Baseball Association" was formed in 1876. The two groups merged two years later, with establishment of the first "Athletic Association." The Association was controlled by the students, with the only input from the administration being in the form of advice. The "Athletic Association" as such lasted for six years.

In 1890, the "Athletic Association of the University of Michigan" was established to once again oversee all athletics. Membership was open to anyone willing to pay an annual fee of three dollars, no small sum for the times. The Association was administered by a Board of Directors: five officers and nine directors, all of whom were elected by the students.

The inability of the Association to properly oversee athletic teams resulted in subsequent changes in the system. In 1893, a "Board in Control of Athletics" with full powers of oversight was established. The Board consisted of five faculty and four students, all selected by the students. In 1898, the position of Graduate Manager of Athletics was established, eventually to be called simply Director of Athletics. Charles Baird, an 1895 graduate of the University, was the first appointee to the position. It was common for both Baird, as well as his successor, Philip Bartelme, to appear in photographs with the athletic teams.

Director	Years
Charles Baird	1898–1908
Philip Bartelme	1909–1920
Fielding H. Yost	1921–1941
Herbert "Fritz" Crisler	1941–1968
Don Canham	1968–1988
Glenn "Bo" Schembechler	1988–1990
Jack Weidenbach	1990–1994
Joe Roberson	1994–1997
Tom Goss	1997–2000
William Martin	2000–

Bibliography

Newspapers:

The Ann Arbor News
The Chicago Times-Herald
The Detroit Free Press
The Michigan Argonaut
The Michigan Chronicle
The Michigan Daily
The University of Michigan Daily

Books and Articles:

Frommer, Harvey. *Rickey and Robinson*. New York: Taylor Trade Publishing, 1982.
Humphrey, Edwin. *The Michigan Book*, Ann Arbor: The Inland Press, 1898.
Michigan Baseball Media Guide
Michiganensian
Morris, Peter. *Baseball Fever: Early Baseball in Michigan*. Ann Arbor, MI: University of Michigan Press, 2003.
Pack, Philip. *100 Years of Athletics: The University of Michigan*. Ann Arbor, MI, 1937.
Palladium
Proctor, Donald. "The Blacklisting of Baseball's Ray Fisher" *Baseball Research Journal*, pp. 34–45; 182–188, 1981.
Ratermann, Dale. *Big Ten: A Century of Excellence*. Champaign, IL: Sagamore Publishing, Inc., 1996.
Sagendorph, Kent. *Michigan: The Story of the University*. New York: E.P. Dutton & Co., 1948.
Seymour, Harold. *Baseball: The People's Game*. New York: Oxford University Press, 1990.
Shaw, Wilfred. *The University of Michigan*. New York: Harcourt, Brace and Howe, 1920.
Tekulsky, Joseph. "Elmer Gedeon." *The National Pastime*, #14, pp. 68–69, 1994.